A TRADITION OF TEACHERS

A TRADITION OF TEACHERS:

Śaṅkara and the Jagadgurus Today

WILLIAM CENKNER

MOTILAL BANARSIDASS PUBLISHERS
PRIVATE LIMITED • DELHI

First Edition: Delhi, 1983
Reprint: Delhi, 1995

ISBN: 81-208-0932-7

Also available at:
MOTILAL BANARSIDASS
41 U.A. Bungalow Road, Jawahar Nagar, Delhi 110 007
120 Royapettah High Road, Mylapore, Madras 600 004
16 St. Mark's Road, Bangalore 560 001
Ashok Rajpath, Patna 800 004
Chowk, Varanasi 221 001

PRINTED IN INDIA

BY JAINENDRA PRAKASH JAIN AT SHRI JAINENDRA PRESS,
A-45 NARAINA, PHASE I, NEW DELHI 110 028
AND PUBLISHED BY NARENDRA PRAKASH JAIN FOR
MOTILAL BANARSIDASS PUBLISHERS PVT. LTD.
BUNGALOW ROAD, DELHI 110 007

TABLE OF CONTENTS

NOTE TO 1994 EDITION vii
INTRODUCTION ix
ABBREVIATIONS xv

PART ONE : THE TRADITION

Chapter

ONE — ANCIENT TRADITION : VEDIC AND UPANIṢADIC ROOTS ... 3-28
- The Teacher in the Upaniṣads ... 8
- The Guru-Śiṣya Relationship ... 15
- Pedagogy in the Upaniṣads 19

TWO — ŚAṄKARA AND THE TEACHING TRADITION 29-59
- The Nature of the Guru 32
- The Personality of the Religious Seeker ... 45
- The Guru-Śiṣya Relationship ... 55

THREE — ŚAṄKARA'S PEDAGOGY IN RELIGIOUS LIFE 60-83
- Self-Inquiry 61
- Triple Method : Hearing, Reflection, Concentration 65
- The Place of Meditation 71
- Practice of Meditation 77
- The Independence of Self-Realisation ... 80

FOUR — THE TEACHING HERITAGE AFTER ŚAṄKARA 84-106
- The First Disciples of Śaṅkara ... 85
- Works of the Late-Śaṅkara 90
- Diversity within Advaita Vedānta ... 96
- The Threshold of the Present 103

PART TWO : PRESENT DAY ŚAṄKARĀCĀRYAS

Chapter

FIVE — THE ŚAṄKARĀCĀRYAS AND THE SEATS OF LEARNING 109-134

	The Vidyāpīṭhas Today	112
	The Pāṭhaśālās and Traditional Education	117
	The Present Śaṅkarācāryas	122
	The Ministry of the Śaṅkarācāryas ...	127
	The Capacity of a Jagadguru ...	132
SIX	THE TEACHING OF THE ŚAṄKARĀCĀRYAS ...	135-153
	The Dharma Path ...	136
	Themes of Special Interest	142
	The Supreme Teaching : Advaita Vedānta ...	146
	The Exaltation of Ādi Śaṅkara ...	152
SEVEN	THE TEACHER-STUDENT RELATIONSHIP TODAY	154-174
	The Meaning of the Student Today ...	161
	The Experience of a Guru	168
	The Path of the Student	170
EIGHT	THE GURU IN THE MODERN WORLD	175-188
	Hymn to Śrī Dakṣiṇāmūrti	175
	The Guru in the Historical Order ...	177
	The Guru in Modern Life	181

BIBLIOGRAPHY	189
GLOSSARY	202
INDEX	209

NOTE TO 1994 EDITION

Since the first edition of this study in 1983, more recent scholarship has focused upon aspects of this work. The reader is referred to the following: Jonathan Bader, *Meditation in Śaṅkara's Vedānta,* New Delhi: Aditya Prakashan, 1990; Patrick Olivelle, *Renunciation in Hinduism, A Mediaeval Debate,* Vol. I, *The Debate and the Advaita Argument,* Vienna: Institute for Indology, University of Vienna, 1986; Yogshitsugu Sawai, *The Faith of Ascetic and Lay Smārtas: A Study of the Śaṅkara Tradition of Śṛṅgeri,* Ann Arbor, MI: University Microfilms International, 1984; Yogshitsugu Sawai, "Śaṅkara's Theory of Saṃnyāsa", *Journal of Indian Philosophy*, 14 (1986), pp. 371-87. Two of my own works advance this study: "The Hindu Guru and Zen Roshi in Comparative Study", *Proceedings of the Seventh International Symposium on Asian Studies,* Hong Kong, 1985; "The Śaṅkarācārya of Kanchi and the Kamaksi Temple as Ritual Center", *A Sacred Thread: Modern Transmission of Hindu Traditions in India and Abroad,* edit. Raymond Williams, Chambersburg, PA: Anima Publications, 1992.

The four traditional Vidyāpīṭhas, namely Śṛṅgeri, Dwārakā, Puri and Jyotirmaṭha have new ācāryas. The most recently installed Śaṅkarācārya is Śri Bhāratī Tīrtha of Śṛṅgeri who became reigning ācārya in late 1989. Following the brief *yātrā* in 1987 of Sri Jayendra Sarasvatī of the Kāñchipuram Kāmakoṭi Pīṭha, Śri Vijayendra Sarasvatī became the leader of *pūjā* and administrator of the Maṭha. The Sage of Kanchi, the retired senior *ācārya* and most popular and beloved Śaṅkarācārya of this century, died in early 1994 but not before celebrating his centenary of birth.

The Śaṅkarācāryas have become increasingly social and political figures in the past decade and especially in recent years. Śrī Jayendra of Kāñchipuram has taken as his primary task the raising of social consciousness and advancing social projects in south India. The northern ācāryas have consistently gained public attention due to their actions and utterances on national issues. As recently as in 1990 Śrī Svarūpānanda Sarasvatī was arrested and imprisoned over the Ayodhya affair.

Thus contemporary developments support the thesis that the Śaṅkarācāryas visibly reflect the ongoing growth of the Śaṅkara tradition.

Washington, 1994 WILLIAM CENKNER

INTRODUCTION

The rise of interest in the religious guide within contemporary religious society parallels, paradoxically, the decline of interest in and the increasing skepticism toward religion as a normative factor in social life. A religious figure is no longer esteemed for his or her capacity to articulate a religious tradition or administrate a religious group, but there is expectation that he or she be a guide in the developing life of the human spirit. There is a conviction, among many religious seekers today, that an advanced religious personality is still a reality in today's world, that such a person can guide the religious seeker through the ambiguities of modern life, that he or she can transform both personal history and world history to some significant degree. In Western Europe and the Americas, this is evidenced by the presence of the Sufi pirs, Hindu gurus, Zen masters, Tibetan lamas, and even Christian and Jewish men and women who have become guides in religious experience and community. In India today, the context of this study, criticism of the traditional holy man, and holy woman to a lesser degree, is sometimes harsh and iconoclastic; but this has not prevented the emergence of new gurus, such as the popular Bhagavan Rajneesh or the more typical Swami Muktananda, who capture the imagination of some people. The devotion expressed toward more traditional guides, such as the Madhvācāryas and the Śaṅkarācāryas, or those gurus inspired by the late Swami Sivananda and the saintly Ramakrishna, has not diminished.

There is instant recognition of who these individuals are, but there is little clarity as to what they are as spiritual guides. The uniqueness of the Indian guru rests upon the uniqueness of the Indian teaching tradition, which for some gurus means a relation to a figure in Indian history 500 years or 2,500 years ago. More than in most religious teaching traditions, the Hindu guru has been esteemed as a catalyst of experience and expression in religious life. But the Hindu figure of sanctity is fundamentally a teacher. Before anything else, the saint and the spiritual guide are teachers of tradition. The gurus, whether orthodox or heterodox, emerge from a particular teaching tradition. This gives specificity to the Hindu guru which is not necessarily common to other religious groups. An understanding of a religious figure in India can be achieved only within the framework of the teaching tradition from which that individual has come. This is not a simple endeavor because there exists in India even today a broad range of teaching traditions. But this does not lessen the necessity to define a guru in these terms. If clarity is to be achieved in understanding a particular guru in modern times, it can only result from examining the meaning of teacher as instanced within his lineage. This need not detract from the genius or originality of the figure; on the contrary, this critical examination makes the teacher's qualities stand out.

This study attempts to specify the role of the guru as it is understood within one classical tradition in Hindu life. Moreover, it seeks to describe the special relationship between teacher and student, the guru-*śiṣya* relationship, as the didactic locale where guidance is given, where spiritual transformation is initiated and consummated. Consequently, this study selects one way of understanding the guru in classical Hindu life in the belief that this articulation offers something normative for an understanding of guru in the wider Hindu development and history. The version of guru and the guru-*śiṣya* relationship investigated here is taken from one of India's most classical and respected thinkers : Śaṅkara. Śaṅkara gave the first comprehensive articulation to the Vedānta system in the eighth century C.E. He has been selected because he closely identified with the scriptural tradition of the Upaniṣads and the early Vedānta system, a context for many Indian gurus even today. Śaṅkara, as the exponent of nondual experience and expression, Advaita Vedānta, articulated a conception of guru that continued for the following 1,200 years. His importance to the guru tradition, therefore, rests upon his own exposition, an Advaita and scriptural understanding, and the emulation of it by his followers. This study consists of two parts. The first part is drawn from texts that trace the role of guru and the guru-*śiṣya* relationship in the writing of Śaṅkara, who is placed within the greater framework of the history of Indian education and the Upaniṣadic literature.

It is not possible to verify historically the breadth and depth of Śaṅkara's own role as guru either in his own lifetime or in the centuries immediately after him. It would have been desirable to test Śaṅkara's conception of the guru in his personal history or the history of his times. But such a reconstruction of Indian history is virtually impossible. Philosophical texts and law books are still the major source for discovering belief and practice within an ancient Indian teaching tradition. These do not offer sufficient historical analysis. What is disclosed in the first part of this study remains very much on the ideal plane because it cannot be tested in eighth century Indian history. It is the concern of this study, however, to find out whether today's gurus stand within this conception of the spiritual guide and whether their self-understanding has continuity with Śaṅkara.

Consequently, the second part of this study is an investigation of five major gurus, or *ācārya*-s,[1] of the Śaṅkara *sampradāya*, teaching tradition. The leap from Śaṅkara, as an eighth century teacher, to the reigning Śaṅkarācāryas of this century is great. However, the five Śaṅkarācāryas, as they are called, were selected because they are the principal teachers among the Śaṅkara ascetics who now reign over the five major Vidyāpīṭhas, or seats of learning, throughout India. These figures fulfill a teaching role superior to that of other Śaṅkarācāryas in India, who head secondary *maṭhas*. In short, this study looks to the articulation of guru in the writings of Śaṅkara and tests this ideal in the concrete among the major figures of the Śaṅkara tradition today. The importance of the study rests upon the significant place of Advaita Vedānta as an articulation of a scriptural tradition and the extensive role taken by a group of traditional teachers who reflect most concretely the teaching and life of Śaṅkara for a large number of Hindu devotees.

Several problems were confronted in this study. The first was the textual problem of determining from a large corpus of writing what was authentically of Śaṅkara's authorship. In most cases, I have followed S. K. Belvalkar (1927), Mario Piantelli (1974), Sengaku Mayeda (1965) (1979) and Robert E. Gussner (1976), in narrowing the body of literature.[2] Belvalkar's principle of

1. Once these terms have been established in the first part of the study, they will be used interchangeably. Gonda (1965) has made a comprehensive study of this vocabulary in early Indian literature, but the history of the broader tradition uses the vocabulary somewhat indiscriminately. This present study indicates the need to specify the meaning of the terms within a particular teaching tradition.

2. Citations are in the Bibliography. A fuller discussion of this question takes place in Chapter Four.

authentication is based primarily upon nondual (*advaita*) meaning and its centrality in the texts. Mayeda and Gussner employ more sophisticated stylistic and stylometric methods in authenticating a text. Even within the Advaita corpus, some texts are contested, which indicates need for further textual study. Outside the Advaita literature of Śaṅkara, however, exists a much larger body of literature attributed to the master Advaitin reflecting *bhakti* and Tantra interests. I have not ignored this body of literature, which I call late-Śaṅkara, but I draw upon it sparingly and within the context of the immediate followers of Śaṅkara. In resolving this textual problem, I have taken a typical academic approach; it should be recognized, however, that the Śaṅkara tradition, and especially the Śaṅkarācāryas today, usually accept as authentic the larger corpus of Śaṅkara writings, whether the texts emphasize *advaita*, *bhakti* or Tantra.[1]

In the second part of this study, I have not limited myself to what is generally considered the tradition of the four *maṭha*s founded by Śaṅkara, but I have included the Kanchi Kāmakoṭi Pīṭha and its two living *ācārya*-s. The controversy whether there were four or five major *maṭha*s founded by Śaṅkara continues and does not appear near resolution.[2] I have accepted the tradition of the Kāmakoṭi Pīṭha itself and the judgment of several contemporary scholars who have researched the problem, both convincing me that I should accept the more inclusive tradition. This decision gave me a wider sampling of the Śaṅkara tradition and its major teachers today. Other than these five *maṭha*s and their *ācārya*-s, I have drawn upon several secondary Śaṅkara *maṭha*s in Maharashtra as further testing, but I do not include them within the present study in any substantive way.

The second part of the study is based upon field research that draws upon a range of informants and published materials that pertain to the five reigning Śaṅkarācāryas and the Vidyāpīṭhas under their supervision. I had the opportunity to speak with and

1. Gussner (1976) speculates on the reasons for the large number of hymns attributed to Śaṅkara. He notes the piety and the growing medieval tradition to attribute theistic hymns and *ṣaṇmata* worship to the Advaitin. Gussner believes that medieval India tried to harmonize knowledge and devotion for the sake of national unity which was being threatened by the challenge from Muslim incursions.

2. This is discussed in Chapter Five.

observe five of the major teachers, and to spend time with their students, attendants, *paṇḍita*s, and academicians who are associated with the five centers. My informants also included devotees of the *ācārya*-s from different sectors of Indian society. The published materials that frequently record sermons, lectures, and biographies of the *ācārya*-s are a further resource. This writing is somewhat polemical but reveals how a particular teacher perceives himself and his tradition and how others perceive him. The discourses of the Śaṅkarācāryas, especially those delivered to a wider public, reveal more accurately than most sources the breadth of their personalities. On the other hand, the biographies belong to hagiography and attest more to the devotion and esteem of their authors.

Sanskrit words and proper Indian names and places are employed in this study. I have reduced the use of Sanskrit wherever possible for the ease of a wider readership, and I have used diacritical marks as found in contemporary usage. Regarding geographical sites, I have followed, as consistently as possible, *The Times Atlas of the World*,[1] A list of Abbreviations introduces the study, and I append a Glossary that should overcome any difficulty for the general reader.

I express my appreciation to the many individuals who made this study possible and who have helped to sustain it to completion. My greatest appreciation is extended to the teachers who met with me and who were so gracious to me : His Holiness Jagadguru Śrī Śaṅkarācārya Abhinava Vidyātīrtha of the Sringeri Śāradā Pīṭha; His Holiness Jagadguru Śrī Śaṅkarācārya Candraśekharendra Sarasvatī of the Kanchipuram Kāmakoṭi Pīṭha; His Holiness Jagadguru Śrī Śaṅkarācārya Jayendra Sarasvatī, also of the Kanchipuram Kāmakoṭi Pīṭha; His Holiness Jagadguru Śrī Śaṅkarācārya Abhinava Saccidānanda Tīrtha of the Dwaraka Śāradā Pīṭha; His Holiness Jagadguru Śrī Śaṅkarācārya Śāntānanda Saraswatī of the Jyotirmaṭha, Joshimath.[2] The frankness I met with from the secretaries, attendants, *paṇḍita*s and devotees of the Śaṅkarācāryas made the second part of this study a reality; I sincerely thank them. I also thank Professor T. M. P. Mahadevan and Professor V. A. Devasenapathi of the University of

1. London : Times Newspapers Limited, 1973.

2. For the sake of brevity, the full titles of the Śaṅkarācāryas, as found here, will not be used in study itself.

Madras; Sri V. S. Ramachandra Sastry, Bangalore; Professor M. A. Mehendale and Sri B. M. Deo of Deccan College Post-Graduate Research Institute, Poona; Sri M. D. Bhandare, American Institute of Indian Studies, Poona; the officials and librarians of the Deccan College Post-Graduate Research Institute, the Bhandarkar Oriental Research Institute, the University of Poona, the University of Madras, and the Adyar Library and Research Centre. In the United States, my colleagues in the School of Religious Studies, The Catholic University of America, Washington, D.C., receive special thanks for allowing me time away from university duties to pursue research. Finally, I express gratitude to Dr. Sally Sutherland, Ms. Marianne Sawicki, and Mr. Dennis Doyle for editorial assistance.

In the Upaniṣadic tradition, the first teachers are one's father and mother. Accordingly, I dedicate this book to my father and mother, my first teachers.

LIST OF ABBREVIATIONS

Upaniṣadic sources and the major works of Śaṅkara are cited as noted in the List of Abbreviations. Other Sanskrit sources are generally listed by the first word of the title; works of classical Indian philosophers are preceded by author's name. Secondary sources are cited by the author's last name only (and date of publication for several works by the same author). Full bibliographical information appears in the Bibliography.

Bhagavadgītā	*B. Gītā*
Bṛhadāraṇyaka Upaniṣad	*B. U.*
Chāndogya Upaniṣad	*C. U.*
Kaṭha Upaniṣad	*Kaṭha*
Kena Upaniṣad	*Kena*
Māṇḍūkya Upaniṣad	*Māṇḍ. U.*
Muṇḍaka Upaniṣad	*M. U.*
Śvetāśvatara Upaniṣad	*Śvet. U.*
Taittirīya Upaniṣad	*Tait. U.*
Śaṅkara's *Commentary on the Aitareya Upaniṣad*	S. *Ait. U.*
Śaṅkara's *Aparokṣānubhūti*	S. *Aparok.*
Śaṅkara's *Ātmabodha*	S. *Ātma.*
Śaṅkara's *Commentary on the Bhagavadgītā*	S. *B. Gītā*
Śaṅkara's *Commentary on the Brahma Sūtra*	S. *B. Sūtra.*
Śaṅkara's *Commentary on the Bṛhadāraṇyaka Upaniṣad*	S. *B. U.*
Śaṅkara's *Commentary on Chāndogya Upaniṣad*	S. *C. U.*
Śaṅkara's *Śrī Dakṣiṇāmūrtistotra*	S. *Dakṣiṇ.*
Śaṅkara's *Commentary on the Kaṭha Upaniṣad*	S. *Kaṭha*
Śaṅkara's *Commentary on the Kena Upaniṣad*	S. *Kena*
Śaṅkara's *Commentary on the Māṇḍūkya Upaniṣad*	S. *Mānd. U.*
Śaṅkara's *Commentary on the Māṇḍukyakārikā*	S. *Māṇḍ. Karika.*
Śaṅkara's *Commentary on the Muṇḍaka Upaniṣad*	S. *M. U.*
Śaṅkara's *Commentary on the Praśna Upaniṣad*	S. *Praśna.*
Śaṅkara's *Commentary on the Taittirīya Upaniṣad*	S. *Tait. U.*
Śaṅkara's *Upadeśasāhasrī*	S. *Upadeśa.*
Śaṅkara's *Vivekacūḍāmaṇi*	S. *Viveka.*

PART ONE

THE TRADITION

Chapter One

ANCIENT TRADITION : VEDIC AND UPANIṢADIC ROOTS

Few civilizations possess an educational system as continuous and unmodified throughout history as India's. Education began in India with technical knowledge of language and religious hymns, handed down from father to son. The Brāhmaṇa class studied, transmitted and preserved in an unaltered form the wisdom of the past. It is believed that, in ancient times, a quarter of Indian society was involved in this form of higher study. An early text traces the line of teachers who had transmitted the sacred lore back to the creator-god Prajāpati.[1] The learned tradition of ancient India was preserved by an unbroken succession of teachers.

In ancient times, the transmission of learning was oral. Teachers repeated to their students texts that they themselves had received orally. In the whole of Vedic literature there is no reference to writing because that literature was transmitted entirely by word of mouth. The oral transmission of the sacred literature continued longer in India than in any other civilization. Although writing was known by about 800 B.C.E. and the Sanskrit alphabet and grammatical principles took written form by 500 B.C.E., still India reserved writing for commerce and trading. No prejudice existed against the written word except for scriptural literature. Writing became an art for the non-Vedic literary tradition in the early years of the common era. Palm leaves were in use by 200 C.E., and leaves dating from 600 C.E. are still extant. Later religious literature explicitly forbids the writing down of the Veda. The *Mahābhārata*, for example, condemns to hell anyone who would write the Veda; the *Nārada Smṛti* claims flatly that learning the Veda from a book, unlike learning it from a teacher, is utterly worthless.[2] Sāyaṇa quotes the adage that the text must be learned from the lips of a teacher and not from a manuscript because religious education takes

1. *Śatapatha Brāhmaṇa* X.6.5.9.
2. Mookerji, p. 27.

place through hearing and memorizing sacred wisdom. Kumārila Bhaṭṭa (eighth century C.E.) describes the writing of the Veda as sacrilege. For him, to learn the Veda from written sources is equal to not comprehending it.[1] The oral transmission of the Veda continued into the eleventh and twelfth centuries C.E. before the texts were commonly committed to writing, but it is believed that Vasukra, a Kashmiri, first wrote out the Veda in the eighth or ninth century C.E.

The hymns of the *Ṛgveda* are now classified according to families of authors. Each unit of the *Ṛgveda* authored by a particular family possesses a significant homogeneity of authorship. While there existed no system that could be identified with a single teacher, the poets and philosophers of India's earliest religious literature did achieve a marked individuality. The religious preferences of each family of authors can be detected in the hymns by their references to cult deities and by peculiarities in ritual and prayer. Each family guarded its oral tradition with great secrecy as a sort of family inheritance. Some of the Vedic authors were domestic priests, and it is in their families especially that the process of generation-to-generation transmission arose. Although 407 authors of the *Ṛgveda* have been traced,[2] all the collections were brought together and collated, orally, by 1100 B.C.E.[3]

Thereafter, it was incumbent on the priestly class to commit the whole of Vedic literature to memory in order to ensure its transmission. It took from twelve to twenty-four years to completely master a particular text. Consequently, most education was repetitive, and oral tradition was transmitted by means of recitation and repetition. The *Ṛgveda* mentions the monotonous repetition in education and compares it to the croaking of frogs excited by an approaching rain.[4] Since recitation was regulated by meter, the early seers placed value in the sounds of syllables, words and phrases. The success of the oral tradition rested upon faith in the efficacy of sacred words. I-Tsing, one of the first Chinese intellectuals to visit India, writes : "There are two tradi-

1. *Tantra Vārttika* 1.3.
2. Confer Rahurkar; also Kunhan Raja.
3. Keay, pp. 12-14.
4. *Ṛgveda* VII.103. It is estimated that one-fifth of the *Ṛgveda* is repetitive.

tional ways in India of attaining to intellectual power : committing to memory; and the alphabet fixes one's ideas."[1] Religious knowledge in the ancient tradition is first heard; scripture (śruti) is knowledge heard by the Vedic sages. The *Ṛgveda* speaks of education as hearing and repeating another's language.[2] Although ancient Indian education consisted basically in memorization, education without understanding is held up to ridicule in the Veda. Effective learning, for Kauṭilya, author of the *Arthaśāstra*, is progressive : "From hearing ensues knowledge; from knowledge steady application is possible; and from application, a self-possession (*ātmanvatā*) is possible. This is what is meant by efficiency in learning."[3] The vehicle of this entire process is the teacher.

Teaching was a religious duty placed upon the Brāhmaṇa class. The creation of a hereditary class of teachers enabled Indian civilization to make vast strides in education. In early times, the teachers usually were householders who took no fees for their task; they understood themselves to be fulfilling their personal *dharma* as they transmitted the sacred heritage. Settlements of Brāhmaṇa teachers became the basis of the educational system. The teachers frequently were called together into assemblies in order to maintain purity of knowledge and integrity in transmission. The *Dharmaśāstra* and the *Gṛhya Sūtras* lay down rules for the teacher, rules minute in detail. The professional teacher often became a functionary in the government. The *Arthaśāstra* ranks the preceptor (*ācārya*) as second in the king's cabinet, followed by the priest, the military commander, the heir-apparent, the queen-mother and finally the queen, in that order.[4] From the time of Aśoka, a priest was the cabinet adviser in religious duty, and in later centuries a priest served as minister of education and religion.[5]

Various types of teachers existed in ancient India; guru, *ācārya*, and *upādhyāya* were common types. The guru, after performing

1. *I-Tsing*, quoted in Keay, p. 101
2. *Ṛgveda* VII.103.
3. *Arthaśāstra*, quoted in Keay, p. 65.
4. Confer Patwardhan, p. 45.
5. By the 11th cent. C.E., the minister of education and religion was a recognized institution in India. The *purohita* in the cabinet of King Bhoja was ranked second, following the royal preceptor (*rājaguru*).

various rites, gave instruction in the Veda; the *ācārya* initiated a student through the *upanayana* rite and instructed in any one or possibly each Veda. The *upādhyāya*, although frequently called the first-teacher along with a student's father and mother, was a secondary sort of teacher because he taught only a portion of the Veda and took a fee for his instruction.[1]

An early hymn describes a student bringing firewood and alms to the home of the teacher, an action that signified the youth's desire to become a student and to participate in domestic ritual.[2] The rite of *upanayana*, which literally means "leading towards," suggests the student's approach to the teacher. More specifically, the teacher holds "the pupil within him as in a womb, impregnates him with his spirit, and delivers him in a new birth." A ritual text states : "The teacher lays his right hand on the head of the pupil whereby he becomes pregnant with him (*tena garbhī bhavati*), and then in the third night the embryo issues out of the teacher and (the pupil) being taught the Sāvitrī obtains true Brahmanhood."[3] Although knowledge was open to all classes, *śūdra*-s and women alike, only the young of the upper three social classes were permitted and obliged to undergo the *upanayana* rite, which introduced a youth to Vedic study. In this rite, the youth announces to the teacher, "Let me be a student." The teacher replies, "What is your name ?" Taking the student's right hand, he says, "You are Indra's disciple; Agni is your teacher; I am your teacher." He then commits him to the cosmos : "To Prajāpati I commit you; to the God Savitṛ I commit you. . . . to the waters, to the plants, to the heaven and earth I commit you. . . . to all beings I commit you for protection from injury. You are a brahmacārī . . . sip water, sip ambrosia . . . do your work . . . . put on fuel . . . .do not sleep." Enclosing him on both sides with ambrosia, the teacher then recites the sacred Gāyatrī

1. An *upādhyāya* is one who taught for a living; a female preceptor or the wife of a teacher are also referred to by this word. The tradition abounds in other names for teacher : *adhvānka* is a preceptor or instructor of sacred knowledge; *prādhyāpaka* is a seasoned teacher instructing advanced students and other teachers; *pravaktā* is a generic word for teacher or guru; *prācārya* is a retired teacher. Confer Mitra, pp. 16-17.

2. *Atharvaveda* XI.5.

3. *Śatapatha Brāhmaṇa* XI.5.4., quoted in Mookerji, pp. 91-92.

mantra.[1] From this moment, education is based on *brahmacarya.* Studentship implies consistent association with the teacher.

In ancient India, according to the Veda, the student would live in the home of the teacher for twelve years; some advanced students frequently remained with the teacher until they were twenty-five years old. The *Ṛgveda* says that the decision to admit a student (*śiṣya*)[2] is to be made by the teacher according to the simple criterion of moral fitness. Later literature, however, heightens considerably the qualifications of the prospective student.[3] Begging alms for the teacher, tending the ritual fire and meeting his daily needs are mentioned as conditions based upon a sense of service to the teacher expressed in thought, word and deed.[4] Although residence in the home of the teacher was common, day students also were admitted. By living an intimate life with the teacher, a youth began to imbibe the method of the teacher, the secret of his efficacy and the spirit of his life and work. At the core of the educational system in ancient India, therefore, was the living relationship established between teacher and student.

It was left to the discretion of the teacher to judge the capacity of the pupil and to set out a course of study. At the primary level, education consisted in phonetics and the logical science of grammar. These impressed upon the youth from the beginning the importance of method, order and principles, organized into a system. While there existed much rote recitation, in which intonation, accent and pronunciation of the teacher were imitated, nevertheless the etymology of words and the interpretation of texts

1. Ibid. The Gāyatrī *mantra* is the most sacred verse of the *Ṛgveda* and is addressed to the sun god Savitṛ. Only the twice-born may utter this verse and should do so in the mandatory daily prayers. Other than the ceremony of initiation, it is used in the marriage ritual.

2. *Śiṣya* signifies any student; *śaikṣa* is a student who has just begun study of the Veda, a novice; *vidyārthī* is a student-scholar who desires further learning. Confer Mitra, p. 16.

3. *Manu* II.149 ff. According to Manu, the teacher selects the following types for studentship : the son of one's own teacher; one who does personal service; one who teaches some other subject; a good man; a pure man in mind and heart; a reliable friend, one capable of comprehending and applying knowledge once acquired; a patron; a recluse.

4. The student's daily life was rigorous with early rising, prayer, regulations of dress, food and sleep, celibacy, and moral and mental disciplines. Confer Kumar Das, pp. 76 ff.

were also stressed. In the Vedic scheme of education, phonetics and metre are to be taught by simple recitation; grammar and etymology initiate understanding; astronomy and ceremonial, completing the primary curriculum, are applied to practical ritual. From this core curriculum other subjects develop. Education is regarded as a means and never as a goal in itself. The goal of classical education is far beyond mere mastery of a curriculum. The formation of character and the development of personality are the primary objectives. The preservation of tradition and the performance of religious and social duties are secondary goals.[1]

Since every student was duty-bound to honor the teacher as one honored a father and mother, the teacher had to cultivate in the student an esteem and love for knowledge. In ancient India, education was called *vidyā*, a word whose root meaning connotes five distinct perceptions: knowledge, reality, attainment, discrimination and sublime emotion. *Vidyā* is any knowledge, science, learning, lore or philosophy that formed character and developed individual personality. Knowledge is traditionally spoken of as the third eye that unleashes insight into all life and human activity. In worldly affairs, knowledge leads to progress and prosperity; in the affairs of religion it leads to spiritual liberation and release.[2] Not only does the individual mature in knowledge, but also knowledge is experienced as a living power within the cosmos as within the human person. The traditional Indian teacher who establishes a youth in knowledge is transmitting, it is believed, an ancient and frequently eternal knowledge. There is a classical axiom in this vein that indicates that the status of the teacher is higher in India than in most civilizations : "A king is worshipped in his own kingdom, but a learned man is worshipped everywhere."

The Teacher in the Upaniṣads

Although early Indian literature reveals a brilliant lineage of individual teachers, little is known of their personal histories. The teacher was an educational leader at the inception of India's ancient history, but for the seers of the *Upaniṣads* he becomes both an intellectual and a spiritual figure. In fact, scripture (*śruti*) and the later Vedānta tradition define the teacher in terms

1. Altekar, pp. 326 ff.
2. Mitra, pp. vii ff, 34 ff.

of both dimensions, while revered literature (*smṛti*) emphasizes the spiritual component of the teacher's role almost exclusively.

The two sides of the teacher's identity are expressed in the principal Upaniṣadic definitions of the teacher. The *Muṇḍaka Upaniṣad* describes the teacher (guru) as one versed in Veda and absorbed in Brahman.[1] One who has heard the Veda and more specifically has heard the meaning of the Veda fulfills the intellectual aspect, while one who stands in Brahman fulfills the spiritual dimension of teacher. A teacher, according to the Upaniṣads, is a self-realised person whose realisation has come through the wisdom of the Vedic tradition. This is the basic perception of the teacher to be found in Upaniṣadic literature. The esteem given to the guru in the Indian tradition grows out of this initial conception of the teacher as both a knower of Brahman and a dweller in Brahman.

The Upaniṣads depict teachers steeped in knowledge of Brahman (*brahmavidyā*) who possess an exclusive wisdom, which originated long ago in the experiences of particular sages who then established a custodianship over it and passed it on to their pupils. Those pupils, in turn, began a lineage in a specific type of knowledge (*vidyā*).[2] Religious knowledge is to be sought only from a teacher who has mastered it and who has made it a part of his own life. A significant portion of early Indian literature is enigmatic; namely, it is a *sūtra* literature that lends itself to the skill and imagination of the teacher.[3] The early teachers sharp-

1. *M.U.* 1.2.12., *śrotriyam brahmaniṣṭham*. *Śrotriyam* : proficient or versed in the Veda; teachable; a learned Brāhmaṇa, well versed in sacred learning (confer Apte, p. 934). It comes from the Sanskrit root *śru*, to hear, which is the distinctive feature of Upaniṣadic and Vedāntic education. *Brahmaniṣṭham*, literally, is one who stands in Brahman, that is, one who has fully realised Brahman; it comes from the Sanskrit root *sthā*, to stand, which implies to dwell, live, abide, exist in a particular state (confer Apte, p. 1007). The *Bhagavad Gītā* reiterates this notion (*B. Gītā* 2.54 ff); *Kaṭha* 2.7-8, implies the same. Confer Sarmah, pp. 87-108 for the place of the teacher in Upaniṣadic education.

2. *Brahmavidyā* is the science of understanding Brahman. *Vidyā* is from the verbal root *vid* (to know, to understand, to feel, to experience, to teach, to expound) and is understood as knowledge or learning in the sense of a science, especially a religious science (confer Apte, pp. 856-857). It corresponds to Greek wisdom and the Christian scholastic notion of theology.

3. *Sūtra* literature is aphoristic, brief catch-words which leave the teacher

ened their skills in debates and in the larger discussions for which numbers of them would gather. A ritual text cites a discussion between two teachers, one of whom was found to be poorly versed in a particular area of learning. That teacher closed his classes, dismissed the students and began to study and master the subject in which he was weak before he returned to teach.[1] But the teacher described in the Upaniṣads is no mere intellectual. He is a spiritual figure as well. Since teaching was a religious duty in India, the teacher from early times was looked upon as a spiritual leader. The wisdom of a particular lineage and the teacher himself who mediated it were sources of personal transformation, illumination and power to others. The very sight of a learned man was believed to be sacred, because he possessed salvific knowledge; he was a transformed individual, a realised person. Teachers thus occupied a special place in Indian society as masters of sacred wisdom.

The *Chāndogya Upaniṣad* speaks of the teacher as one who removes the bandages from the eyes and gives direction.[2] By the end of the Upaniṣadic period, the role of the teacher had become an absolutely essential one, so that sacred wisdom required a teacher for its transmission. The teacher became indispensable once the difficulty of attaining knowledge of Brahman and self-realisation by oneself was openly admitted. In the early Veda, it seems relatively easy to reach Brahman, because symbols of the Absolute are of a ritual nature. With the decline of ritual in the later Upaniṣadic texts, the Absolute is discussed in more negative terms; the merely suggestive and enigmatic formulations of the sages indicate that Brahman was understood to be more difficult of access. Self-realisation, therefore, was difficult to attain and called for a teacher in relationship with a qualified student. In the latest Upaniṣads, liberation is virtually impossible without the knowledge and grace of the guru. It is heard in India today that the importance given to the *alma mater* in modern times was given to the guru in ancient times. As the

the task of amplifying the meaning and applying it to the conditions of the time and the circumstances of the pupil. For complete understanding, *sūtra* literature is dependent upon a tradition for transmission of meaning.

1. *Gopatha Brāhmaṇa* 1.1.31.
2. *C.U.*VI.XIV.1.

Upaniṣads move from ritualism to mysticism, the necessity of the teacher and the consequent reverence for him increase, since liberation depends more and more upon the knowledge he transmits. The Brāhmaṇas, who were the primary ritualists of early Vedic society, became a teacher class in the Upaniṣads.

Although Upaniṣadic literature contains cosmological, moral, mystical and metaphysical insights and approaches, the psychological cultivation of the individual for self-realisation distinguishes the Upaniṣads from every other body of Indian literature. The liberation of the mind is the goal of Upaniṣadic education. Since self-realisation is principally a psychological reality and achievement, the necessity of a preceptor becomes doubly important. R. K. Mookerji, India's most significant historian of education, has said that "the guru takes the place of what Freud defines as the Super-Ego of the individual pupil, i.e., the embodiment of the ideals and traditions in which he is brought up."[1] The Upaniṣads highlight the absolute position of the guru not only for the liberation of the individual but also for the psychological growth of the human person.

During the times when the Upaniṣads were composed, teachers could be both householders and ascetics. In contemporary Jain and Buddhist education, however, only an ascetic (*sannyāsī*) might be a teacher; this became the general rule by the end of the Upaniṣadic period. The teacher of sacred wisdom usually transcended social class, and Upaniṣadic teachers were confined neither to the Brāhmaṇa class nor to ascetical life. For example, Gārgī and Maitreyī, two women, take part in spiritual discourses; another woman, Umā, gives spiritual direction. One teacher is called *mahāśāla*, a great householder, to signify his eminent place in social affairs. During the Upaniṣadic era, the environment for teaching was the home, which implies both domestic context and personnel. Some teachers were kings like Janaka. Yājñavalkya, who has been the model of the ideal teacher since early times, was a householder who instructed his wife and others. He exemplifies a major characteristic of the guru, namely, to teach fully, holding nothing back. Although different teachers use different methods, the authentic guru holds nothing in reserve; he teaches all that he knows and experiences. According to the texts, Yājñavalkya ex-

1. Mookerji, p. xxviii.

posed principles relentlessly until understanding took place. These early teachers, though their teaching was frequently obscure and esoteric, were not part of a closed society. There was no bar to a free exchange of ideas even among the teachers themselves. Above all, they were concerned for the lineage of sacred wisdom and the necessity of its transmission. The *Taittirīya Upaniṣad* imparts a final instruction from the teacher to his pupil with the admonition : "Do not cut off the line of progeny."[1] One who advances the tradition to another generation is a true teacher. Self-realised individuals experience this imperative.

Every religious seeker had to have an instructor in the scriptures. "One who has a teacher knows," for "only knowledge as acquired from a teacher is best," observes the sage of *Chāndogya Upaniṣad.*[2] Ordinarily, a youth would approach a teacher early in life. Great importance is given to the student's approach to the teacher. The *Muṇḍaka Upaniṣad* instructs students to meet the teacher "with sacrificial fuel in hand" and confidence that "this one will certainly tell us about Brahman."[3] The proper approach to the teacher is crucial, for if the preceptor refuses to accept the youth and teach him sacred wisdom, there is usually no other way for him to gain it. The first stage in religious education is the acceptance of the student in the *upanayana* ceremony, by which he begins a life of *brahmacarya.* In ancient times this ceremony was open to both male and female youths. The *upanayana* rite in classical Hinduism is not only initiation into formal education but also introduction into knowledge of Brahman. Through the *upanayana* rite and *brahmacarya* the student pledges himself to the guru and to the path of self-realisation. A life of learning and discipline is begun. The learning, however, would frequently be postponed until service to the teacher was firmly established and a high level of discipline was acquired. Upakosala tends the ritual fires of his teacher and performs religious austerities for twelve years before Satyakāma-Jābāla will impart religious instruction to him.[4] A more reasonable time is prescribed by the

1. *Tait.* U. I.XI.1.
2. *C.U.* VI.XIV.2; IV.IX.3; confer Sarmah, pp. 123-140, for the place of the student in Upaniṣadic education.
3. *M.U.* I.II.12; *Praśna* U. I.1.
4. *C.U.* IV.X.2-3; *C.U.* IV.IV.5.

sage of the *Praśna Upaniṣad* : "Live here for a year in a fitting manner, with control over the senses and with *brahmacarya* and faith. Then put questions as you please. If we know, we shall explain all your questions."[1]

One of the most decisive factors for the acceptance or rejection of a student during Upaniṣadic times was to establish his eligibility (*adhikāra*) for instruction in sacred wisdom.[2] Eligibility means the presence of superior moral qualifications which one needs in order to perform specific duties and to pursue self-realisation. Until a high level of moral and psychological discipline is acquired, one is not fit for the sacred wisdom of Veda. The *Muṇḍaka Upaniṣad*, more specifically, requires a ceremonial approach to the guru, a calm heart and control of the senses, personal discipline, and finally that one be versed in the Veda already and devoted to Brahman.[3] The guru, having satisfied himself that the prospective student meets all these requirements, is to ask several questions concerning family, class and self-understanding in order to determine the level of competency. The preceptor can either admit or reject a student, or admit him provisionally but withhold advanced knowledge until he is assured of the student's competency.

The *Taittirīya Upaniṣad* begins with a discussion of the comprehensive development of the student; this Upaniṣad above all others fully outlines the integral cultivation of the religious student. Upaniṣadic spirituality means growth toward self-realisation. It is based upon a gradual development of fundamental human qualities. For a youth to be qualified, his parents should be versed in the Veda and should perform specific rites. A qualified father, mother and guru are the three gifts due to the grace of God. With this background, the youth then detaches himself from progeny, property and even spiritual satisfaction. He begins

1. *Praśna U*, I.2.

2. *Adhi* in the adjectival sense (*adhika*) is a superlative indicating more, greater, surpassing in quantity, copious, abundant; *adhikṛ* means to authorize, to qualify for the discharge of some duty, to be entitled to a right; *adhikāra* in its primary sense is to watch over and superintend religious matters and secondarily a duty, office or charge because of right, authority, privilege or title. It implies the presence of qualifications in order to perform specific duties. Confer Apte, pp. 43-44.

3. *M. U.* I.II.13, III.II.10; *Śvet. U.* 6.XXII.23.

the life of a mendicant and ascetic.[1] A list of qualifications for discipleship can be compiled from these early texts : truthfulness in speech, following one's *dharma* in conduct, religious disciplines (*tapas*), dedication to study, and respect for parents, teachers and guests. These qualities result from faith and a desire to understand. Self-realisation, for the early seers, is due not only to understanding but also to a life of purification and penance. After watching the conduct and determining the caliber of the student for some months, the guru normally begins instruction. The Tantras, however, speak of a period of five to thirty-two years before secret and esoteric doctrine is transmitted.[2] For the Upaniṣadic tradition, instruction begins much sooner. But once begun, education continues for at least twenty-five years among the more committed religious seekers.[3]

The duties of the student show how close his association with the teacher should be. To render service to the teacher is the primary obligation of the student, seemingly more important than study itself. Through service a strong bond is established between the guru and the student. The interior disciplines of self-restraint and self-denial, calm and patience, recollection and silence are cultivated. The vow of celibacy is to be observed rigorously and universally among students. Sacrifice, study and charity are the ideals. The pupil must have intellectual discipline to master the meaning of sacred texts; growth in moral discipline brings the meaning of the sacred texts into the student's daily life.

The qualifications a student must fulfil and his consequent duties gradually will bring about an introversion, a catharsis, and a capacity for greater personal experience.[4] Naciketas is mentioned as the ideal religious seeker in the Upaniṣads. He is characterized as one who through mounting catharsis achieves extraordinary intellectual experience. Upaniṣadic wisdom calls for the student to look within himself for dominion over sense life; a new direction is given to human life. A call for a change

1. *B.U.* III.V.1.
2. Mitra, p. 54.
3. In Buddhism a young monk is required to choose a *bhikkhu*, a monk who is a full member of the order as his teacher (upajjhāya). Their relationship usually grows into a father-son relationship; the association of the two monks usually lasts for ten years.
4. Ranade (1926), p. 328.

of life takes place. As the student confines himself to association with the teacher and pursues the cultivation of his personality, a new life emerges. In the Upaniṣadic view of the educational process, the teacher is the source and context of this new life.

The Guru-Śiṣya Relationship

The living relationship between guru and student (*śiṣya*) is looked upon as the source of true education. The educational goals of the teacher-student relationship were shaped by the cultural context of Vedic India and the Upaniṣadic period. The *gurukula* system made the student a member of the teacher's family, which stimulated the youth to intellectual growth. The association with the teacher was a source of both moral and spiritual development. Not only did the student experience the heritage of language, literature, ritual and the training of memory, but also he experienced the teacher as a transmitter of knowledge. He participated in transmission to the degree that he entered into a personal relationship with the guru. A spiritual relationship was the highest ideal of both the religious seeker and the guru. Their relationship lead to wisdom. The *Taittirīya Upaniṣad* states : "The teacher is the first letter. The student is the last letter. Knowledge is the meeting-place. Instruction is the link."[1]

The basic attitude toward knowledge is what determines the nature of the teacher-student relationship. The Upaniṣads contain multiple paths of knowledge, but only the path of *brahmavidyā* (knowledge of Brahman) elicits a salvific relationship between teacher and pupil.[2] The preparatory discipline and service on the part of the student are foundational for the relationship; by requiring competency, the guru prepares for a relationship wherein knowledge is gained. The desire of the religious seeker and the commitment of the guru to guide him toward self-realisation draw upon the effort of each in forming the relationship.

A filial relationship is the basis for growth. From the perspective of the teacher, the *gurukula* system meant filial care of the student. Both Hindu and Buddhist teachers of this period in

1. *Tait. U.* I.III.3. Confer Sarmah, pp. 141-145, for the student-teacher relationship in Upaniṣadic education.

2. Mukhopadhyaya, pp. 41 ff. Over seventeen *vidyā*-s are listed in this place from the *C.U.* and *B.U.* principally.

Indian history cultivated filiality. From Vedic times, he who imparted the Gāyatrī *mantra* was regarded as father, and the *mantra* itself was looked upon as mother. The tenor of this filial relationship between teacher and student reflects the traditional esteem with which both father and mother were regarded as teachers of their children. The most ancient literature was first transmitted from father to son, and the Upaniṣads also give evidence that spiritual wisdom was passed on from father to son. When Bhṛgu, the son of Varuṇa, approaches his father for knowledge of Brahman, the value of the knowledge imparted is heightened because it passes from father to son.[1] A moving passage relates a dying father's final instruction to his son, in which he urges the son to take up the teaching duty and its accompanying burden in his place.[2] The son becomes an embodiment of both the father and the teaching tradition. The concept of the teacher's spiritual fatherhood is common to all the religious traditions of India, but the Upaniṣads, with their philosophical orientation, achieve a balance between intellectual and spiritual fatherhood. The filial relationship usually built up a strong human bond as well, so that the friendship between teacher and student continued even after the completion of studies. There was no remuneration for spiritual teaching. Teacher and pupil both regarded themselves as being in debt to the ancient seers and the heritage, and they paid this debt by constantly pursuing wisdom even after the years of formal education. Filiality was a spiritual reality and a religious duty eliciting life-long effort.

The invocatory and valedictory prayers found in the Upaniṣads give some insight into the quality of the teacher-student relationship. A typical invocation calls repeatedly upon Brahmā for the protection of guru and student : "Of the perceptible Brahman will I speak. I will speak of the Right. I will speak of the True; may that protect me; may that protect the speaker. Let that

1. *Tait. U.* III.I.1.

2. *B.U.* I.V.17 : "When a father who knows departs from this world, he penetrates his son with the organ of speech, the mind and the vital force. Should anything be left undone by him through any slip, the son exonerates him from all that. Therefore he is called a son. The father lives in this world through the son. Divine and immortal speech, mind and vital force permeate him."

protect me; let that protect the speaker."[1] A prayer may end an Upaniṣad with a view toward removing faults which teacher or student may have committed inadvertently during the course of instruction. The *Kaṭha Upaniṣad* ends : "May He protect us both. May we attain vigour together. Let what we study be invigorating. May we not cavil at each other."[2] Such common prayers point to a relationship even more profound than filial association. The teacher-student relationship presents the possibility of intimate union and at its highest stage identification. The *Taittirīya Upaniṣad*, the most significant text for identifying the nature of the teaching tradition, implies a type of union between guru and student : "May we both attain fame together. May spiritual eminence be vouchsafed to both of us together."[3] This verse is from a prayer of a student who desires to establish more intimate association with his preceptor. In the Hindu tradition there is no intervening factor between guru and *śiṣya*. The guru is the source of knowledge that leads to self-realisation. There is no other medium.

In the Upaniṣadic view of the educational process, the teacher tries to evoke in his student the sort of experience that previously liberated the teacher himself. By evoking a corresponding experience, the guru gently transforms the disciple into one like himself. At its end the teaching process leads to identity between the participants. After the pupil achieves self-realisation, he and the teacher stand as equals. This advanced moment is foreshadowed from the very beginning of their association, in the formula the teacher uses as he admits the student to education. The formula raises up an ideal which the early seers strove to realise : "Your heart shall dwell in my heart; my mind shall follow your mind; my word you shall rejoice in with all your heart; to me alone you shall adhere; in me your thoughts shall dwell; upon me your veneration shall bend; when I speak you shall be silent."[4]

1. *Tait. U.* I.I.1; I.XII.1.
2. *Kaṭha U.* II.III.19. This verse is not contained in all editions of the *Kaṭha U.*
3. *Tait. U.* I.III.1. This prayer, observes Śaṅkara, is only appropriate for the student since the teacher has already achieved fulfilment.
4. *Hiraṇyakeśī Dharmasūtra* i,2,5,11, quoted in Mookerjii, p. 181.

It is axiomatic in Indian thought that the grace of God and the grace of the guru are one and the same for the graced disciple. Although only the late Upaniṣads, for example the *Śvetāśvatara*, clearly stress devotion (*bhakti*) and a grace tradition, many instances among earlier texts imply the favor of the guru. Self-realisation is said to occur by one's following the instruction and grace of the teacher. Since the teacher dwells in Brahman and is identified with Brahman, he becomes an immediate source of favor.[1] The *Śvetāśvatara Upaniṣad* along with *smṛti* literature explicitly looks upon the guru as God. Meditation is made upon either the guru or God; for this purpose they are interchangeable. The teacher in the *Śvetāśvatara Upaniṣad* is exalted to the point of worship.[2] Because the teacher loves Brahman while dwelling in Brahman, the student reciprocates with devotion toward the preceptor and this devotion is usually expressed in an extraordinary manner. The later devotional tradition in the epics, Purāṇas and medieval poets emphasizes the love relationship. The love relationship stands behind the service which the Upaniṣads describe as being rendered by the devotee to the guru. Even in Vedic times, the student's service to his teacher and the forming of a filial relationship became the basis for a love relationship. However, since the early sages took a more intellectual direction than those of later Hinduism, they neither stressed nor developed a love relationship. Self-realisation was achieved through intellectual disciplines, and intellectual discrimination became the general pedagogy of the Upaniṣads. Knowledge and austerity predominate in spiritual training and the teacher-pupil relationship. Nonetheless, total dependence upon the guru—developed because of the difficulty of achieving salvific knowledge alone—is conducive to a love relationship. In the later Upaniṣads, dependence is given to God, but the intellectual and psychological quality of the guru-*śiṣya* relationship is retained throughout the early period.

The *Bṛhadāraṇyaka Upaniṣad* recounts the extraordinary story of a competition called among the great teachers to which Yājñavalkya, the exemplar of all teachers, sends his pupil.[3] The

1. Confer *M.U.* III.II.9.
2. *Śvet. U.* VI.23.
3. *B.U.* III.I.5.

story hinges on the fact that Yājñavalkya identifies himself with his student. Upaniṣadic thought implies that once a religious seeker achieves self-realisation, he is equal to his guru. A relationship of perfect equality in wisdom and realisation is the final goal of this tradition. The later Vedānta tradition will make much of this factor, which these early texts pass over lightly. Buddhist tradition speaks more explicitly of equality between teacher and pupil in its early scripture.[1]

After self-realisation, the teacher is not forgotten. The necessity to keep alive the lineage is foremost in the mind of the newly liberated individual. An early text warns : "Do not teach one who will not himself teach."[2] The new adept is conscious of both his former teacher and the imperative to advance the heritage. Offering a final instruction to his student, one preceptor says : "Speak the truth. Practice righteousness. Make no mistake about study. Having offered the desirable wealth to the teacher, do not cut off the line of progeny. Do not be careless about learning and teaching."[3] The history of the tradition has shown that when the relationship between preceptor and disciple is vibrant, lineage is maintained and in many cases significantly enhanced.

Pedagogy in the Upaniṣads

The relationship between teacher and student arises from a specific pedagogy in spiritual development. Two parallel strands can be identified in this developmental process, beginning in the *Ṛgveda* with its multiform world-views and approaches to reality. The most common was the way of sacrifice and worship (*karmakāṇḍa*), and the other was the way of meditation and ascetical discipline (*jñānakāṇḍa*). Both traditions—sacrifice (*yajña*) and ascetical discipline ((*tapas*)—were received by subsequent ages. *Tapas* has a range of meaning, for it implies the pursuit and realisation of

1. Alāra Kalāma, the Buddha's teacher, says : "The doctrine which I know, you too know, and the doctrine which you know I too know. As I am so are you, as you are so am I. Pray, Sir, let us be joint wardens of this company." The Buddha replied : "In such wise did Alāra Kalāma, being my master, set himself on precisely the same footing as me." *Ariya-parivesana Sutta*, quoted in Altekar, p. 73.
2. *Aitareya Āraṇyaka* III.2. 6.
3. *Tait. U.* I.XI.1.

the highest truth not only through ascetical practice but also through concentration and meditation. The Upaniṣadic tradition drew upon *jñānakāṇḍa* in developing an educational method that brought about knowledge of the Self (*ātman*). This was no mere rejection of Vedic sacrifice, but rather its fulfilment and finally its transcendence in the pursuit of self-knowledge.

Ascetical discipline and the *upanayana* rite prepare the way in the student for a new method of achieving wisdom. Without preparation, the pursuit of knowledge is nothing but idle curiosity. The goal of education, for the Upaniṣads, cannot be mere intellectual knowledge achieved through reasoning and study : "That (Brahman) is surely different from the known; and again, It is above the unknown."[1] The Upaniṣads specifically claim that logic and argumentation do not achieve wisdom,[2] but the "Self (*ātman*) reveals Its own nature."[3] Pedagogy only creates the conditions wherein wisdom emerges by the strength of its own nature.

The different objects of knowledge (*vidyā-s*) discovered by the Upaniṣadic sages, representing a diversity of preference and attitudes, inspire a variety of approaches. A wide range of literary methods is employed : the enigmatic, the aphoristic, the etymological, the analogical, the dialogical and the monological.[4] The *Īśā Upaniṣad* exemplifies enigmatic pedagogy, with its use of oppostion, knowledge and non-knowledge (*vidyā-avidyā*), and skepticism. The enigma may point to a synthesis of opposites that transcends the verbal contradiction, but it need not necessarily do so. The *Māṇḍūkya Upaniṣad* and the later *sūtra* literature of the philosophical schools abound in aphorisms that are open to a wide range of interpretation. Etymological arguments, which became popular among later commentators, also occur in the Upaniṣads. Analogy is frequently employed to advance the process of self-discovery. The dialogical method is used constantly throughout every stage of Upaniṣadic development. Yājñavalkya employs it every time he engages in discourse. The soliloquy is usually contrasted with dialogue. After the initial

1. *Kena* I.4.
2. *Kaṭha* I.II.9.
3. *M.U.* III.II.3; *Kaṭha* II.23. Confer Sarmah, p. 54.
4. Mukhopadhyaya, pp. 41 ff.; Ranade (1926), pp. 34 ff; also confer Sen, pp. 111 ff.

dialogue of Yama and Naciketas, for instance, an eloquent monologue on the nature of reality unfolds. A variation on the dialogical method that might be termed regressive discourse can also be identified, where there is a series of questions and each new question probes behind the answer of the previous one.[1] These diverse literary methods entail different approaches to reality, for reality may be understood from a metaphysical, a cosmological, a psychological or a mystical perspective. The student is imbued with his preceptor's own particular literary method and particular understanding of reality.

The Upaniṣads employ both analytic and synthetic approaches to pedagogical practice (and to meditational practice, as will be seen later). The *Bṛhadāraṇyaka Upaniṣad* offers the clearest example of analytic method in this body of literature as it pursues discrimination (*viveka*) verse upon verse; on the other hand, the *Chāndogya Upaniṣad*, which draws upon a galaxy of methods, follows a more synthetic approach to teaching. Both approaches may appear in one and the same Upaniṣad, indicating that both could be called on at a particular moment. The diversity of methods indicates the diversity of teaching traditions in this single body of literature. Few teachers were able to master multiple methods, but they did become specialists with expertise in one or several methods. The teaching tradition was still an open field during the Upaniṣadic era, so that teachers freely shared and perfected their methods among themselves.

The unique contribution that the Upaniṣads make to educational method in religious development is the three-fold operation of hearing (*śravaṇa*), reflecting (*manana*), and concentrating (*nididhyāsana*). This is the new pedagogy that follows upon purification and the *upanayana* rite, both of which originated in an earlier period. Yājñavalkya tells Maitreyī, his wife, "By the realisation of the Self, my dear, through hearing, reflecting and meditation, all this is known,"[2] and he then proceeds to lead her through these three stages. The process of hearing, reflection and concentration is not defined with precision in these texts; the application is left to the individual teacher. The later philosophical and yoga traditions give precision—and varying meaning—to these terms.

1. *B.U.* IV.3; *Śvet.* U. II.
2. *B.U.* II.IV.5.

The Upaniṣads share a general understanding of the three moments of the educational process. Hearing (*śravaṇa*) comes through the agency of the teacher, for it consists in listening to and receiving oral tradition.[1] This is instruction in its most basic sense. Reflection (*manana*) is intense deliberation over the meaning of the truths heard, to such a degree that truth is appropriated by the individual. This second moment grasps the meaning of Upaniṣadic texts through intellectual apprehension and reasoning. It is sometimes understood as discursive meditation (*dhyāna*). The third step, concentration (*nididhyāsana*), is described as advanced meditation; it is a unitive stage of understanding. *Nididhyāsana* is not a mental process like ordinary meditation (which entails reflecting, imaging and analysis), but simply concentration upon the meaning of the great Upaniṣadic axioms. Paradoxical as it may seem, hearing, reflection and concentration are independent of self-realisation, for knowledge of the Self arises spontaneously through its own power.

The Upaniṣads give a significant place to remembrance in educational method.[2] Both hearing and reflection call for rigorous use of memory. Gauḍapāda's *Māṇḍūkyakārikā* gives the instruction that after one understands non-duality one should fix the memory on it.[3] This implies that memory is used even in concentration, which follows upon reflection and reasoning. Memory thus takes on a major role in religious development: "On the purity of the inner nature, memory becomes strong; and on strengthening of memory follows freedom from all ties."[4] There is the fundamental presupposition that liberating knowledge exists in memory. Religious development unleashes memory through hearing, reflection and concentration. Hearing and memorization, the core of education in ancient India, were thought by the early seers to possess a spiritual efficacy. The oral word is more important than the written word precisely because the former has an effect upon the memory which the latter does not. To educate according to the Upaniṣads requires silence and

1. *Kaṭha* I.II.13.
2. *Smṛti* (memory) is implied as a source of knowledge in the Upaniṣads, and in subsequent schools it is explicitly listed as a *pramāṇa*. Confer Sarmah, pp. 227 ff. for the role of memory in Upaniṣadic education.
3. *Māṇḍ. Kārikā* II. 36.
4. *C.U.* VII.XXVI. 2.

meditation, the prerequisites for the exercise of memory. Although this tradition does not go so far as to raise memory above the other sources of knowledge, still memory alone is integral to the entire method. Since self-realisation is the work not of the empirical individual but rather of the Self revealing Itself through Its own power, memory is of paramount importance because it is the faculty that conditions the mind for illumination.

Yājñavalkya instructs his student, Kahola : "Therefore let a Brāhmaṇa, having known all about learning, try to live as a child; having known all about this strength as well as learning, he becomes a silent meditator."[1] The Upaniṣads, like the earlier Veda, prescribe meditation along with ritual. The *Praśna Upaniṣad* recommends meditation as the means to attain either the immutable truth or Brahman as the first born.[2] He who knows meditation becomes Brahman, according to the early sages. Again, Yājñavalkya, instructing his wife, says, "As I explain it, meditate (upon its meaning)."[3]

Meditation, however, is not the same as the threefold method; it stands apart from hearing and reflection upon the Veda. Even the gods meditate upon Brahman.[4] The Upaniṣads do not offer a technical definition of meditation. It is left to individual commentators within the tradition to specify precisely what meditation entails. The Upaniṣads use various words for meditation, of which the most common are *upāsanā* and *vidyā*. Repetition is the common factor in all meditational vocabulary. *Upāsanā* literally means to come near a thing, in this case, to approach the realisation of the Self through concentration on an object of meditation. Human speech—an ordinary word—is the usual object of meditation.[5] Meditation may be made on a syllable, such as *OM*, or on a more material symbol. In either case, it involves deliberation and rational analysis. Meditation consists in focusing

1. *B.U.* III.V.1. The word *muni* is used in this place and is translated as silent meditator.
2. *Praśna* V.1 ff. The word *abhidhyāna* is used in this place for meditation.
3. *B.U.* IV.V.5. The word *nididhyāsana* is used in this place for meditation.
4. *Tait. U.* II.V.1. The word *upāsate* is used in this place for meditation.
5. *B.U.* I. III. 2. ff.

repeatedly upon the meaning-content of the symbol or syllable.[1] The *vidyā*-s in the Upaniṣads specify the type of meditation more concretely by determining its object, whether it is Brahman, *ātman*, Agni, or Puruṣa. *Upāsanā* may be a form of concentration pursued devotedly in reflection (*manana*) and perfected in the more advanced stages of *nididhyāsana*.[2] Many objects of meditation are suggested in the Upaniṣads, but overall importance is given to repeating them with devotion after having reflected upon them. In the *Śvetāśvatara Upaniṣad*, *upāsanā* really means devotion (*bhakti*) to God or to the guru. The literature is in agreement, however, that acts of meditation are to be repeated successively and focus upon Brahman as the inner Self.

The most substantive factor in meditation is constant remembrance. In some instances the Upaniṣadic text maintains a difference between the meditator and the object, but in other cases the object of meditation is the meditator himself.[3] Although each meditation is described as involving subject, object, and the act of meditating, the meditator seeks ultimately to identify himself with the object. The act of meditation is conditioned by faith, understanding and repetition, a combination that keeps it from degenerating into a senseless and mechanical practice.[4] Meditation is neither pure knowing nor pure activity.[5] It embraces both subject and object, and it advances gradually to transcend both subject and object by penetrating to the Self. In some meditations the object predominates—for example, when some god is the object. But the subject predominates when the Self becomes the center of meditation. "Meditate on the Self thus with the help of *OM*," instructs one sage.[6] To realise the Self through meditation is the general orientation of the Upaniṣads.

1. Unlike the later yoga of Patañjali, it attempts neither to stop mental activity nor to separate the mind (*manas*) from the Self. Confer Sen, p. 122. I disagree with Sen who too closely identifies Patañjali's yoga with that of Upaniṣadic meditation.

2. Confer Madhusūdana, *Siddhāntabindu*, Preface, p. xv, of the translator, Prahlad Chandrashekhar Divanji.

3. Contrast *C.U.* I.I.1 with III.XIV.1 ff.

4. *C.U.* I. I.10.

5. Mukhopadhyaya, p. 82. It is neither *jñāna* nor *karma*.

6. *M.U.* II.II.6. The word *dhyāna* is used in this place for meditation.

The method is synthetic insofar as the Self is sought through some symbolic center that holds in harmony subject and object. But the major contribution of the early sages was to attain an analytical grasp of the Self through a rational analysis of the states of consciousness. As the analytical method is pursued, extrinsic symbols are discarded and meditation is made on the different conditions of the Self. "The Self alone is to be meditated upon."[1] The dialogue between Gārgya and King Ajātaśatru shows the utter weakness of symbols and a preference for analytical meditation.[2]

Devotional meditation centering on a love object is recommended, but it places limits on achievement.[3] Some Upaniṣads explicitly hold that neither good acts nor meditation bring an end to the saṃsāric world; ritual and meditation are held within the world of duality. Agentship remains, for one still experiences the difference between the doer and that done. Pointing to instinct, reason and intuition, the Upaniṣads urge the religious seeker on toward higher knowledge. The *Muṇḍaka Upaniṣad* distinguishes higher from lower knowledge.[4] The latter is communicated through scholarship, the Veda, and meditation upon objects. Only lower knowledge can be gained through meditation, while the higher intuitive knowledge simply reveals itself to the religious seeker. Whenever a text refers to the higher and immediate knowledge of Brahman, it suggests that discrimination (*viveka*) will continue until spontaneous and intuitive knowledge reveals itself. What is most distinctive in Upaniṣadic meditation, beyond the use of a multiplicity of objects to lead to the conditioned Absolute, is the notion that intellectual discrimination most immediately prepares one for spiritual liberation.

Consciousness of the guru is neither lost nor obscured in the process. The final step in both ritual and meditation is to recall the lineage of teachers. Not only does each Upaniṣad conclude with a litany of teachers from whom the previous wisdom has been transmitted, but the seeker also concludes each religious

1. *B.U.* I.IV7. The word *upāsate* is used in this place.
2. *B.U.* II.I.I. ff.
3. "The aspirant, by taking himself to devotional exercises, subsists in the conditioned Brahman." *Māṇḍ. Kārikā* III.1.
4. *M.U.* I. I. 4 ff. The Advaita tradition highlights this distinction; the following interpretation of mine is true to an Advaita interpretation.

activity and "returns the way he went, sits behind the fire, and repeats the line of teachers."[1]

Expansion of the Tradition

With the emergence of the *smṛti* literature and the parallel growth in the yoga, the Tantra and the *bhakti* schools, everything in the teaching tradition of India expands with vast pluriformity.[2] The guru in the Upaniṣadic tradition is a realised individual, one who intellectually knows the Veda and experientially dwells in the Absolute Brahman. The epics, however, highlight the divinity of the guru and the consequent reverence and worship of him. Kṛṣṇa in the *Gītā* is addressed as father, lord and most venerable guru.[3] In the Purāṇas the guru is the highest divinity in a particular sect; the *Bhāgavata Purāṇa* regards the guru as a deity who is worshipped because liberation comes only from him.[4] The action of the guru is the action of God in much of this literature.

Yet the law books, drawing upon the wealth of early custom, try to define sharply the various types of teachers. Manu, especially, gives specific definitions to the kinds of teachers.[5] Still, the range of vocabulary for the preceptor is often used synonymously in this expanding body of literature. Thus it is necessary to look to the specific function of a religious teacher and the type of ideal he projects in order to discover his meaning. The tradition produces a plurality of teacher-student types.

The ascendency of the *brāhmaṇa* class along with the heterodox teachers of Buddhism and Jainism gives impetus to the ascetical groups within Hinduism from which come most of the religious

1. *B.U.* VI.III.6.

2. Confer Gonda, Mookerji, Chakraborty for the specification of these developments.

3. *B. Gītā.* 11.43; 18.75.

4. *B. Purāṇa* XI. 3; X. 86.

5. *Laws of Manu* II. 140 ff. In *Manu* II.140 *ācārya* initiates in and teaches the Veda; in *Manu* II.141 the *upādhyāya* teaches only a portion of the Veda for money; in *Manu* II.142 a greater distinction begins to take place between *ācārya* and guru, the latter who also instructs in the Veda and initiates with certain rites. *Manu* attributes to the *ācārya* the teaching of socio-religious duties and to the guru the teaching of more spiritual realities. The sharpest distinction is drawn between guru and the ritual priest (*purohita*).

teachers of the tradition. Both the *Mahābhārata* and the *Rāmayaṇa* refer to *āśrama* life where ascetics teach. *Smṛti* texts admit women into Vedic study and life, into the use of the Sāvitrī *mantra*, and into the *upanayana* rite. An increase among the wandering ascetics from which come the popular teachers of religion increases during the Gupta period (320 C.E.-647 C.E.). Yet the Upaniṣads uphold the teacher as the indispensable means for liberation because the path of knowledge is acutely difficult. The *Kaṭha Upaniṣad* sounds the imperative : "Arise, awake, obtain your boons (teachers) and understand them. The wise describe the path to be as impassable as a razor's edge, which when sharpened is difficult to tread on."[1] The indispensability of the guru is spoken of in all *smṛti* literture, but only among the gurus of Tantra is this imperative equally as strong as in the Upaniṣads because the esoteric and secret aspects of their salvation process is made known only through the preceptor. The Tantra draws a distinction between those who teach the *śāstra*-s (*śikṣā*-guru) and those who initiate in and teach the practical means of liberation (*dīkṣā*-guru), the latter of whom are indispensable for spiritual liberation. The ideal teacher in the Upaniṣads is a figure of intellectual astuteness, while in the Tantra his personality is dominated by mysterious power. This contrast is sharply set against both the love-personality of the guru who dominates the epics, Purāṇas and devotional literature, and the teacher of religious duties who dominates the law books.

The relationship between teacher and pupil is determined in the Upaniṣads by the type of knowledge sought. In the case of the religious seeker who pursues knowledge of Brahman or knowledge of the Self (*ātmavidyā*), a personal association between the guru and *śiṣya* is established. The goal of such a relationship is transformation whereby the student, after his self-realisation, becomes a guru himself. The law books, on the other hand, reflect a basic parental relationship between teacher and student because obedience to the teacher and observance of duties are paramount injunctions.[2] The epics, Purāṇas and the early *bhakti* literature establish the basis for a refined love relationship between

1. *Kaṭha* I.III. 14. Śaṅkara interprets boons as teachers (*ācārya*-s); the word '*kavi*' is understood as the wise.
2. *Laws of Manu* II.171; II. 69 ff.

teacher and student that reaches its highest articulation in the medieval devotional poets. The *smṛti* literature is not without older notions concerning the outstanding teachers, for even the *Gītā* speaks about the chain of disciplic succession.[1]

The Upaniṣadic contribution to both educational and spiritual growth is the process of hearing, reflection and concentration. This pedagogical tool may be applied synthetically or analytically, and its use in the latter mode is the unique Upaniṣadic contribution to the pursuit of spiritual liberation. The highest form of meditation is an analytical process that discards symbols in its advanced stages. Direct concentration on the Self, achieved by rational discrimination and insight, is the context in which the Self reveals its own reality to the meditator. There is also diversification in religious pedagogy in the expanding tradition. The Tantra places significance in ritual incantation (*mantra-japa*), elaborate worship of images, along with meditation on ritual diagrammatizations (*maṇḍala-yantra*). The devotional development, taking its cue from the *Gītā*'s notion of self-surrender, places equal stress upon symbolic meditation and especially upon the divine aspects of the guru-*avatāra* as a love object. Popular yoga, stemming from Patañjali's *Yoga Sūtra*, elaborates complex methods of posture, breathing and withdrawal in order to concentrate the mind and to bring an end to mental activity. Impressive in the Upaniṣadic tradition is the fact that pedagogy has a direct relationship not only to self-realisation but also to the role of the student following self-realisation. The Upaniṣadic student is taught to be a teacher himself; this is not as apparent in the other teaching traditions of India.

The preceptor in the Upaniṣads is an intellectual guide, teaching through analysis a method and wisdom leading to intuitive experience. This is not generally the case in the *smṛti* literature and is found with similar importance only in Buddhist teaching systems and some few schools of yoga. But the Vedānta tradition and Śaṅkara, especially, build upon these early Upaniṣadic foundations.

1. *B. Gītā.* 4. 2.

Chapter Two

ŚAṄKARA AND THE TEACHING TRADITION

From the end of the Upaniṣadic period to the advent of Śaṅkara, the teaching tradition developed within the classical religions and philosophical systems. The philosophies of India are systems of spiritual liberation, and as such they are bound to educational and spiritual discipline. The six orthodox philosophical systems expanded the learned tradition, but only the *Mīmāṃsā* and the Vedānta accepted entirely the authority of scripture and the wisdom of the ancient sages. The Vedānta, drawing upon the Upaniṣads more than on any other portion of the scripture, followed in principle the Upaniṣadic teaching heritage. The Vedānta has been defined by some as a religion, while others describe it as an art.[1] All philosophers agree that it embraces a total way of life.

Bādarāyaṇa (fourth-second century B. C. E.) and Jaimini (fifth-fourth century B. C. E.), the early systematic and authoritative thinkers, provide an exegesis of the scripture along the lines of Vedānta and Pūrva Mīmāṃsā respectively. Recognizing the many schools of thought in the Upaniṣads, Bādarāyaṇa refers to other teachers of the Upaniṣads whose understanding differs from his. The *Brahma Sūtra* of Bādarāyaṇa is the major articulation of the Vedānta, and it is upon this text that Śaṅkara bases his major commentary. Continuity between the Upaniṣads and the Vedānta is easily recognized.[2] Śaṅkara maintains continuity with the Upaniṣads and Bādarāyaṇa on such issues as the absolute reality of Brahman, the relative phenomenality of the created world, and the unity of the Self and Brahman.[3] Gauḍapāda's *Māṇḍūkyakārikā* (seventh century C.E.), a sources of thoroughly Advaita thought, more directly influenced Śaṅkara, who expressed a special reverence for Gauḍapāda above all the sages of the past. The early Advaita tradition,

1. Bhattacharya, p. 118; Hiriyanna, p. 2.

2. The *Brahma Sūtra* of Bādarāyaṇa quotes the *C.U.* 127 times and the *B.U.* 57 times.

3. Śaṅkara's frequent formulation is : *Brahma satyam jagan mithyā jīvo Brahmaiva nāparaḥ*.

however, does assimilate divergent opinions to a certain degree. Gauḍapāda accommodates aspects of Upaniṣadic thought by stressing the extraordinary use of reason employed in the grand Advaita vision.[1] He uses, for example, the classical notion of the silent sage (*muni*) that Śaṅkara understands as one who meditates, discriminates and contemplates. Śaṅkara specifies the silent sage as one primarily pre-eminent in knowledge and secondarily an accomplished ascetic.[2]

There is a consistent attempt in early Advaita to integrate the meditative process with *karma* yoga, so that religious activity is ultimately displaced by knowledge. While Śaṅkara himself rejects any compromise between *karmakāṇḍa* (ritual acts) and *jñānakāṇḍa*, this is not the case with his older contemporary Maṇḍanamiśra, who produced major works on Mīmāṃsā and even authored a work on Advaita. Maṇḍanamiśra compromises Advaita in ethics, ontology and espistemology, favors the conjoining of knowledge and *karma*, and raises up meditation over every other pedagogical tool.[3] Unlike Śaṅkara, Maṇḍanamiśra reduces the role of guru to a minimum and leaves the individual completely responsible for his spiritual growth.[4] It is clear, then, that although there is considerable continuity between the Upaniṣads and Śaṅkara, the old scriptural tradition was frequently accommodated to new insights from the developing Vedānta system.

Śaṅkara's appearance in the late eighth century is not a sudden outburst of genius but presumes meaningful lineage. There is

1. Kuppuswami Shastri (1946), pp. 17 ff.

2. Ś. *Māṇḍ. Kārikā.* I.29 and II.35. This notion is found in *B.U.* III.5.1, which modern commentators such as Radhakrishnan interpret as the silent meditator (Śrī Ramana Maharshi in this century is an example of this sage figure); in Ś. *B. Sūtra* III.4.47, *muni* is a synonym for the state of *sannyāsa*; in this place Śaṅkara also advances a third meaning for silent meditation, namely, as a means to knowledge itself; confer Bhagat, pp. 107-112, for the history of the term *muni*. Not infrequently, Śaṅkara uses *muni* synonymously for an ascetic.

3. Kuppuswami Shastri (1946), p. 23. According to Shastri and other recent scholars of Maṇḍanamiśra, there is no foundation from textual evidence that Maṇḍanamiśra became a disciple of Śaṅkara and is the same person as Sureśvara, Śaṅkara's extraordinary disciple. It is a common belief in the Śaṅkara tradition that Sureśvara and Maṇḍanamiśra are the same person. Confer Sastri (Shastri) (1937).

4. Biardeau (1969), p. 122.

little possibility of historically determining definitive lineage, but Śaṅkara himself is acutely conscious of his own dependence on teachers of the past. Various attempts have been made to establish Śaṅkara's predecessors. In one case the list of *ācārya*-s from Kapila to Śaṅkara is forty-six; between Gauḍapāda and Govinda, Śaṅkara's teacher, four are traced.[1] Another list of Advaita teachers numbers twelve between the author of the *Brahma Sūtras* and Śaṅkara.[2] It has even been argued that Gauḍapāda was really the teacher of Govinda, the guru of Śaṅkara.[3] The most that can be said is that Advaita comes from many sources, most of which are reflected in the commentaries of Śaṅkara in passages where he deals with their thought.

There exists internal evidence that many Advaitins preceded Śaṅkara, but the fact that his commentaries are the only extant ones indicates his pivotal influence on the Vedānta system. He refers to earlier commentaries on the *Brahma Sūtra*, the *Bhagavad Gītā* and the Upaniṣads, and he criticizes them rigorously, accepting the views of some and rejecting others. Although he bases his major commentary on Bādarāyaṇa, Śaṅkara credits Gauḍapāda with the recovery of classical Upaniṣadic thought.[4] In Gauḍapāda, Śaṅkara first confronted Advaita as he himself understood it. Śaṅkara was aware of his own dependence upon the Upaniṣads, of his predecessor's lineage, and of the different traditions in the *Brahma Sūtra*. From the frequency with which he quotes the Upaniṣads in his commentary on the *Brahma Sūtra*, it is

1. Sahasrabudhe, p. 207.

2. Devaraja, p. 21, quotes from M. M. Pt. Gopinath Kaviraj, "Introduction to Hindi Translation of *Brahma-Sūtra-Bhāṣya* of *Śaṅkara with Ratnaprabhā*,' reproduced in *Acyuta*, Vol. LLL, N. 4, pp. 8-19, in which the *ācārya*-s are : Bhartṛprapañca, Brahmanandī, Ṭaṅka, Guhadeva, Bhāruci, Kapardī, Upavarṣa, Bodhāyana, Bhartṛhari, Sundarapāṇḍya, Dramidācārya and Brahmadatta. Yet, Gopinath Kaviraj, *The Quarterly Journal of Mythic Society*, Vol. 24, No. 1 & 2, 1933, argues that Śaṅkara's system developed from ancient Śivādvayavāda.

3. Belvalkar & Ranade (1927). p. 96.

4. Dasgupta believes that Gauḍapāda was living when Śaṅkara was a student; confer Dasgupta, Vol. 1, pp. 422-423. Devaraja, pp. 22 & 39, denies authenticity of the fourth *prakaraṇa* of *Māṇḍ. Kārikā* and its commentary as Śaṅkara's work; he also says that there is no conclusive evidence that the first three parts are from Śaṅkara.

evident that he esteemed the Upaniṣads, especially the *Chāndogya*, the *Bṛhadāraṇyaka* and the *Taittirīya Upaniṣads* above all other scripture.[1]

The eighth century Vedāntist systematizes the main tenets of the Upaniṣads in a coherent presentation It is hard to assess how faithful he is to Bādarāyaṇa and other Advaita teachers. Radhakrishnan has observed : "It is indeed difficult to decide whether Śaṅkara's philosophy is a continuation or reinterpretation of, or an addition to, the old teaching."[2] Although earlier literature gave him freedom for interpretation, it is certain, that the Upaniṣads had the most formative influence in Śaṅkara's understanding of the teaching tradition and the nature and role of both guru and student.

The Nature of the Guru

Śaṅkara's Vedānta is a scriptural tradition to which the individual applies his highest reason. Other literature may reveal an absolute of extraordinary qualities (*saguṇa* Brahman), but only the scripture, and for the Vedānta only the Upaniṣads, bring one to the nonduality of the absolute (*nirguṇa* Brahman). In his commentary on the *Brahma Sūtra*, Śaṅkara states : "The scripture is the only source of the knowledge of the truths regarding the suprasensible."[3] Reason encounters scripture rationally and analytically. The necessity of the teacher for the Vedānta system arises from the extraordinary role given to reason in the Vedānta scheme of understanding. One can attain knowledge by oneself only after long and arduous effort, according to Śaṅkara; he therefore urges constant reliance upon the guru. Analysis of scripture is difficult, and if it is to lead to liberating knowledge, that knowledge depends upon others for its emergence. To approach the Upaniṣads means to receive understanding through the instruction of a teacher. The knowledge that leads to liberation can be achieved only through traditional authority, and

1. In his commentary on the *B. Sūtra*, Śaṅkara quotes the *C.U.* 810 times, the *B.U.* 567 times, the *Tait. U.* 142 times, the *B. Gītā* 56 times, the *Mahābhārata* 34 times, and the *Ṛgveda* 15 times. Confer Mayeda (1965), p. 187.

2. Radhakrishnan, Vol. 11, pp. 467, 469-470.

3. S. B. *Sūtra* II.3.1; II.1.27. Scripture is verbal testimony (*Śabda pramāṇa*) concerning truths beyond normal experience.

Śaṅkara believes that authority has come through a line of teachers.[1] Traditional authority is the way of effective teaching. Commenting upon the Upaniṣadic advice that one go to a "teacher alone" (*gurum eva*), Śaṅkara extends that norm even to those students already versed in scripture. There is no pursuit of wisdom independent of a guru.[2]

The master Vedāntist attributes a special efficacy to knowledge gained from a teacher. The ancient sages were "endowed with the power of Viṣṇu,"[3] he writes. In the *Upadeśasāhasrī*, his singular exposition of the teaching art, he lists intellectual power as the foremost mark of the teacher : "The teacher is one who is endowed with power of furnishing arguments pro and con, of understanding questions and remembering (answers) . . . "[4] The teacher is the pilot and his wisdom is the raft.[5] Since the guru has crossed over death and rebirth, he has the capacity to lead others along the same path. The Upaniṣads teach that the guru's authority is established on the superiority of his knowledge and experience. Śaṅkara, however, accepts the dependence upon the guru primarily because the role of reason is paramount in his system, and secondarily because the teacher's knowledge is superior. Human development for Śaṅkara presupposes three factors, all due to God's grace : a human birth, desire for liberation and the protecting care of a perfect sage. The teacher becomes indispensable, like the scripture itself. Śaṅkara reflected an already existing belief in the need for a guru, and he solidified this belief

1. S. *Kena* I.3-4. Śaṅkara uses the word *āgama*, which means traditional teaching.

2. S. *M. U.* I.II.12. The use of *gurum eva* (teacher alone) is consistently found in Śaṅkara's thought.

3. S. *B. Gītā* 10.6.

4. S. *Upadeśa*. I.6. Śaṅkara uses a cluster of words for teacher : *ācārya*, *guru*, *sadguru*, *mahāpuruṣa*, *sādhu*, *muni*, *sannyāsī*. The most common usages are *guru* and ācārya. When commenting on a text, he follows the usage within the original text; in his own texts the context usually determines the choice of usage, e.g., *ācārya*, confer *Upadeśa*. 1.26, 1.40; *S. Tait*. I.II.I, I.11.4; *guru*, confer *Upadeśa*. 2.46, 2.48, 2.50, *S. Tait*. I.4.1, *S. Muṇḍ*. I.2.12, *Viveka*. 15, 25, 28, 34, 576-77; *sadguru*, confer *Viveka*. I, which refers to Govinda; *Mahāpuruṣa*, confer *Viveka*. 3; *sādhu*, *Viveka*. 42; *muni*, confer *Viveka*. 70, S. *B. Sūtra* III.4.47, S. *B. U.* III. 5.1; *yati* (renouncer), confer *Viveka* 567. *Yati* and *sannyāsī* may refer to either teacher or student.

5. S. *Upadeśa*. I.3.

for the next 1200 years among those who followed his system of the Vedānta. In his own formation, he went to a teacher Govinda, at an early age. Learning traditional wisdom with extraordinary speed, he quickly passed through the stage of studentship. The moment came, moreover, in his own teaching career when he could place his pupils in charge of religious centers as teachers themselves. Once one is liberated, there is no need for a guru; nevertheless, the need is incumbent upon those not yet self-realised.

Accepting the Upaniṣadic notion that only one versed in Brahman and dwelling in Brahman is a true teacher, Śaṅkara insists that education in scripture follow a particular lineage and a particular path of knowledge. A most significant contribution of this, which constitutes an advance beyond Upaniṣadic thought on the nature of the guru, is to identify teacher and scripture. Whenever he refers to the scripture as a source of knowledge, he invariably mentions the teacher. In the *Gītābhāṣya*, he says that the Self is seen when one is equipped with teachings of the scripture and the teacher.[1] In commentaries on the Upaniṣads he consistently links the two, observing that the mind "is purified by the teacher and the scripture,"[2] and "those alone who follow both scripture and teachers transcend ignorance."[3] Scripture and the teacher function together as a single cause for Śaṅkara; the teacher in the Vedānta is differentiated from other teachers by this close identification with scripture. Teacher and scripture are an integral unit, because the former embodies the latter and the latter articulates the experiences of the former. The guru dwells in Brahman because he is versed in scripture, and he is knowledgeable in scripture because he dwells in Brahman. The guru is the living embodiment of the highest truths of the scripture because he is one with Brahman. The guru is a master of theory because he is versed in scripture (*śrotriya*), but as a dweller in Brahman (*Brahmaniṣṭha*) he is a master of experience and life. The union of scripture and teacher is the foundation for whatever else Śaṅkara may contribute to the concept of guru and the

1. S. *B. Gītā* 2.21; also 8.8, 16.1, 18.55. This formulation is the most obvious phrase to be found in all of Śaṅkara's commentaries, Upaniṣads, *B. Gītā*, *B. Sūtra*, even in his original works such as *Upadeśa* and *Viveka*.

2. S. *Kaṭha* II.I.11; also confer S. *C. U.* VIII.I.5, VIII.IV.3.

3. S. *B. U.* II.V.15; also confer IV.IV.21; confer Sarmah, p. 96.

learned tradition. As the embodiment of the scripture, the guru is both an exemplar and an authentic articulator of the heritage.

Śaṅkara, commenting on the sage who loosens the bandages from the eyes of his pupils, describes the liberated teacher as having his own bandage removed, and as such resting in Brahman.[1] A teacher identified with Brahman does not exerience duality but is beyond the world of dual experience.[2] Although one teaches within the world of duality, one's underlying and perduring experience of the world of people, of nature and of the Absolute is nondual. Śaṅkara pens the refrain in one of his hymns : "He who has learnt to look upon all as Brahman is really my guru, be he a *caṇḍāla* or *brāhmaṇa*."[3] A teacher of the scripture is different from a mere logician or from one who has grasped only the meaning of the scripture.[4] A guru in Śaṅkara's estimation lives in the nonduality of the self and Brahman, but for the sake of his disciples he teaches within a differentiated and dual world. Gurus "emancipate, by their teachings, all those who are fortunate enough to stand in their presence, from the three kinds of misery and the three kinds of sins."[5]

The singular aim of the teacher is to impart knowledge of Brahman. According to Śaṅkara's reflection on the Kṛṣṇa of the *Gītā*, teaching establishes "both the text itself and its meaning as I (Kṛṣṇa) have established it in you," for to hand down the scripture is the "dearest work."[6] The master Vedāntin and the Advaita tradition place priority on the teaching of the Upaniṣadic

1. S. *C. U.* VI.XIV.2.
2. S. *Kaṭha* I.II.8.
3. S. *Manīsha Pañchaka*, in Atmananda. In a work attributed to Śaṅkara but considered spurious, titled "My Guru" in Subrahmanya Sarma, the writer reflects on the legend in which Śaṅkara met the chandals : "That consciousness which shines forth most distinctively in waking, dream, and sleep · · · that I am. Whoever possesses such a firm conviction is my Guru. This is my conception of Guru." Throughout the hymn, the refrain "He is my Guru. This is my conception of Guru," occurs after identifying the guru as : (a) one who is firmly convinced that he is supreme consciousness; (b) one whose mind is rooted in the highest reality; (c) one who has a pure, tranquil mind and contemplates pure consciousness; (d) one who has realised his identity with Brahman.
4. S. *Kaṭha* I.II.9.
5. S. *Śataślokī* 2, in Venkataraman, p. 86.
6. S. *B. Gītā* 18.68-69.

texts. Yet, the teacher's threefold role is to disclose the meaning of the scripture, to eradicate ignorance, and finally through the prior tasks to transmit liberating wisdom. The guru disabuses the pupil of the notion that he knows himself sufficiently well, and works toward removing ignorance. To save the student from ignorance is the primary task the teacher takes on when he accepts a student. In the practical order, he dispels the causes of ignorance : past and present sin, laxity, courting popular esteem and vanity, lack of firm knowledge of what constitutes discrimination of the Self and non-self.[1] Ignorance is removed through a study of scripture and especially an understanding of the great sayings (*mahāvākya*-s) of the Upaniṣads. If the teacher is an authentic transmitter of sacred wisdom, he will impart the meaning of the essential doctrinal texts of the Upaniṣads through which ignorance is dissipated. Śaṅkara was a peripatetic teacher, travelling the length and breadth of India, debating and dialoguing with friend and opponent alike. He spent a greater portion of his life teaching verbally than he spent writing his great commentaries. Whether in debate or in dialogue, he was exposing Upaniṣadic texts whose meaning, he believed, removed the binding force of ignorance. He was both a transmitter of traditional knowledge and a guru.

The Vedānta preserves in memory the import of Upaniṣadic wisdom. This is what lineage means, to store in memory and to transmit the knowledge that leads to self-realisation. Throughout his works, Śaṅkara begins and ends each treatise with praise and salutations to the teachers of the past. He follows this pattern and intersperses his texts with praise to his personal teacher. The teacher has awakened those asleep and has "completely saved me,"[2] he writes. He bows before those teachers and his own teacher who have been sources of knowledge. He reverently salutes his own guru and attributes to him liberation from births and deaths.[3] He views his teacher as part of the Vedānta lineage : "I bow down to my teacher, a knower of Brahman, who collected for us the nectar of knowledge from the Vedāntas like a bee collecting the best honey from flowers."[4]

1. S. *M. U.* I.II.13; S. *Upadeśa* I.4.
2. S. *Viveka*. 51 ff.
3. S. *Upadeśa*. XVII.2-3, XVII.89.
4 S. *Upadeśa*. XVIII.233. In a text considered spurious, Śaṅkara

In the beginning of the commentary on the *Taittirīya Upaniṣad,* he bows before "the wonderful teachers by whom was explained this Upaniṣad in the past," and twice invokes God to protect the teachers.[1] Both Govinda and Gauḍapāda are singled out by Śaṅkara for special reverence. He praises at one and the same time the triad of Brahman, the line of teachers and his own teacher.[2] The old teachers hold special authority for Śaṅkara. Repeating the line of teachers serves as *mantra*, which heightens consciousness and becomes a source of power. In one place he traces lineage through the mothers of the teachers to indicate the creative principle and efficacy in the life of a teacher.[3]

Aware that lineage indicates traditional knowledge, Śaṅkara uses it to enhance doctrine itself for it refines, strengthens and clarifies knowledge. Lineage increases the value of doctrine as it passes through the memory of the ages. Since the Vedānta proposes a rational understanding of the Self as a prelude to an intuition of the Self, initiation into tradition comes from memory of the past. Initiation into knowledge is a familiar point of departure in Indian religion, and in the Vedānta it extends into a life-long practice of bringing to memory the line of past teachers. Śaṅkara believes the yoga of the *Bhagavad Gītā* to have been "handed down in regular succession" beginning with the Lord Himself but broken over the course of time.[4] He views the teacher as one who sustains and transmits lineage. He strongly advocates an intellectual path based upon past understanding. The transmission of sacred wisdom, the specific function of the guru, takes place with the help of traditional authority, which is harnessed to the present educational situation by sustaining in memory the lineage of teachers. The memory of the past is gathered together through a *mantra* of gurus, but the impact of accumulated wisdom is brought into present instruction by the living teacher.

Part of the *Chāndogya Upaniṣad* was handed down through a line of Kṣatriya teachers, a fact that indicates the wide social

salutes the holy feet of his master, which action destroys duality and doubt : "Whose two feet reveal oneness as the meaning of That." Confer *Svātmanirūpaṇa* 1 & 2, in Venkataraman, p. 198.

1. S. *Tait. U.* Intro. & I.I.1.
2. S. *Māṇḍ. Kārikā* IV.100; S. *B. U.* Intro.
3. S. *B. U.* VI.V.1-4; II.VI.3.
4. S. *B. Gītā* 4.1-2.

base from which early teachers came. Although Śaṅkara opened religious instruction to all, irrespective of social status, the teacher was most frequently a renunciant, a *sannyāsī*. It has generally been the case in Hinduism that the self-realised individual transcends social class and social conformity. The *sannyāsī* is free from ritual and class obligations. The fundamental characteristic of the guru is his living beyond duality. From this point of view, a twiceborn or one of any class or *gotra* could become a teacher. The four classical stages of life are helpful in acquiring knowledge, and Śaṅkara insists that those bound to social class (*varṇāśrama*) pass through the stages. Yet it is easier for a renunciant, who is not bound to ritual or household duties, to pursue the demanding path of the Vedānta. Recalling the Upaniṣadic advice to renounce wealth, progeny and worldly goals, Śaṅkara maintains that only a *sannyāsī* can be fully meditative.[1] Since the guru must be an exemplar of contemplative life who is given to Brahman and to instruction in sacred wisdom, Śaṅkara says, he should generally be a renunciant, a *sannyāsī*. The teacher who is self-realised does not usually remain in domestic life; he is no longer bound to the duties of such a life. To sustain himself, though, he may follow domestic pursuits.[2] Śaṅkara, however, restricts the teacher to a life of perpetual renunciation : ". . . it can only be understood by those highly worshipped persons . . . who are *paramahaṃsa*, wandering mendicants, who have reached the final life-stage and are totally devoted to the philosophy of the Vedānta and none others, who carry on this teaching."[3] The obligation to carry on the teaching tradition transcends both household and family. The teacher in the tradition of Śaṅkara is an ascetic who has renounced normal society.

Śaṅkara established the teacher-*sannyāsī* as a model within the Advaita lineage. In the Upaniṣads, the spiritual teacher could be an ascetic or a householder or even a king or a woman; but Śaṅkara, by stressing the high intellectual personality of the guru, made renunciation in its most rigorous expression, *sannyāsa*, the norm for following generations of Advaitins and, in fact, for all Vedānta teachers. Renunciation is a central theme from the

1. Confer S. *B. U.* III.1.
2. Confer S. *Ait. U.* Intro.
3. S. *C. U.* VIII.XII.1, Concl.

scriptural period through classical and popular Hindu development. A recent study maintains that *sannyāsa* is the most fundamental trait of the Indian religious spirit.[1] Hindu, Buddhist and Jain ascetical traditions looked to renunciation as a means of release from desire and a means of realising higher orders of reality. What distinguishes renunciation in Advaita Vedānta is that *sannyāsa* is "an extension of knowledge into the realm of practical living."[2] The teacher-*sannyāsī* is a singular way for a self-realised personality to live in harmony with the metaphysical identification of the Self and Brahman.[3]

Equally significant is the direct institutionalization that resulted from this teaching model. The teacher-*sannyāsī* became part of the Vedānta lineage from this moment forward because Śaṅkara established *maṭha*-s throughout India and laid the foundation for the custom of having religious teachers come from orders of ascetics. Śaṅkara is credited by tradition with the establishment of major *maṭha*-s, geographically placed throughout India, and the organization of ten religious orders of ascetics.[4] This was not an innovation in India, because by Śaṅkara's time the Buddhists and Jains had had an established learned tradition within their monastic centers for a thousand years. Śaṅkara initiated a similar custom within the entire Vedānta tradition to such a degree that *maṭha*-s were extensive in Hinduism by the tenth century C.E. An important difference exists between Śaṅkara's *maṭha*-s and the earlier forest hermitages and *āśrama*-s during the period of the Veda and the epics, namely, a teacher-*sannyāsī*, a self-realised figure, headed a *maṭha* in a somewhat monarchial fashion. Even in the earlier *pariṣad* system, which brought together learned laymen and ascetics, a custom also continued by Śaṅkara, the role of one self-realised teacher-*sannyāsī* as its head distinguishes Śaṅkara's reformed institutionalism. This clearly differentiates Śaṅkara's form of monasticism from the previous

1. Tiwari, p. 123; confer pp. 21-22 for a brief historical development of the concept. Bhagat and Chakraborty devote exhaustive studies to asceticism and are in basic agreement with Tiwari.

2. Ibid., pp. 10-11.

3. Ibid.

4. Ibid., p. 128; The earliest *maṭha*-s recorded in epigraphy are 7th century, C. E.; these were Śaiva *maṭha*-s in the Chola and Pāṇḍya areas; confer Das, p. 335; also confer Chakraborty, pp. 180 ff.

Buddhist tradition where the monasteries, although centers of learning, were more a federation of individual educational communities with a republican structure of government and teaching. Buddhist teachers (*ācārya*-s and *upādhyāya*-s) multiplied within a particular monastic center because their positions were primarily based upon seniority in monastic life; however, each local community had its own head.[1] The Buddhist ascetics, those pursuing meditation alone, tended to live in isolated forest hermitages, a custom true of Indian *sādhus* even to the present day; likewise, the Jain ascetics stressed seclusion, although they were more itinerant.

The new institutionalism in Vedānta was the result of the guru-*sannyāsī* who taught within an ascetical context and from a religious center. Śaṅkara's personal history may have influenced him to set this new direction within Hinduism. Legends reveal that he desired to be an ascetic at an early age, and at a critical moment in his youth he took a vow of asceticism and mendicancy. As a mature teacher, he recommended a life of asceticism and monastic environment for teachers of the Vedānta. The *maṭha* provided discipline, which was imperative for the religious seeker and helpful for the religious teacher. From his own experience of instruction with Govinda, who according to tradition was an ascetic and renunciant, Śaṅkara saw the need for a style of life that transcended everyday society. A secluded life with Govinda during the period of studentship fortified him for the years of peripatetic teaching. In addition, the tradition of *maṭha*-s that Śaṅkara established provided for a succession of teachers. By redefining the guru tradition in this manner, he more firmly rooted his lineage and the transmission of the Vedānta. Other groups of teachers within Hinduism, following the master Advaitin, sought greater organization and began centers of teachers and ascetics along similar lines. With the advent of Rāmānuja and Madhva and the expanding Vedānta, the institutionalism around a guru in a *maṭha* became a norm for orthodox Hindu asceticism and its characteristic theme of renunciation. Thus Śaṅkara may be credited for the greater discipline and organization in the Hindu teaching profession.

1. Mookerji, pp. 420 ff; also confer Chakraborty, 199 ff. In Buddhism the *ācārya* is a senior monk who instructs in monastic rules; the *upādhyāya* is the spiritual master.

The guru, in Śaṅkara's conception, is both an intellectual and a moral personality. He is thoroughly versed in the Veda, and he is able to discourse publicly on Brahman. His mind is penetrating and "calm as fire."[1] The intellectual qualities of the teacher are paramount. Since the guru's principal function is to remove the causes of ignorance and lack of understanding among his students, he must have a superlative degree of intellectual acumen. The Vedānta system and the early Upaniṣads consistently select the discipline of understanding as the primary means for liberation, making intellectual virtues the foremost ones. Śaṅkara speaks of "the learned teacher" and "instruction by a proficient teacher," and considers learning one of the three major qualities distinguishing the *sannyāsī*.[2] Learning especially designates the teaching function of the guru, for it implies not only that he has wisdom but also that he has the capacity to communicate it and to awaken a corresponding understanding in his student. The learned man (*paṇḍita*) is an intellectual figure who embodies an intellectual heritage.[3]

Whenever Śaṅkara speaks of the qualities of the liberated person, qualities necessarily possessed by the authentic guru, he lists both intellectual virtues and moral virtues, the latter invariably more numerous and comprehensive but not more important. The moral virtues suggested by Śaṅkara for the teacher describe a particular state of mind. A teacher is calm, tranquil, childlike, silent and free from distracting motivations.[4] Although learned, he should be as a child (*bālya*), parading neither wisdom, nor learning, nor virtue itself. Employing the image of a child, the master Vedāntin suggests a particular childlike quality that does not display pride, conceit or egotism.[5] The absence of ostentation and attachment to sensual or social pleasures distinguishes a figure who is correctly motivated. Such a preceptor is endowed

1. S. *Viveka* 33; this *śloka* is an accommodation of *Śvet. U.* VI.19. The image of fire for the mind is common to both Hindu and Buddhist literature.
2. S. *Upadeśa.* 1.3; S. *Kaṭha* I.II.7; confer S. *B. Sūtra* III.IV.47-50. The three qualities are *bālya* (childlike), *pāṇḍitya* (learned) and *mauna* (silent). *Pāṇḍitya* is used here.
3. Guenon, pp. 174-175; *paṇḍita* means learned, wise, cleaver, skilled and proficient in a scholarly manner (Apte, p. 581).
4. Confer S. *Upadeśa*. 1.6; S. *Viveka*. 37; S. *B. Sūtra* III.IV.50.
5. S. *B. Sūtra* III.IV.5.

with physical and mental self-control.[1] The guru is portrayed as a magnanimous and merciful individual. Śaṅkara uses the term magnanimous to indicate the teacher's desire to teach. He compares the magnanimous teacher to the moon, which "voluntarily saves the earth parched by the flaming rays of the sun."[2] He is a "reservoir of mercy" who teaches out of compassion for the multitude; he does "good to others as does the spring," unobserved, unasked and unsought.[3] The teacher is not merely morally good but is called the excellent one, the adorable one, the wise one.[4] His goodness is visible in the act of teaching. He is sympathetic to the condition of the student and is able to act with empathy toward him. He is a friend to his pupil. The notion of the teacher as friend resonates throughout Hindu and Buddhist educational theory, and this perception serves as the basis for the Vedānta's description of the moral personality of the guru.

The role of devotion (*bhakti*) in Advaita Vedānta is not easy to ascertain, but it is clear that the preceptor is portrayed as a loving personality who freely elicits devotion from his followers. Śaṅkara invariably speaks of grace and devotion in the context of the teaching tradition, especially when he is defining the personality of the guru. The guru's favor and the devotion he elicits constitute him as a love-personality. He inculcates knowledge "out of sheer compassion";[5] the aim of life is to be achieved through the teacher's grace. Delusion is dissipated by the grace of the master. After referring to the grace of Govinda as the source of his own wisdom, Śaṅkara begins many of his works by combining renunciation and the grace of the teacher as equal sources of knowledge.[6] He follows closely the Upaniṣads on this point and brings together the instruction and the grace of the teacher as a single cause disposing the student for self-

1. S. *M. U.* I.II.12.
2. S. *Viveka.* 38.
3. S. *Viveka.* 33, 37.
4. S. *Kaṭha* I.III.14.
5. S. *Viveka.* 42. Śaṅkara uses the word *karuṇā*, compassion, in this place. A spurious work reads that the Self cannot be realised by those "devoid of the grace of the Master." *Svātmanirūpaṇa* 41, in Venkataraman, p. 216.
6. S. *Tait. U.* Intro; S. *M. U.* Intro.

realisation. In the *Gītābhāṣya*, he uses the triad of teaching, the master's grace and initiation as generative of self-knowledge.[1] The gracious guru is unique and incomparable[2], according to Śaṅkara.

Significantly absent in Śaṅkara's description of the intellectual and moral qualities of the teacher is reference to mystical or yogic powers. Although there may be some carefully guarded references to his own yogic capacities in his writing, such powers are apparently neither important nor contributive to the personality of the teacher. The Śaṅkara legends, however, abound in tales about his powers. These powers, it seems, did strengthen the relationship between him and his disciples, but they were not a source of knowledge and self-realisation.

This does not mean that Śaṅkara denies divine qualities to the guru; the guru who dwells in Brahman is not merely god-like but one with the divine. The hymns of Śaṅkara, especially the revered *Śrī Dakṣiṇāmūrtistotra,* extoll the divine qualities of the teachers. They raise the teacher above the moral and intellectual order and make him an exalted spiritual figure. The significance of one living beyond duality is grasped for a moment in poetic image. Although the *Dakṣiṇāmūrti* is a hymn to Śiva as world teacher, the author intends to sing of any self-realised teacher in the line of the Vedānta. He speaks of divine qualities incarnate in the guru, for he believes that all great teachers embody Śrī Dakṣiṇāmūrti, Śiva, the nondual Brahman. A refrain sings out "to that Śrī Dakṣiṇāmūrti in the form of the revered teacher, be this salutation." The qualities of the guru are proclaimed verse upon verse : he who is self-realised, one without a second; he who projects the differentiated and undiffentiated universe; he who enlightens his pupil directly with the Vedic text, "That you are"; he who destroys the play of the powers of delusion; he who recognizes the Self in sleep, dream and awakened state; he who reveals to his pupil his own Self; he who perceives the whole universe as a manifestation of the Absolute Self; he whose identity of Self and the whole universe has been made clear.[3] The guru in Śaṅkara's theistic hymns embraces both God and the human order. He identifies with total subjectivity, which is the

1. S. *B. Gītā* XIII.33. The word *śāstra* is used here for teaching.
2. S. Śataślokī, in Seshadri, p. 117.
3. S. *Dakṣiṇ.* V.1-10, in Subrahmanya.

immanent principle of the human person, the world and Brahman, and he also identifies with total objectivity, which is radical transcendency. Following a fundamental perception from Hindu theistic traditions, Śaṅkara understands the action of the guru as the action of God.[1] Śrī Dakṣiṇāmūrti, as the transcendent Brahman, teaches through silence but breaks his silence through the instruction of the guru, namely, Śiva in manifestation. The legends of Śaṅkara refer to him as the reincarnation of Śiva, Śrī Dakṣiṇāmūrti who has broken the eternal silence.[2] Hari and Viṣṇu are invoked as Teacher and Supreme Lord,[3] and even Brahman is addressed as the Prince of Teachers.[4]

Śaṅkara in effect praises the teacher as divine : "I praise Śrī Dakṣiṇāmūrti, my youthful teacher / Who, through silent instruction, reveals the truth of the Parabrahman/I praise the Supreme Teacher . . ./The Silent One, whose hand is uplifted in the benediction of knowledge."[5] Nonetheless, the poet-philosopher singles out his own guru in many verses: "I bow to Śrī Dakṣiṇāmūrti in the form of my guru."[6] The Vedānta follows Upaniṣadic thought in that the knower of Brahman is Brahman; the real guru is Brahman. Śaṅkara and the Vedānta, drawing upon a belief common in Hinduism long before the eighth century, fully divinize the teacher. Every human being is potentially Brahman; the self-actualised person is, indeed, Brahman. The religious seeker because of his innate divinity, holds the possibility of becoming a teacher himself.[7]

1. Date, Vol. II, p. iii; Gonda, Vol. II, pp. 240-41.

2. In Śaṅkara's *Śivānandalaharī*, a hymn considered spurious, Śiva is addressed as world teacher (*lokaguru*) which is also a title given to Śaṅkara. The hymn implies an autobiographical note and hints of an identity between the two teachers, the extoller and the extolled.

3. S. *Aparok.* 1. Śaṅkara uses the word *upadeśa* for teacher in this place.

4. S. *Viveka.* 519. Śaṅkara uses *guru* in this verse as well as 517.

5. S. *Dakṣiṇ.* 15, in Nikhilananda (1967), p. 243. The word *guru* is used consistently in this hymn.

6. S. *Dakṣiṇ.* 1-9, 11, in Nikhilananda (1967).

7. The notion of inner guru is not explicit in Śaṅkara, but it is common to most of the Hindu tradition. In one hymn, spuriously attributed to Śaṅkara, the concept is present; confer *Śivrāprarādhakṣamāpanāstotram*, 9. In another hymn, authenticated by some scholars as a Śaṅkara work, he speaks of "the Lord within your heart.". .Confer *Dvādaśapañjarikāstotram*, 12.

The spiritual master is an intellectual and venerable figure, and the venerable teacher who bestows instruction is believed to be far greater than a philosopher. From what can be surmised about Śaṅkara's life, it seems that he himself personified this conception of the preceptor. In fact, the master Vedāntin himself was essentially neither a speculative philosopher nor a private researcher, but a true guru.[1] He is revered in the Hindu tradition as a guru and not merely as an expositor of the Vedānta. He was the transmitter of a lineage, an authoritative and sacred lineage, which constituted him as guru. Behind his writing and the manner of his teaching is the self-illumined teacher who instructs out of his own experience.[2] The tradition that Śaṅkara advanced looks to him primarily as guru and invariably as a divine guru, the embodiment of Śiva.

The imperative to teach is exemplified in his writing and in the legends of his life. The ideal teacher continues to teach even after a disciple's liberation.[3] The guru's whole life without other preoccupation is committed to instruction. The period of Śaṅkara's own short life that was given to writing scriptural commentaries was relatively brief, four to five years; during the remainder of his life approximately fifteen years, he established religious centers and gave verbal instruction as a wandering ascetic. One particular legend highlights his desire to teach. While travelling in the Himalaya Mountains, he came upon Vyāsa and Gauḍapāda, both deeply enveloped in *samādhi*. He awakened them from their rapture with the imperative to go forth and teach by singing to them the Dakṣiṇāmūrti : "I bow to Śrī Dakṣiṇāmūrti . . . I bow to Him who bestows on the sages direct knowledge of ultimate truth/I bow to the teacher of the three worlds.. . ."[4]

The Personality of the Religious Seeker

Śaṅkara, following the Upaniṣads, holds that even if a religious seeker is versed in the scripture, he still must go to a teacher for liberating knowledge. Both scripture and teacher, as an integral

1. Confer De Smet (1956), p. 1; S. *Śataślokī*, 1.
2. Confer De Smet (1960), p. 27.
3. Confer S. *Viveka*. 520 ff.
4. S. *Dakṣiṇ*. 11.

cause, must be confronted if the student is to transcend binding ignorance. The necessity to become a formal student of a guru arises from the subtlety of the goal of knowledge, which is Brahman, and from the difficulty of the path. That path is rational analysis of reality, and it results in intuitive understanding that in turn enhances the subtlety of both means and end. The master Vedāntin speaks vividly of taking refuge in a teacher as one withdraws into self-discovery and begins the internal search for the true Self. There can be no transmission of liberating knowledge unless one has been a regular student, first undergoing normal academic training and then advancing to the spiritual search of a committed *śiṣya.* To become a student in the Upaniṣadic and Advaita traditions is to follow a particular code of conduct, a code stipulated by the intellectual nature of the pursuit and tested down through the ages. Although the code of conduct is supported by social and moral custom, it becomes the foundation for religious growth and even for final liberation.[1]

Again closely following the Upaniṣads, Śaṅkara speaks of approaching the teacher in the proper way. In listing the basic characteristics of the student, the master Vedāntin consistently includes the requirement that he approach the guru in the prescribed manner. In a discussion of the word *upaniṣad,* Śaṅkara elaborates the theme of approaching the scripture as an approach to knowledge itself.[2] Since scripture and guru are one in his thinking, the approach to scripture is at the same time an approach to the teacher. This approaching entails much more than the initial introduction to the teacher; the notion of approaching also connotes a continual process of seeking liberation and knowledge through the teacher.[3] Direction under a master preceptor is a consistent endeavor until liberation emerges; this is fundamentally what the approach to the teacher implies. Śaṅkara intends far more than the Upaniṣadic injunction to bring wood to the sacrificial fire. While that classical instruction expresses the notion of serving the preceptor, Śaṅkara extends the approach to the teacher throughout the whole developmental process, thus

1. S. *B. U.* II.I.14.
2. S. *Kaṭha.* Intro.
3. Confer S. *Viveka.* 33-34; also S. *B. Gītā* 4.34.

making it the basis for competency to hear, to meditate upon and to realise the wisdom of the highest reality.[1]

It is not surprising that competency (*adhikāra*) plays such an important role in the Vedānta, for the same emphasis is found in most gnostic paths that consist in the transmission of sacred wisdom. Those Hindu sects that give a high place to the guru also give him the prerogative to accept or reject a person as his disciple. This prerogative is based upon the concept of eligibility. A *śiṣya* is any student who can be taught, while an *antevāsin* is one who waits upon and serves the teacher. Only an *adhikārin*, a competent student, is truly qualified for sacred wisdom[2]. In

1.. S. *Kena*, Intro.

2. As will be established later in the text, Śaṅkara's most significant concept for a student is *sannyāsī*, which includes the long history of enunciation and especially *brahmacarya*. The Indian tradition employs a cluster of words for student as it does for teacher. *Brahmacarya* (confer Gonda, 1965, pp. 284 ff) is the most common, an early Vedic concept which refers to studentship and devotion to Brahman. In its full expression it places the seeker of Brahman within a state of renunciation and especially a state of celibacy; this term is the most consistent in meaning and has retained even in modern times the fundamental meaning of a life-long seeking of Brahman as a renunciant, (Gonda, 1965, pp. 311 ff). *Śaikṣa* is a novice in Vedic study; *vidyārthī* is a student desirous to learn. The Upaniṣads use *avakīrṇa* in reference to a student; *antevāsin* (e.g., *Chānd U.* III.2.5) as a worthy student (Śaṅkara's commentary on the *B. Sūtras* 12.1.1. interprets this as one who dwells in a teacher's house); *naiṣṭhika* is perpetual studentship (*Chānd. U.* 2.23). More vocabulary is developed from the *smṛti* literature, for example, *gurukulavāsa* (*Mahābh.* 12.184.8), which refers to studentship for the entire period of purification; *snātaka* or *adīkṣita* for the uninitiated student. Gauḍapāda uses *upāsanāśritaḥ* (*Māṇḍ Kārikā* 111.2), which Śaṅkara interprets as one who performs devotional exercises, and *antevāsika* for one who lives with a teacher (in the Buddhist tradition antevāsika is a pupil involved in a significant teaching relationship). The Vedānta further expands the vocabulary : *mumukṣu* for the seeker of liberation; *sādhaka* for a spiritual aspirant; *madhyama adhikārins* for mediocre students and *adhama* or *manda adhikārins* for inferior students. Śaṅkara's basic use of *adhikāra* is set out in his intrduction to the *B. Sūtra* 1.1.1; this foundation serves as the basis for the variety of vocabulary he takes from the Indian tradition. Yet Śaṅkara uses such words as *śiṣya, brahmacārin, adhikārin, antevāsin,* somewhat synonymously. Sometimes he is governed by the text under commentary; in his own texts the context gives specificity to the meaning; e.g., adhikārin, confer *Viveka.* 14; *śiṣya,* confer *Upadeśa.* 1.18, 2.49, 2.53; *brahmacārin,* confer S. *Tait.* 1.4.3, 1.5.2, and *Upadeśa.* 2.45; *antevāsin,* confer S. *Tait.* 1.11.1.

addition, Śaṅkara situates competency within the broader context of social and ascetical development. The teacher imparting instruction is constrained by the special quality of the knowledge itself.[1] The principle of competency presumes that people differ in what they bring to religious education, that is in their capacities, needs and desires. The spiritual master does not compel his pupils, but rather he gives instruction according to the individual's capacity at a particular time. Śaṅkara argues that one must possess special attributes to be qualified for sacred wisdom. In his introduction to the *Kaṭha Upaniṣad,* he writes : "Thus these cantos themselves are (meant) for special persons (competent for their study), and have a special subject matter, a special purpose, and a special connection .... The knowledge is (meant) for a man of special competence and has a special subject matter, a special purpose, and a sepcial connection[2]..." Whether competency is rare in Śaṅkara's estimation or in the judgment of the tradition preceding him is not easy to ascertain.[3] Śaṅkara requires extensive human development on the part of the student before any serious pursuit of knowledge is undertaken; he opens studentship to a broad spectrum of religious seekers. Nevertheless, the proper conjunction of social and moral prerequisites appears to be a rare achievement, attained by only a few students.

A competent student must be endowed with intelligence. Śaṅkara believes that the first recipient of wisdom is the intelligent and learned individual skilled in argumentation, who not only supports the scripture but also refutes arguments against it.[4] In another place he states that the intelligent person acquires competency for scriptural duties by knowing the relationship of the Self to another world.[5] He does not intend here the realisation of the Self, but he certainly implies a recognition of one's personal inner life. Śaṅkara can thus say that having approached the guru, the religious student immediately takes to reasoning.[6] The teacher, upon the student's approach, questions

1. S. C. U. III.XI.6.
2. S. *Kaṭha,* Intro.
3. Confer De Smet (1956), p. 2; also Kenghe, p. 42.
4. S. *Viveka.* 16.
5. S. *B. Sūtra,* Intro. Śaṅkara uses the term *paraloka* for a world beyond this one.
6. S. *Viveka.* 15.

the novice thoroughly. In the *Chāndogya Upaniṣad*, Satyakāma Jābāla, who out of honesty and frankness reveals his low status in society, is deemed eligible because of his forthright manner and is immediately taught by the preceptor. Śaṅkara observes that the teacher must ask about the family and examine the student regarding caste, profession, conduct and learning.[1] The master Vedāntin is obviously concerned with the social, moral and intellectual capacity of the student.

Śaṅkara insists upon the fulfilment of the stages of life for those who are bound by duties, but at the same time he extends religious instruction beyond any social restriction. Social status does not stand in the way.[2] Even *śūdra*-s and non-Aryans have the need and the capacity for scriptural knowledge, according to Śaṅkara. Whereas Bādarāyaṇa excludes the *śūdra*-s, Śaṅkara opts for the liberality of the earliest Upaniṣads which include them.[3] Believing in the four stages of life Śaṅkara stresses education during the first two stages. Those who belong to the *varṇāśrama* may be encouraged to become *sannyāsī*-s, for renunciation is an easier path in which to pursue liberation. One who has renounced everything for the religious search is already a *sannyāsī*.

Śaṅkara struggled with the notion of eligibility, because significant spiritual development for him is brought about not by effective activity (*karma* yoga) in social and ritual life, but knowledge alone. Renunciation suffices to make one eligible and constitute one a *sannyāsī*. By establishing guru-*sannyāsī*-s in religious centers throughout India, Śaṅkara also introduced the corresponding notion of the student-*sannyāsī*. The student

1. S. *C. U.* IV.IV.1; S. *Upadeśa* 1.2.
2. S. *B. Sūtra* III.IV.36-39.
3. Contrast S. *B. Sūtra* III.IV.37, where Śaṅkara opens eligibility broadly, to S. *B. Sūtra* I.III.34-38, where *śūdras* are prohibited from Vedic study because they are not twiceborn. Yet in S. *B. Sūtra* I.III.38, he admits that those *śūdras* who led a good life in the past cannot have knowledge withheld from them. It is contested among some scholars whether Śaṅkara is liberal or rigid in this matter. In my judgment, he is liberal in opening sacred wisdom to all, but he is rigid in denying *sannyāsa*, seemingly the great access to sacred wisdom, to those outside the higher classes. The paradox of the matter is that *sannyāsa* itself transcends caste.

ascetics were recruited, in the beginning, from all castes; some individuals soon tran scended caste by the quality of their lives and were called *ativarṇāśramī*-s (superior to caste and the stages of life). Śaṅkara's liberality, nonetheless, had its limits, for although he admitted *śūdra*-s and widowers to formal studentship, he did not open the *maṭhas* to women and did not make provision for them. He seems, in fact, to limit female scholarship to domestic affairs.[1] This stands in strong contrast to Buddhist asceticism which accepted women in monastic life from the time of the Buddha. It also constrasts sharply with the tradition of the early Veda, which identifies at least twenty-six learned women among the ancient seers. Śaṅkara attempts to build a foundation for eligibility with criteria that can be grouped around two poles : intellectual acumen and renunciation. In regard to the former, three things are to be accepted : scholarly discipline, strength arising from knowledge, and meditativeness. As for the latter, three things are to be rejected : progeny, property, and the achievements of other worlds.[2]

Śaṅkara mined the ascetical tradition of India for insight into renunciation. There are four classical requirements which that tradition demands of the renunciant, and Śaṅkara consistently elaborates upon them as sure signs of competency in the student. The four are discrimination (*viveka*) between the real and the unreal, renunciation (*vairāgya*) of worldly desires, the conjunction of six ethical virtues (*ṣaṭ-sampatti*), and longing for spiritual liberation (*mumukṣutā*).[3] They qualify one as a religious seeker. They constitute the moral preparation and the moral personality of the religious seeker. By placing discrimination at the head of the list, Śaṅkara again suggests the intellectual nature of Advaita Vedānta. Discrimination, according to Śaṅkara, is an understanding of reality as propounded by Advaita. It is a rational analysis that differentiates Brahman as real (*satya*) from the false (*mithyā*) universe.[4] It is the mental capaciy to distinguish between eternal and ephemeral values and reality. The

1. S. *B. U.* VI.IV.17. Confer Sarmah, pp. 251 ff.
2. S. *B. U.* III.V.1. As an example of other worlds, Śaṅkara, in this place, gives the example of the world of Hiraṇyagarbha.
3. S. *Viveka*. 17 ff; S. *Aparok*. 9.
4. S. *Viveka*. 20. Discrimination (*viveka*) is Śaṅkara's term, which I interpret as rational analysis.

individual attains liberation because he has the capacity to discriminate with understanding. Each of the four requirements is causative of another. Discrimination gives rise to renunciation; one is able to reject transitory enjoyment once one has attained the right knowledge of objects by perceiving their ephemeral and transitory condition. Renunciation is the classical Indian concept of non-attachment. The discriminatory mind is turned away from the world of sense objects. Renunciation implies a life of austerity. The practice of religious austerities (*tapas*) is renunciation in the mundane order. Śaṅkara believes that the religious seeker must live upon the strength of knowledge alone. Renunciation and discrimination are absolutized in the thought of Śaṅkara to the degree that they are indispensable for liberation. Discrimination, the one-pointed direction of the mind, and renunciation structure the moral personality.

A cluster of ethical virtues, the third prerequisite, strengthens the two previous requirements. Ethical virtues bring about a greater control of the mind and the senses. The first virtue is calmness (*śama*), and it is described as resting the mind in the pursuit of Brahman. The second is self-control (*dama*), which withdraws the intellect and the senses from their objects. Following upon them are forbearance (*titikṣā*), the capacity to bear anxieties and afflictions; faith (*śraddhā*), an intellectual confirmation and acceptance of the truth of scripture and the guru; withdrawing the mind from distractions (*uparati*) that prevent the seeker from reverting to previously rejected objects; and finally the concentration of the mind (*samādhāna*) upon Brahman.[1] From an intellectual perspective, these virtues create a personality with pure motivation, one dispassionate and controlled.

Śaṅkara speaks in different contexts of the desire, the thirst and hankering for liberation (*mumukṣutā*), which is the fourth and last of the requirements for studentship. The thirst for liberation seeks freedom from the body, the physical world, the uncertain mind and even egotism; on the other hand, it is a positive desire for true knowledge of the Self and Brahman.[2] Desire for liberation means active faith in Brahman and belief in the possibility

1. S. *Viveka*. 22-26; this is confirmed in S. *Ātmānātmaviveka*, a contested work, in Chaterjee, p. 37.

2. S. *Viveka*. 27.

of self-realisation. The *Muṇḍaka Upaniṣad* teaches that the Self is attained neither by study nor by the intellect; rather, when one seeks the Self, it reveals its own reality. Commenting on this, Śaṅkara observes that actual pursuit of the Self is the principal human effort and the achievement "consists in praying for this consummation to the exclusion of everything else."[1]

The four ascetic requirements point to qualities that are present only in seminal form at the beginning of student life, but that grow throughout the development of the individual until they attain a perfect form with the emergence of liberating wisdom. Śaṅkara also includes in his scheme several practices that were common in religious training, for instance, that a student could not turn back once he had begun his duties. Commenting upon the three branches of knowledge listed in the *Chāndogya Upaniṣad* (study, living in the teacher's house and mortification of the body), Śaṅkara notes that the second, service to the teacher, implies a life of austerity but not the life of a wandering ascetic. Service means an ascetical life lived with the preceptor. An absolute observance of celibacy, mortification and penance is also prescribed. The student undertakes three practices : sacrifice, study and service.[2] Knowledge is not imparted unless one is obedient, controlled and dispassionate. The teacher expects service and elicits devotion, but the concrete meaning of service and devotion to the teacher is the ascetical life. The requirements of student life are clearly demanding. In the four prerequisites, Śaṅkara stresses intelligence along with religious austerities, but elsewhere he places emphasis upon service and devotion to the guru.[3] Student life, consequently, embraces both the pursuit of intellectual goals and the formation of an ascetical personality. The quality of student life is measured by the degree to which these requirements are fulfilled.

The moral traits that modify the personality of the student have an intellectual aspect to them as well. When Śaṅkara speaks of tranquility, calmness and a pacified mind, he means to add an intellectual element to what is ordinarily understood by these terms. Discrimination and renunciation are to purify the

1. S. *M. U.* III.II.3.
2. Confer S. *C. U.* II.XXIII.1; S. *Kaṭha* I.I.17.
3. S. *B.' Gītā* 18.67

mind so that "liberation is as easy of access as a fruit on the palm of one's hand."[1] The religious seeker dissipates ignorance through self-control, forbearance, calm, and withdrawal of the mind from the realm of the senses. The mind is refined by calmness (*śama*) and self-control (*dama*).[2] Virtue tends toward the creation of a new mind. For Śaṅkara, purity of mind is essential because self-knowledge occurs only among those who are mentally pure.[3] The master Vedāntin, in fact, looks upon the whole period of student life as a time of purification. All yoga, even the eight-limb yoga of Patañjali, purifies the mind as it kindles "the fire of knowledge."[4]

All of this does not mean that the student of Śaṅkara's conception is solely an academic. Śaṅkara cautions against excessive infatuation with the scripture and a passion for too much study. The many words of scripture frequently cause the mind to ramble, he observes.[5] The kind of personality he envisions in the student is wholly centered upon self-discovery and the repudiation of all other concerns. Śaṅkara rejects, for example, concern over social formalities, concern for "trimming the body" and physical comforts.[6] He sternly rejects the physical order and denigrates the body with severe language. To throw off the physical is a common injunction.[7] Śaṅkara inculcates an indifference toward everything but self-realisation.

In spite of these uncompromising strictures, Śaṅkara does not eliminate from the moral personality softer characteristics such as pious generosity, compassion, noninjury, contentment, dispassion and simple obedience. His emphasis upon the more rigorous virtues stems from his conviction that they prepare a student for realisation more than any other qualities can. Śaṅkara would create, however, neither a severe character nor a cerebral one. Three basic qualities that he atrributes to the ideal *sannyāsī*, be he student or teacher, are childlikeness (*bālya*), learning

1. S. *Viveka*. 181.
2. S. *B. Gītā* 2.21.
3. S. *Ātma*. 1, 2.
4. S. *Haristotra* 41.
5. S. *Viveka*. 270-271; also 60-61.
6. S. *Viveka*. 270.
7. This is especially prevalent in S. *Viveka*.

(*pāṇḍitya*) and silence (*mauna*)[1]. Childlikeness means concentrating upon one pursuit only, upon a return to simplicity and a primordial condition of receptivity. Learning involves the comprehension of scripture and the instruction of a teacher. And the stage of silence and reflection, the condition of the *muni*, suggests the sort of receptivity from which knowledge of the Self emerges. It is significant that in Śaṅkara's conception, the personality of the religious student is not substantially different from that of the teacher. One is distinctively formed in the image of the other. Since communication of knowledge takes place between teacher and student, a communion of personalities is anticipated.

What is the role of devotion (*bhakti*) in the formation of the religious personality ? Although there is ample use of devotional vocabulary in the writing of Śaṅkara, it must be understood within the more general context of Advaita Vedānta. Faith arises from knowledge. Faith is an intellectual acceptance of the truth of instruction from the teacher and the scripture. The mind in faith attains reliance on the truth of instruction.[2] Devotion, like faith, is also intellectualized, in terms of seeking one's real nature or inquiring into the truth of one's inner Self.[3] Devotion renders one worthy of scriptural instruction.[4] In his commentary on the *Gītā*, the master Advaitin distinguishes devotion to knowledge from devotion to activity; the latter can be a means to the former, which alone leads to liberation.[5] Both faith and devotion are interpreted in relation to knowledge. A more traditional conception of *bhakti*, however, is also present in Śaṅkara's writing and in the personality of the student that he articulates. His hymns attest to his profound love for the gods and his gurus;

1. S. *B. Sūtra* III.IV.46-50; in S. *B. Sūtra* III.IV.46, *bālyam* means childlike innocence which is the basic sense of the passage cited. In S. *B. Sūtra* III.IV.50, *bālya* is a childlike state. These three states are prefigured in the *āśrama*-s, that is childlikeness as student, learning as a householder, and silence as a forest dweller (Guenon, p. 176).

2. S. *Viveka*. 25. Śaṅkara defines faith (*śraddhā*) in this place as a result of judgment and any blind belief is ruled out. For a Hindu concept of faith, confer Wilfred Cantwell Smith, *Faith and Belief*. Princeton : Princeton University Press, 1979, pp. 53 ff.

3. S. *Viveka*. 31-32.

4. S. *B. Gītā* 18.68.

5. S. *B. Gītā* 2 & Intro.

his commentaries, likewise, reflect an affectionate regard for the gurus of the past. He instructs students to worship their teachers with devotion, prostrations and humility, with virtues that resonate the love tradition.[1] He illustrates devotion to his own teachers in poetic terms, for example in a reference to Govinda "who like the gods churned the great ocean and gathered nectar."[2] Śaṅkara's disciples, as early legends testify, reciprocated with equal devotion. In the initial stage of religious formation, Śaṅkara recommends devotion to a personal god, but devotion becomes gradually intellectualized as the disciple progresses along the path of knowledge.

The nature of the religious student in Advaita Vedānta is firmly rooted in the tradition of *jñāna* yoga (the yoga of knowledge). He "walks in accordance with the instructions of a well-wishing and worthy guru as well as his own reason."[3] Śaṅkara's conception of religious formation rests upon the conviction that knowledge of the Self arises in a particular type of mind, a mind formed by discrimination and renunciation. Discrimination and renunciation further characterize the student. The development of an Advaita personality, in Śaṅkara's vision, leads to realisation of one's own spiritual nature. K. C. Bhattacharya, the modern Indian philosopher, speaks of the student's securing a spiritual attitude : "To know the truth about himself can be the only way of attaining freedom, and the discipline, therefore, is primarily that of knowing (*jñāna*) and secondarily that of willing and feeling (*karma* and *bhakti*)."[4] The life prescribed for the student is a distinct spirituality, in which the Self is accepted initially in faith and then confirmed, formulated and clarified by reason and the guru. The student interiorizes knowledge, whereupon understanding of Self emerges as vision. He walks with the guru but stands in the strength of his own reason and experience.

The Guru-Śiṣya Relationship

The relationship between guru and *śiṣya* begins in what the two

1. S. *Viveka*. 34.
2. S. *Upadeśa*. XIX.28; also confer XVIII.233.
3. S. *Viveka*. 81.
4. Bhattacharya, Vol. 1, p. 118.

hold most in common, namely, a life of discrimination and renunciation. Those qualities that are initially required of the student and constitute his competency eventually will bring teacher and student together and advance their relationship. Since service to and attendance upon the teacher are more important than other duties in the scripture, they structure a filial relationship. From a filial relationship develops a love relationship as attendance upon the guru elicits affection, esteem and ultimately devotion. Service to the teacher is a form of devotion, and deep devotion results in worship. Devotion to the guru implies devotion to God in Śaṅkara's estimation, a belief that accords with the Hindu classical tradition. The student enters an intimate union with the preceptor wherein his mind and life are conentrated upon him. Their relationship attains higher expectation in the greater concentration of the student upon the knowledge imparted by the teacher. The highest moment of the guru-*śiṣya* relationship in Śaṅkara's Vedānta is in the order of knowledge, which distinguishes it within the guru tradition.

There emerges an important difference with the Buddhist teachers where the relationship between student and *ācārya*, united by mutual purpose and community of life, appears set within a filial framework. Likewise, the relationship between the Buddhist *upajjhāya*, the teacher of doctrine, and the student is governed by spiritual dependence (*nissaya*) to such a degree that both the student and even the ordinary teacher remain in filial obeisance. The Indian epics and *Purāṇas* naturally highlight a love relationship resulting from service done in devotion or from intense worship of the guru. The Tantra, on the other hand, places such stress upon initiation that all practice done by a disciple is centered solely on the guru. One study maintains that the guru-disciple relationship in Tantra exists only when divine *śakti* (energy) is not communicated in initiation. Gathering all orthodox Hindu traditions, the *Dharmaśāstra* offers the most composite picture of the varieties of guru-disciple relationships, from master-servant, father-son, even to lover-beloved. The Laws of Manu, when drawing upon the Upaniṣadic heritage, may come closest in articulating a relationship raised to the level of wisdom.[1]

1. Confer Bhagat, Chakraborty and Mookerji, on *Tantra*, Woodroffe, pp. 38, 206.

The Advaita student reaches a point where there is no difference between the teacher, the teaching and the taught : this is the condition of nonduality. In each teaching tradition in India, the guru forms the student in his own image.[1] For Śaṅkara, this means that the disciple is brought to the nonduality of the teacher, the teaching and the disciple himself.[2] The teacher, however, directs the student neither to imitate him nor to seek the divine in him. Following the Upaniṣadic axiom, the guru does not ask the disciple to verify that "I, the guru, am Brahman," but to verify instead that "You, the student, are Brahman."[3] Śaṅkara speaks of the teacher who "creates equality with himself in the disciple."[4] Śaṅkara's delineation of the spiritual relationship between guru and *śiṣya* that culminates in the equality of the two is one of his important contributions to India's teaching tradition. This is more implied than explicit in Śaṅkara's thought, but it logically follows from his emphasis on the student's own knowledge and experience. Equality is achieved in a relationship experienced in and expressed from the order of knowledge. With the experience of liberation, the disciple becomes equal to his guru. He becomes a guru himself due to his own experience.

A contradiction may appear in Śaṅkara's thought between the importance accorded to the teacher on the one hand and that given to the experience of the student on the other hand. Śaṅkara insists, for example, that knowledge depends on others for its emergence, and at the same time maintains that liberation is due to oneself. "The true nature of things is to be known personally, through the eye of clear illumination, and not through a sage," he writes.[5] A primary factor in Śaṅkara's system is the role of personal experience and intuition in the liberation process. Self-realisation takes place in consciousness through discrimination, personal experience and intuition. What separates Śaṅkara from other Hindu teachers is that he leads the

1. Confer S. *Śataślokī* 1. This concept, however, is extremely rare in Śaṅkara's writing and is absent in his major commentaries.

2. S. *Māṇḍ. Kārikā* 1.18. Śaṅkara explains that the diversity of instruction, instructor and instructed exists only for the sake of the instruction; ultimately the diversity ceases to exist (*dvaitam na vidyate*).

3. Confer Date, p. 458.

4. S. *Śataślokī* 1.

5. S. *Viveka*. 54.

student beyond the experience and knowledge of the guru. The guru is finally transcended by the experience (*svānubhava*) of the disciple.[1] Personal experience is the norm and source of liberating wisdom; such experience emerges from a relationship deeply formed in knowledge, but it is raised to nondual experience. In his commentary on the *Gītā*, the master Vedāntin distinguishes between knowledge acquired from scripture and the teacher (*jñāna*), and knowledge acquired from personal experience (*vijñāna*).[2] Although Śaṅkara places personal experience beyond the teacher and scripture in the developmental process, experience and higher wisdom (*vijñāna*) come about in the context of a relationship in the order of knowledge (*jñāna*). The living relationship is, in this sense, a source of liberating experience and wisdom.

The spiritual relationship between the teacher and the disciple culminates in a permanent nondual union between them. Therefore, the time during which it is properly called a teaching relationship is limited. The time of the guru's teaching ends once self-realisation is achieved. Then, Śaṅkara urges the student himself to "establish by teaching both the text itself and its meaning as I have established it in you."[3] The student himself is called to a teaching mission. Three distinct phases can be detected in Śaṅkara's relationships with his disciples. There was the initial period of association and instruction wherein the filial, devotional and intellectual relationship was cultivated. This was followed by a period when his disciples began to write treatises and commentaries of their own but were still in close contact with him. The third and final stage occurred when he created the major teaching centers, in each of which he placed a disciple to take over its leadership. Having established his disciples as teachers in their own stead, he left them to continue the teaching tradition they had received from him. They became gurus. Nonetheless, their spiritual relationship with Śaṅkara continued as one of love, esteem and lineage.

Śaṅkara's contribution to the teaching tradition consists especially in the quality he gives to the relationship of teacher and

1. Confer Date, p. 457.
2. S. *B. Gītā* 3.4.
3. S. *B. Gītā* 18.68.

student. He places reason on a par with scripture in the religious quest, and reason even becomes a test for scripture. He gives a special role to reason and personal experience because of the unique place of the guru in the life of the disciple. The guru establishes continuity between scripture and reason. He calls forth the experience of the student to test and to verify whatever is taught by himself or scripture. Placing confidence in the power of reason and human experience, Śaṅkara gives efficacy to the teaching relationship. The great discovery is that in relationship one transcends his own limitations, individuality and even his guru.

CHAPTER THREE

ŚAṄKARA'S PEDAGOGY IN RELIGIOUS LIFE

The relationship between teacher and student is fostered by an educational method, and the discrete pedagogic tools making up that method imprint the relationship with its distinctive characteristics. For Śaṅkara and for much of Hinduism, the educational method itself comprises a spirituality within which the relationship between guru and disciple can be perfected and the disciple can achieve liberation. Śaṅkara uses the word *sādhana* to signify that his educational method is both a singular means of teaching and a means for spiritual liberation.[1] Educational method in Advaita Vedānta is more than pedagogy: it is carefully executed program of spirituality whose goal is the development of the religious student. When the master Vedāntin speaks of pedagogy, he always presumes that the student has already achieved a high level of personal growth and has progressively refined his total person—mind, senses and body.

This pedagogy, conceived here as a spiritual path, is preceded by a thorough preparation in religiously motivated activity. Śaṅkara does not eliminate *karma* yoga; rather, he posits it as a precondition for religious education and spiritual growth. In performing religious duties, a capacity for knowledge is cultivated. The selfless activity sanctioned by the *Bhagavad Gītā* prepares the student for commitment to knowledge (*jñāna-niṣṭhā*) and subsequently for more advanced religious growth.[2] As he observes injunctions from scripture, duties and rituals, the student gradually learns that knowledge of the Self is beyond human activity.[3] Śaṅkara speaks of the elimination of ritual and religious duties after the rise of knowledge. The *karma* yoga of the

1. S. *Upadeśa*. 1.1. *Sādhana* is from a root signifying that which leads straight to a goal or that which guides one to it; most literally, it is the effective means toward a goal. The Hindu *mārga*-s (paths) and yogas are frequently called *sādhana*-s; *sādhana* generally refers to a spirituality, that is a religious discipline based upon a religious vision.

2. S. *B. Gītā*, 18.46.

3. Ibid., 12.2.

Gītā, which consecrates activity as selfless and altruistic, is but the initial path in spiritual development. Such activity serves as a means to achieve educational competency, a means prior to advanced religious instruction, a preparatory moment, to perfect intellectual capacity. Once this moment is past, the religious seeker renounces such activity and commits himself wholly to the path of knowledge.[1]

Further growth is brought about through the teachings of scripture and of the teacher. Achievement in nondual experience and understanding follows upon the instruction begun by the teacher and scripture. Instruction consists in a practical plan of self-inquiry on the one hand, and an equally practical understanding of the Self on the other, both of which are cultivated by hearing, reflection and concentration.

Self-Inquiry

Knowledge arises by inquiry. Śaṅkara's commentary on the *Brahma Sūtra*, which is written presumably by a self-realised teacher, is an inquiry into the nature of Brahman, but from the perspective of the religious student it is an inquiry into the Self. Self-inquiry is rooted in an understanding of scripture. The Upaniṣadic and pre-Śaṅkara traditions view scripture as a source of knowledge precisely because it invariably turns the student inward to self-inquiry, to an analysis of experience and understanding. Understanding achieved through the Upaniṣads is singularly true knowledge for Śaṅkara. An analytical understanding of Brahman is available only from the Upaniṣads, because these texts alone, according to Advaita, articulate reality as it truly is.[2] This does not mean that one goes to the Upaniṣads indiscriminately, but rather that the four great axioms (*mahāvākya-s*) of scripture are employed in self-inquiry.[3]

The structure of Śaṅkara's metaphysics is reflected in the four axioms, which contain his educational method for self-inquiry as well. "That Thou Art" (*tat tvam asi*), the first axiom, is a metaphysical statement that is to be substantiated in direct experience through self-inquiry. "I am Brahman" (*ahaṃ brahmāsmi*), the

1. Confer S. B. *Gītā* 18.55 ff; S. B. *Sūtra*. 4.26.-27.
2. S. *B. Sūtra*. II.I.11; II.I.27.
3. Confer *Māṇḍ U.* 11; *C. U.* 6.8.7; *B. U.* 1.4.10; *Ait. U.* III.1.3.

second axiom, is the counterpart or subjective expression of the former great saying. "That" (*tat*) is perceived and encountered outside the body, extrinsic to the individual, but it is interiorized and experienced immanently and finally expressed by "I am Brahman" (*aham brahmāsmi*). The objective "that" is correlated with the immanent "I". The "I" (*aham*) perceived within the human person as immanent and subjective is reciprocally exteriorized as transcendent and finally expressed by "That thou art" (*tat tvam asi*). Although the four great Upaniṣadic sayings are metaphysical statements, they pass through an epistemological process in self-inquiry wherein they are perceived, experienced and understood.[1] The other two axioms, namely "*Ātman* is Brahman" (*ayaṃ ātmā brahma*) and "All is Brahman" (*sarvaṃ khalvidaṃ brahma*), are variations of the first two axioms and function in the same way.[2] The first metaphysical statement, "*Ātman* is Brahman," is epistemologically substantiated as the "All is Brahman" of direct experience. The objective state is again perceived and interiorized. While the four axioms have the grammatical structure of synthetic *a priori* propositions, they are really analytic statements supported by experience. That is to say, the four axioms are identity judgments rather than attributive judgments, and self-inquiry tries to attain such identity. Śvetaketu in the Upaniṣads is instructed with "That thou art" nine times before the great axiom passes from a mere propositional statement to one fully perceived and finally caught in intuitive vision. In each of the nine stages, Śvetaketu comes to a deeper understanding of reality, reality remaining always the same.

Śaṅkara follows a traditional pattern of education in the *Upadeśasāhasrī*, his classical treatise on teaching. He first gives instruction on the important scriptural texts, then he proceeds to definitions of Brahman culled from the texts, and finally he begins a series of questions leading to more radical self-inquiry.[3] The definitions of Brahman are taught from descriptive texts such

1. Date, Vol. II pp. 467-470.

2. Confer S. *Upadeśa.* 1.6; also confer S. *C. U.*, VII.XXV.2. The variation on the axiom, "All is Brahman" is "Consciousness is Brahman" (*prajñānam brahma*)." Confer *Ait. U.* III.1.3.

3. S. *Upadeśa.* 1.7. ff.

as "Existence-Knowledge-Infinite," "Not this, not this," "The Brahman that is immediate and direct," "It is the Seer Itself unseen." Each description implies oneness of the Self and Brahman.[1] Śaṅkara does not limit himself to the scripture for definitions of the nature of the Self, but he also includes texts from other religious literature.[2] In the process of self-inquiry, however, there is but one objective as the teacher reveals the meaning of the great axioms and the nature of Brahman : the realisation that the Self is one with Brahman, the unitary principle.

Another method familiar to the Upaniṣadic seers that Śaṅkara takes up is the use of questions as pedagogical tools for self-discovery. After teaching the scriptural texts that establish the nature of the Self and Brahman, Śaṅkara recommends a process of questioning to uncover different levels of understanding the reality of the Self.[3] The student is urged to take the initiative and to place before the teacher similar questions that reveal the causes of ignorance and subsequent freedom.[4] For example, the student may ask, "How am I devoid of birth, lineage and ceremonies which are different from the Self ?"[5] Throughout the questioning process between teacher and student, the descriptive understandings of the Self and Brahman are kept foremost in mind. Śaṅkara counsels his students to "remember the characteristics of the Self."[6] Self-inquiry draws upon reasoning and scripture, but difficulties in analysis are usually solved by the scripture. If the scripture itself raises problems of interpretation and understanding, the authority and experience of the teacher carry weight. In fact, the scripture has greater authority when it is supported by the experience of the preceptor.

In addition to following the traditional method of self-inquiry through teaching the classical axioms and the definitions of Brahman and through a probing dialectic, Śaṅkara continues the

1. Ibid., 1.7; confer S. *Tait. U.* II.1; S. *B. U.* II.III.6, III.IV.1, III.VIII.II.
2. S. *Upadeśa.* 1.9.
3. Ibid., 1.9. ff.
4. Confer S. *B. Gītā* 4.34. The *Ātmānātmaviveka*, a spurious work attributed to Śaṅkara, also employs dialogue between teacher and student in the form of question and answer.
5. S. *Upadeśa.* 1.23. Confer S. *Viveka.* 49.
6. S. *Upadeśa.* 16-17.

Vedānta lineage by employing an equally traditional method referred to as "assertion through negation."[1] He advises the use of negation in self-analysis, that is, the negation of every factor progressively experienced and understood that lacks absolute and perduring reality. At the same time a positive assertion is made by the student affirming his oneness with Brahman. Discrimination (*viveka*) is to assert positively what one is, "I am Brahman," and at the same time to deny what one is not, "Not this, not this" (*neti neti*). The student denies, through statements of negation, an identity with the ephemeral nature of all microcosmic and macrocosmic objects; through positive statements, he identifies with the perduring nature of all beings and possibly in a final state with eternal being.[2] This method is employed in Śaṅkara's examination of the states of consciousness and in the examination of the coverings of the Self that are taken up for analysis in typical Upaniṣadic self-inquiry.

The analysis of the states of consciousness in the *Chāndogya Upaniṣad* is a means to perceive and to experience the disengagement of the Self from the states of waking, dream and dreamless sleep. In the awake state, the mind is perceived in close contact with the external world of objects; in dream and dreamless sleep, there is incoherency, and then the mind ceases to function. But the continuity, according to the Vedānta, in the various stages, even in dreamless sleep, is consciousness, independent and free. The *Taittirīya Upaniṣad* speaks of the gross body of the awake state constituted so to speak, by the sheath or covering of matter : the subtle body of the dream state is constituted by the covering of vitality, mind and self-consciousness; and finally the causal body of deep sleep is constituted by the covering of bliss. The last stage of dreamless sleep or bliss (*turīya*), wherein consciousness exists of itself with nothing present to it, comes close to a condition of being that is free and transcendent of all conditions, states and individuality. This analysis, leading to self-understanding and self-discovery, common in Upaniṣadic literature, is employed in Śaṅkara's Vedānta in order to achieve an awareness of the Self. Examination of experience is highly reflective and analytical throughout, and it employs both negative and positive assertions until the inquiry can be pursued no further.

1. Date, Vol. II, p. 459.
2. Krishnananda, p. 125.

The Triple Method : Hearing, Reflection and Concentration

Śaṅkara's contribution to the practice of self-inquiry consists in isolating the four classical axioms and using them not only as metaphysical expressions of Advaita Vedānta but also as pedagogical tools for self-realisation. Other practical means, such as the analysis of the states of consciousness, are taken by Śaṅkara without modification from the Upaniṣads. The triple method, also from the same literature, receives greater definition and specification in Śaṅkara's usage than in the parent literature. His *Ātmabodha*, a concise work used in Advaita for religious training, is basically an exposition of the triple method. This method occurs in Śaṅkara's writing more frequently than any other means to self-realisation. It constitutes precisely the educational framework in which the student is placed for growth in religious life.

The employment of the triple method is supervised by a guru. Hearing, reflection and concentration upon the Vedānta relate directly to Brahman, for they are the causes that remove obstacles to and evoke knowledge of primal reality.[1] They form the context for self-realisation. Śaṅkara insists that these means must be actualized and in some manner combined for true realisation.[2] Although they constitute a single course of development, they are three successive moments that must accord with one another and with the Vedānta. There is one place in his writing where Śaṅkara considers each state superior to the previous one[3] so that each is taught and practiced as an isolated and distinct moment. This one text notwithstanding, the fact that the method is to be treated as a single unit is beyond contention. The student resorts to each of the three means within the same period of time. In proposing the method, Śaṅkara insists that hearing, reflection and concentration are done rationally, with the full resources of the mind. Reflection through reasoning must be in strict accord with scriptural evidence. Concentration, moreover, opposes

1. S. *B. U.* I.IV.2.
2. S. *B. U.* II.IV.5.
3. S. *Viveka.* 364. Since the authenticity of this work is still contested by some, the point should not be considered significant as it is only made here. In the post-Śaṅkara period, hearing is elevated over the other two means by one major Advaita school.

neither reason nor the scripture.[1] The method is used repeatedly. With each use, special attention is paid to the meaning culled from previous hearing, reflection and concentration, until intuitive, nondual experience and understanding arise.

Hearing (*śravaṇa*), listening to the guru and learning the Vedāntic texts, constitutes formal study of the Upaniṣads under the direction of a teacher. It is an academic activity that investigates the texts,[2] especially the classical axioms, in order to determine their meaning. Hearing embodies a conviction that an understanding of the texts leads one to Brahman; its objective is to grasp from the text, context and instruction the meaning of "That thou art." Reflection (*manana*) is a sort of reasoning upon the meaning of the text, wherein a rational critique is applied to the instruction of the guru. It is a mental operation of deliberating upon the instruction and establishing certitude on either the meaning of the text or the instruction. Since Śaṅkara considers scripture and guru to be one integral factor, hearing and reflection are directed toward the texts and the teaching of the preceptor together. In concentration (*nididhyāsana*), the mind dwells consistently on the meaning of the nonduality of Brahman and the Self. Concentration also entails a conscious operation of withdrawing the mind from extrinsic objects and fixing it on the meaning of the Self alone. Concentration is an uninterrupted focus upon meaning or, in Śaṅkara's vocabulary, upon the flow of ideas. Its purpose is to transform the meaning of the instruction, which is mediated and indirect, into immediate and direct knowledge of Brahman. Concentration terminates only in new vision and insight. The triple method is finalized in spiritual liberation.[3]

1. S. *B. U.* II.V.Intro.

2. Six characteristics aid in understanding the text : *upakrama* (beginning) and *upasaṃhāra* (conclusion) usually contain the topic of each text; *abhyāsa* (repetition) is discussion of the topic in repeated variations; *apūrvatā* (originality) indicates that the topic is not considered elsewhere in this particular manner; *phala* (result) points to the conclusion of the study contained in the text; *arthavāda* (eulogy) highlights the value of the study; *upapatti* (demonstration) is the logical argumentation throughout the text. Confer Zimmer, pp. 431 ff.

3. Confer S. *Viveka*. 70, 364; *S. B. U.* IV.V.6. Confer Venkatarama Iyer, pp. 172ff; Satprakashananda, pp. 256ff; Warrier, pp. 445ff; Satchidanandendra Saraswati, pp. 181 ff; Nikhilananda (1967), pp. 121 ff.

Hearing has a unique function within the process. "Teaching becomes useful if it is meant for a hearer," writes the master Vedāntin.[1] The role of the teacher is especially important at this initial moment, for hearing is only from a teacher; one hears only through the favor of a teacher.[2] The Upaniṣads teach that knowledge of scripture is acquired only by the ear, and Śaṅkara upholds this tradition by insisting that one can study only through hearing. To hear is to understand without distraction.[3] It involves two powers, one belonging to the ear, which gathers ephemeral knowledge, and one belonging to the Self, which is an eternal power. The "Self is accepted as the eternal hearer," comments the Vedāntin.[4] He sometimes uses the operation of hearing to signify the entire spiritual process; reflection and concentration may include hearing. In fact, to listen to the teaching and to achieve right knowledge are simultaneous and may result in the eradication of ignorance.[5] Śaṅkara attributes to hearing a comprehensiveness far beyond audile attention to an instructor. The term hearing can be a metaphor for both reflection and concentration. Although he cites in one place the calming of the vitalistic (*rajas*) qualities as a function of hearing, hearing naturally intersects with reflection and concentration.[6]

Nonetheless, understanding from reflection (*manana*) and concentration (*nididhyāsana*) is different from understanding acquired through hearing.[7] Reflection does not take for its object any new knowledge, but that which has been heard and which has its foundation in tradition. For Śaṅkara, "reflections which, without basis in tradition, rest only on the speculation of men are untenable, since such speculation is unbridled."[8] Reflection and concentration involve the recollection of the tradition, even a repetition or re-experience of it. These two moments in the pedagogic method include discrimination (*viveka*). In reflection,

1. S. *Upadeśa*. 18.111.
2. S. *Kaṭha* I.II.13, I.III.16.
3. S. *B. Gītā* 18.72.
4. S. *Ait. U.* II.Intro.
5. S. *Upadeśa*. 18.103.
6. S. *Viveka*. 182.
7. S. *Tait. U.* I.XI.4. Śaṅkara states here that scripture is the primary foundation for reasoning.
8. S. *B. Sūtra* II.I.11.

discrimination signifies rigorous, rational analysis, while discrimination in concentration repudiates all limitations superimposed on the Self. Concentration, unlike typical meditation (*dhyāna*) upon a symbol, presumes a right understanding of the reality upon which one concentrates. Yājñavalkya, a sage in the Upaniṣads, substitutes the word right knowledge (*vijñāna*) for concentration (*nididhyāsana*), and Śaṅkara therefore distinguishes the knowledge (*jñāna*) of meditation (*dhyāna*) from the right knowledge of concentration (*nididhyāsana*).[1] The former (*jñāna*) implies meaning mediated through symbols, while the latter (*vijñāna*) implies immediate and direct experience of Brahman. Knowledge of Brahman, however, is not the result of this intellectual endeavor; it is independent of it. The knowledge (*vijñāna*) of concentration, which follows upon the knowledge (*jñāna*) of meditation (*dhyāna*), is self-revealing. Reflection and meditation imply concentration. But as concentration intensifies, it separates from and advances beyond meditation and reflection.

Three operations hold importance in the triple method and especially in advanced stages of growth : concentration, repetition and memory. Śaṅkara cautions that there is "no greater death than inadvertence with regard to concentration," and affirms that the concentrated individual attains success.[2] The student listens with concentration to the guru's exposition of the scripture with his mind, senses and body focused upon the preceptor while all religious activity and ritual is put aside.[3] The student's attention deepens as he achieves the cessation of perceptions of the external world. For Śaṅkara, yoga means withdrawing the senses from their objects and entering fully into the concentrated mind. The concentration of external and internal senses, of body and mind, is considered the most excellent discipline. It is the highest ascetical discipline, the singular discipline.[4] It is one-pointed attention to hearing, reflection and meditation. Concentration is defined by Śaṅkara in broad terms as "setting up a continuous stream of similar thoughts."[5] While this definition

1. Confer *B. U.* II.4.5; IV.5.6; also Satprakashananda, pp. 288 ff.
2. S. *Viveka*. 327.
3. S. *Kena* IV.8.
4. S. *Tait*. U. III.I.1, III.VI.1. Śaṅkara in these texts refers to concentration as austerity (*tapaḥ*).
5. S. *B. Sūtra* IV.I.8.

is found in many other Indian spiritual traditions, elsewhere it pertains to the nature of reflection or discursive meditation.

Concentration, moreover, is supported by the Vedānta practice of reiteration or repetition. In the *Chāndogya Upaniṣad*, Uddālaka repeatedly teaches the axiom "That thou art" to his student, Śvetaketu. Śaṅkara and the Vedānta also employ repetition throughout the course of hearing, reflection and meditation.[1] In a hymn to Hari, Śaṅkara urges repetition of the sacred syllable *OM*. An entire chapter of the *Upadeśasāhasrī* is devoted to the place of repetition. Instruction is repeated until knowledge is firmly grasped.[2] Repetition recalls and repeats the meaning of the unified nature of the Self.[3] Since repetition is a means to establish equanimity of mind, Śaṅkara calls the "intent and continuous repetition of the Inner-Self" devotion to knowledge.[4] The injunction to repeat instruction implies that the students are attending to the meaning of the instruction. Although repetition is not a direct means to self-realisation, it firmly establishes concentration and a facile memory.

Śaṅkara places a greater emphasis on memory than on any other mental faculty in the educational process. It is the most important faculty because it sustains hearing, reflection and concentration. Memory determines how effective the triple method can be. The student is called upon to exercise memory before, during and subsequent to formal teaching. Throughout instruction, the characteristics of the Self are brought to consciousness through memory. Śaṅkara consistently counsels students to remember the instruction of teacher and scripture. The purpose, moreover, of religious education is to overcome ignorance and to attain remembrance of the Self.[5] The tradition of the Upaniṣadic and pre-Śaṅkara period taught that after a rational analysis of nonduality one should fix the memory upon the new understanding. Śaṅkara, however, heightens the role of memory by saying that one resorts to memory even for the actual realisation

1. S. *B. Sūtra* IV.I.1.
2. S. *Upadeśa*. 1.2.
3. Ibid., 3, 112 ff.
4. S. *B. Gītā* 18.55.
5. S. *B. Gītā* 18.73.

of nonduality.[1] There is no better way to control mental states than through knowledge of the Self and remembrance about it. The Advaitin assigns memory a crucial role in the liberation scheme. Memory is essential in self-inquiry because, the Vedānta holds, the Self is already present and self-realisation is merely experiencing that which is radically present. To remember in self-inquiry is to elicit from memory who you are and what you are, namely, the meaning of "I am Brahman." Śaṅkara has identified memory as the mental faculty that is most vital to pedagogy, but he has not isolated it from the educational scheme. Hearing is to keep instruction in memory, otherwise there is no effective hearing; reflection is to achieve understanding and to hold in memory its meaning; concentration is absorption in the meaning elicited from memory.

The eighth-century Vedāntin writes : "Remembrance means recalling to mind something after its perception, and that can only happen when the agent of perception and memory is the same."[2] Memory is revived perception. By reviving past perceptions, memory clarifies and perfects perception itself. Past perceptions of reality and the Self are made present through the exercise of memory. The effectiveness of the memory depends on the condition of the mind. According to Advaita, the Self is falsified by ignorance. If the mind is burdened by sloth or passion, memory cannot be sustained. But when luminous qualities condition the mind, according to the Vedānta, the memory becomes unwavering. Once luminosity dominates the mind, memory becomes steady and ignorance is rent asunder with ease.[3] Sāṅkhya physics is presumed in understanding the role of memory; within this context, memory recalls a previous moment in evolution when the Self stood in Itself. Memory gives the religious seeker the capacity to resonate with the eternality of the Self.

The master Vedāntin writes that "knowledge of Brahman ends in direct experience and relates to an already existing reality."[4] What is then the purpose of individual effort ? If self-knowledge

1. S. *Māṇḍ. Kārikā*. II.36.
2. S. *B. Sūtra* II.II.25.
3. Confer Seshadri, pp. 69-70.
4. S. *B. Sūtra* I.I.2.

is not new knowledge but a rediscovery of what is already present, what is the purpose of pedagogy in religious development ? It is a basic tenet of Śaṅkara's system that knowledge of Brahman does not depend upon the activity of the individual person. All human activity, even reflection and meditation, is part of the world of ignorance in which the ordinary individual lives. Śaṅkara further maintains that anything acquired through practice is impermanent.[1] Spiritual liberation, consequently, is not achieved by human effort. Nonetheless, the study of Vedic texts, concentration and service to the teacher, although called nescience and products of nescience, are the context for liberating knowledge. Liberation is effected through them. Knowledge is still in some sense the result of rational analysis and discrimination because these means progressively remove ignorance. Each operation within the triple method removes error. Effort is not needed to know the Self, but it is needed to remove the error of identifying the Self with the non-self.[2] Methodological tools in Śaṅkara's system are meant to remove error. For him, the grace of God, religious practices, austerities and meditation are all aids to realisation, while the triple method is a more direct cause.[3] Even though the triple method is rooted in ignorance and the world of duality, it has the capacity to directly create a condition open to new vision.

The Place of Meditation

A Śaṅkara legend has him debating for eighteen days with Maṇḍanamiśra, the exponent of Mīmāṃsā philosophy, which teaches that ritual duty and activity are the principal means of liberation. Historians of Indian philosophy believe that Śaṅkara's major interest in metaphysical debate was to reduce the influence of Mīmāṃsā in the Hinduism of his time. Some of his most outstanding commentaries give considerable treatment to the place and effectiveness of duties, rituals and religious practices. He repeatedly argues that activity and knowledge are not conjoined in the path of liberation. This is a principal theme in his commentary on the *Gītā*. Altruistic and selfless activity is merely a

1. Ibid., II.III.40.
2. S. *B. Gītā* 18.50; confer S. *Ait, U.* Intro.
3. S. *Tait. U.* I.XI.4.

prerequisite for knowledge. Śaṅkara even differs from many modern Hindu philosophers on this point, because he firmly believed that religious activity could not eliminate ignorance, a role assigned only to knowledge. Something brought about by activity is always a perishable effort.[1] Yet activity leaves lasting impressions upon the individual and prepares one for the emergence of knowledge.[2] Radhakrishnan has called Śaṅkara a social idealist on a grand scale, a man of action exhorting his age to follow traditional teaching by study of the Vedas, by sacrifice and gifts to the gods, by prayers and fasts.[3] The Advaitin, for example, recommends such rites as *putreṣṭi* for the birth of a son.[4] One of the most popular stories has Śaṅkara visiting his dying mother and breaking fundamental rules of *sannyāsa* by performing her funeral rites.

Although he believes the path of knowledge to be independent of ritual, Śaṅkara assigns special value to ritual joined with meditation. Ritual with meditation is superior to ritual without meditation, for the former contributes indirectly to the rise of knowledge. Even the latter case, ritual without meditation, does not entirely lack value because the efficacy of a rite consists in achieving its own purpose.[5] The combination of ritual and meditation may attain for an individual the state of one born of Brahmā (*virāṭ*);[6] it may attain human joy.[7] Śaṅkara again follows Upaniṣadic thought by suggesting that ritual and meditation lead to a higher path.[8] Performing ritual along with meditation makes it

1. Activity such as study achieves something in the world of human beings, while rituals and meditations achieve in the world of celestial beings and the gods. S. *B. Sūtra* I.V.16-17. Confer Warrier, pp. 426 ff.

2. S. *B. Sūtra* III.IV.26. Confer Date, Vol. II, pp. 522-523.

3. Radhakrishnan, Vol. II, pp. 614, 658. The study of Tiwari is a convincing statement of the social dimension of Advaita Vedānta from the perspective of renunciation. Confer Tiwari, Intro.

4. S. *Tait*. U. I.XI.1.

5. S. *B. Sūtra* IV.I.18. Śaṅkara uses some form of *upāsanā* for meditation in most of the following text.

6. S. *Kaṭha* I.I.17. This is an obscure passage: it may be understood in terms of the knowledge of meditation conjoined to ritual which achieves knowledge of the Omniscient One who is born of Brahmā.

7. S. *Tait*. U. II.V.1. *Ānanda* (bliss) is an effect of meditation and rites, and *ānandamaya* is constituted by this bliss, writes Śaṅkara.

8. S. *Praśna*. I.10.

more powerful and efficacious.[1] It either removes obstacles to the purpose of the rite or contributes to the fruition of the rite itself. Śaṅkara, nonetheless, retains a limited view of the efficacy of ritual. He excuses *sannyāsī*-s from ritual and maintains that knowledge is discretely independent of ritual.[2] Likewise, the practice of *mantra* and *japa*, prescribed for ritual, and every other religious activity are laid aside in the path of knowledge.[3]

Using the familiar image of the bow and the arrow sharpened by constant meditation, Śaṅkara explains that just as the success of the arrow consists in its union with the target and separation from the bow, so too through meditation one becomes united with the Self by overcoming identification with the body.[4] In meditation one puts aside the objects of the senses and the mind.[5] Meditation disposes the mind by gradually making it devoid of differentiation.[6] Śaṅkara writes that "by constant meditation (compared to the rubbing of firewood) is kindled the flame of knowledge, which completely burns up the fuel of ignorance."[7] With success in meditation and a knowledge of its process, one can become a knower of Brahman. Knowledge of the Self and overcoming the limitations of the non-self are the goals Śaṅkara has in mind when he prescribes the practice of meditation.

The extensive chapter on meditation in Śaṅkara's commentary on the *Brahma Sūtra* is titled *Sādhana*, spiritual practice. Although it is a generic term, *sādhana* describes the role of meditation by referring it to the practice of the religious seeker. Śaṅkara distinguishes meditation from hearing and reflection. In overcoming the diversity of ideas in the mind, the meditator seeks to stabilize concentration. Concentration is directed toward the object of meditation. It is easily learned by meditating upon the form of a personal god. Yet the higher goal is ultimately to concentrate on the Self. "While the perception of the object of meditation, be it God or any other entity, occurs as a result of

1. S. *B. Sūtra* III.III.42, III.IV.22.
2. Ibid., III.IV.25, III.IV.16.
3. S. *B. Gītā* 18.52; Śaṅkara uses *dhyāna* for meditation and *ekāgratā* for one-pointedness in this place.
4. S. *M. U.* II.II.3-4.
5. S. *Śataślokī* 18.
6. S. *M. U.* III.I.8. Śaṅkara in this place is commenting on *dhyāna*.
7. S. *Ātma*. 42.

a single meditation, the other meditations become useless", writes the Advaitin.[1] Meditation is not the same as knowledge of nonduality, which radically removes the distinction between the knower, the known and the act of knowing. But meditation is established upon a certain substratum (*adhiṣṭhāna*) and brings about a uniform awareness, unbroken and undistracted, with regard to the substratum.[2]

Śaṅkara draws on the Upaniṣads and the yoga tradition for the vocabulary he uses to describe meditation. *Upāsanā* and *vidyā* are the two most common terms for meditation in the Upaniṣads. *Upāsanā* denotes the act and state of meditation, while *vidyā* signifies the object of meditation whether it is a ritual, a deity or a metaphysical statement, or any other form of symbol. The Vedānta frequently uses *vidyā* and *upāsanā* interchangeably.[3] Śaṅkara employs *upāsanā* as the most generic term for ritual meditation, by which he means devotional exercises, worship or meditation as a means of spiritual growth.[4] In its core, *upāsanā* is ritual work (*kriyā*), a conventional act.[5] It may be a simple service or devotion, for the man who constantly serves the guru and others is said to be rendering *upāsanā* to them.[6] On the other hand, *upāsanā* also connotes continuous repetition and remembrance, when it is used to refer to the process of concentrating the mind on some support recognized by scripture.[7] In the meaning of this single word, the gulf between activity and knowledge is bridged.[8] Śaṅkara conceives *upāsanā* as the continual awareness of the object of meditation or the flow of consciousness toward it. *Upāsanā*, then, is the act of concentration. The term frequently refers to meditation on a specific object or a form of *saguṇa* Brahman; less often, it signifies a symbol such as *OM* or the *nirguṇa* Brahman. *Upāsanā* has limitations; activity and meditation do not bring an end to saṃsāric experience, for the results of ritual and meditation fall within the phenomenal

1. S. *B. Sūtra* III.III.59.
2. S. *C. U.* Intro.
3. Atmananda, p. 131.
4. S. *Māṇḍ. Kārikā* III.1.
5. Confer S. *B. Sūtra* III.III.42
6. S. *Tait. U.* I.III.4.
7. Confer Venkatarama Iyer, p. 197.
8. Confer Date, Vol. II, p. 521.

world. The injunctions to meditate do not concern themselves with delineating or discriminating principles of truth.[1] Because of the limited nature of meditation (*upāsanā*), other terminology is employed for the principles of the process.

Another common term is *dhyāna*, which also signifies concentration and part of the meditative process. It, too, is understood to be an uninterrupted and concentrated reflection on certain duties mentioned in the scripture. "*Dhyāna* is continuous and unbroken thought like a line of flowing oil," comments Śaṅkara.[2] It is "the condition where there is only the uncontradictable thought 'I am Brahman Itself' and there is no external hold."[3] The term generally describes any act of concentration, similar to *upāsanā*. It withdraws the powers of hearing and the other senses from their objects, and finally centers the mind upon the Self. While *dhyāna* includes meditation on the meaning of the Self,[4] it more frequently refers to meditation on a concrete symbol. Similar in meaning to *dhyāna* but used less frequently by Śaṅkara is *dhāraṇā*, a term culled from classical yoga, which in its most restricted sense means holding the mind firmly to the realisation of Brahman.[5] *Dhāraṇā* points more to the will and the intention to concentrate, while *dhyāna* isolates the act of concentration.

There is significant difference between the three understandings of meditation connoted by *dhyāna*, *dhāraṇā* and *upāsanā*, and the path of knowledge that Śaṅkara conceives. In the former cases, meditation usually is an activity of an extroverted mind that focuses upon an extrinsic image and whose effect rests solely upon the meditator himself. In the latter case, *jñāna* yoga,

1. Confer S. *B. Sūtra* III.III.9.

2. S. *B. Gītā* 13.24. In this place Śaṅkara speaks of *dhyāna* as withdrawing the senses into the mind (*manas*) and then withdrawing the mind into the inner perceiver" (*buddhi*)) and then proceeding with concentration.

3. S. *Aparok*. 123.

4. S. *B. Gītā* 13.24, 18.52. Confer Satprakashananda, pp. 288-291, where *dhyāna* is distinguished from *nididhyāsana*. In "The Chapter of the Self of the Āpastamba Law-book," a work which may be Śaṅkara's, *dhyāna* is used for meditation on the Self; Confer verse 9 in Leggett, p. 44.

5. S. *Aparok*. 122. A recently discovered commentary on the *Yoga Sūtra* of Patañjali, a work which some scholars think may be Śankara's, uses *dhāraṇā*, but the term is still not common in the Advaitin's major commentaries.

meditation is the operation of an introverted mind that concentrates upon knowledge with insights transcending both image and previous reasoning. Śaṅkara maintains the distinction between higher knowledge (*parāvidyā*) and lower knowledge (*aparāvidyā*). Lower knowledge includes the Vedas in general, ritual, grammar, astrology and ancient lore; it is any thing that can be meditated upon. Higher knowledge comprehends Upaniṣadic truth alone; it comes about in meditation that uses only the four great axioms of the ancient seers.[1] There is a difference, according to the Vedānta, between *parāvidyā*, which is liberating knowledge, and *aparāvidyā*, which is non-liberating knowledge. The former is knowledge intuitively grasped, and the latter is knowledge gained through analysis. The path of knowledge in Śaṅkara's system differs from that of most yoga systems both in this distinction of knowledge and in the meditative process.

The master Vedāntin draws upon the concepts of right knowledge (*vijñāna*) and concentration (*nididhyāsana*) more than on any of the previous terms, and they differentiate meditation in his Vedānta from other forms of Indian meditation. Both terms are used somewhat synonymously, although right knowledge refers primarily to the quality of knowledge while concentration refers to the activity of meditation. Together, these terms indicate the highest knowledge and the highest stage of meditation. Concentration does not employ a symbol, but rather it is an activity that gains meaning beyond the limitations of name and form. While contemplating the meaning of the Self in Itself, one also exercises a discriminatory function (*viveka*) by rejecting superimposition ((*adhyāsa*) upon the Self. Concentration is meditation on the meaning of the Self alone. Higher knowledge signifies the immediate and direct apprehension of the Self or Brahman. Both of these terms, culled from Śaṅkara's understanding of the Upaniṣads and early Advaita, are more consistent with his thought than those rooted in classical yoga. Śaṅkara is fully in line with his lineage on the nature of meditation. His deviation from the yoga tradition becomes even more evident in the actual practice of meditation.[2]

1. S. *M. U.* I.1.4.

2. Yoga terms, such as *samādhi* or *nirvikalpa samādhi* to signify the highest state of meditation, are not common to Śaṅkara. In one place he uses *samādhi*

The Practice of Meditation

Śaṅkara sets forth a general meditational method to be followed under the direction of the guru. There is no restriction as to time, place or duration in Vedānta meditation. It occurs at any time, in any place and continues up until death itself.[1] Meditation can be done either with or without symbols, depending on the ability of the individual. In symbolic meditation, one approaches an object of worship or a form of a deity, visualizes it and steadily concentrates upon it. Symbolic meditation consists in three elements : a meditator, an object of meditation and the act of meditating; concentration seeks to identify subject and object. "The meditator assumes the form of the object meditated upon," writes Śaṅkara, for one becomes that on which he resolutely and persistently thinks.[2] The meditator tries to identify with the form of a deity as with one's own body.[3] One may superimpose a higher meaning, for example Brahman, upon the lower, visualized form. Superimposition of the higher meaning upon the inferior meaning contributes to the excellence of the lower form of symbol.[4] Such an exercise merely strengthens the capacity to concentrate. It must contain faith and Upaniṣadic insight if it is to be fruitful for more advanced meditation.[5] When symbol is engaged in meditation, one attains the meaning of the symbol-

to refer to the higher conditions of meditation, and in another place *nirvikalpa* is the highest condition. *Samādhi* is used most generically to mean the whole pedagogical process of hearing, reflection and concentration. Yoga terms with specific meaning are inconsistent in Śaṅkara's thought. Nowhere, for example, does he assert that *savikalpa* and *nirvikalpa samādhi* are the result of *nididhyāsana*, for *nididhyāsana* is itself a direct approach to self-realisation. Confer S. *Aparok*. 124; S. *Viveka*. 364, 365, 408-410; Satchidanandendra Saraswati, pp. 51-53. When the commentary on the *Yoga Sūtra*, attributed to Śaṅkara, becomes generally accepted as authentic, revision in the above judgments may result. Yet the most substantive difference between Śaṅkara and Yoga still remains, that is, the role of *buddhi*. In Yoga there is a disassociation with *buddhi*, while in Śaṅkara the seeker never disassociates with *buddhi*. Confer Satprakashananda, p. 301, and Appendix C, pp. 355 ff. Even the *Kaṭha U*., 1.3.12 states : "The Self is seen through a keen and one-pointed intellect (*buddhi*).

1. S. *B. Sūtra* IV.I.11-12.
2. S. *Upadeśa*. 15.14; S. *Aparek*. 140; Confer S. *B. Sūtra* IV.III.15.
3. S. *B. U*. I.III.9.
4. Confer S. *B. Sūtra* IV.I.5.
5. Confer S. *C. U*. I.I.10.

constituted *saguṇa* Brahman and not of the unmanifested *nirguṇa* Brahman.[1] Symbolic meditation, consequently, has its limits. Identity with the Self does not follow upon identity with the symbol.

Although meditation is a mental operation, meditation on a symbol differs from concentration on the meaning of the Self. The latter cannot be fixed upon or contained by a concrete symbol.[2] The Self, according to Śaṅkara, is marked off from ritual or symbolic concentration.[3] He only gives hints about the practice of this type of meditation. In one instance, it is the guru who shows the disciple "the process of the absorption of parts,"[4] an oblique reference to a common method of withdrawing into oneself and apprehending the universe within oneself. To experience all things in the Self and the Self in all things is a goal of meditational technique common to various Indian traditions. The goal for Śaṅkara is to apprehend Brahman "wheresoever the consciousness reaches."[5]

To withdraw into oneself to the degree anticipated by Śaṅkara requires extraordinary discipline of mind, toward which most ascetical life is directed. The discipline that it calls for effectively restricts this sort of concentration to a few. The universe of Brahman in this form of meditation is experienced not through identification with concrete symbols but through an extension of the empirical self. Hari is realised in the heart "by the expansion of the individual self,"[6] and this conforms with Śaṅkara's philosophy of an acosmic absolute. What is most significant at this stage of meditation is its rational and truly discriminatory nature. In other words, the process of centering on the Self means a deliberate and rational rejection of non-self; the process of self-inquiry extends to this advanced stage of concentration. The seeker by means of the Upaniṣadic axioms, discriminates consistently

1. Confer S. *B. Sūtra* IV.III.15.
2. Ibid., IV.I.4-5.
3. S. *B. U.* I.IV.15.
4. S. *Praśna* VI.5. In this place, Śaṅkara says that one becomes "free from parts" when they are absorbed through knowledge; *nāma-rūpa* (name and form) become absorbed.
5. S. *Aparok*. 122.
6. S. *Hari-stotra* 8.

in order to arrive at radical subjectivity, at the radical meaning of self-immanence. The pursuit of this type of concentration is the highest form of meditation in Advaita Vedānta. Śaṅkara calls this form of meditation concentration (*nididhyāsana*), a direct approach to Brahman that culminates in immediate and intuitive experience. Just as there is a graded meditative process in the Upaniṣads from gross and external objects to the subtle and interior areas of consciousness, so too Śaṅkara moves gradually from symbolic to non-symbolic meditation and finally to the highest levels of the discriminatory work of the mind.

While Śaṅkara departs significantly from the common understanding of yoga, his own conception of the meditative process can be clarified somewhat by analyzing the use he makes of classical yoga and his reconceptualization of it. "Yoga consists in making what has thus been learnt an object of one's own direct perception, by the subjugation of the senses and by one-pointedness," he observes.[1] Although Śaṅkara begins with a common view of yoga, he raises it to a fully rational pursuit in most of his writing. "Converting one's vision (*dṛṣṭi*) into one of knowledge...is the most advantageous vision and not that which is directed to the tip of the nose," he comments.[2] Using the word yoga as a variant for meditation (*upāsanā*) and concentration (*nididhyāsana*), Śaṅkara conceives all yoga as an activity of the mind that seeks intuitive vision. Yoga is one-pointedness of the mind on the Self. He speaks of the eight-limb path, the classical structure of Patañjali's yoga, "as kindling the fire of knowledge."[3] In another text he extends the eight-limb path to a fifteen-fold path of his own reconceptualization. He transforms each stage, even the physical postures (*āsana-s*), into a mental discipline (*rāja* yoga), an intellectual endeavor. But because Śaṅkara treats the fifteen-fold yoga in only one text, the discriminatory nature of meditation and the triple method predominate over any consideration of popular yoga.[4] In this one

1. S. *B. Gītā* 16.1; also confer 18.52.
2. S. *Apąrok.* 116.
3. S. *Hari-stotra* 41.
4. S. *Aparok.* 143, 102-127. Śaṅkara suggests *haṭha*-yoga as a prerequisite for those whose passions have been only partially eradicated. *Yama* is the natural restraint over the senses due to the knowledge that "All is Brahman"; *niyama* is the oneness of consciousness with Brahman and the

text, which briefly summarizes the fifteen-fold path, Śaṅkara retains the classical framework of yoga while substantially changing its meaning by elevating each stage to a mental operation. Śaṅkara's yoga differs from Patañjali's yoga in that the former fully actualizes mental activity while the latter suppresses mental modifications in a fundamental way.[1]

The Independence of Self-Realisation

There is no activity, not even concentration, which establishes the Self, for it is independent of human effort. Śaṅkara is opposed to "thinking" the Absolute so as to create concepts of name and form. As soon as one "thinks" Brahman, he has fabricated something of the phenomenal world with dual existence. Śaṅkara frequently refers to the value of everyday or common sense

separation of the physical universe from Brahman; *tyāga* is the recognition of Brahman everywhere due to the sublation of the material universe; *mauna* signifies that thoughts and words do not reach Brahman and that all doubts have been overcome; *deśa* is the place of the universe with beginning, middle and end; *kāla* is Brahman uninterrupted and unending; *āsana* is that state in which Brahman is unceasingly contemplated with bliss and not postures which disrupt bliss; *mūlabandha*, a posture in classical yoga, is the origin of all existence in whom the mind is fixed; *siddha-āsana* is the Immutable, the beginning of the universe and the reality behind it; *dehasāmya* is that whereby the physical is viewed as Brahman; *dṛṣṭi* is converting one's own vision into one of knowledge; *prāṇāyāma* is the control of all life forces by viewing all creation as Brahman; *dhāraṇā* is steadiness of the mind that views Brahman everywhere; *dhyāna* is the condition, free from all ideas, that "I am Brahman"; *samādhi* is to make thought changeless and to identify consciousness with Brahman. Since the commentary on the *Yoga Sūtra* attributed by some to Śaṅkara (confer footnote 5, p. 75), has not been generally accepted by scholars, I have not contrasted it with this text. Confer Leggett, Part II, whose popular yoga commentary draws upon the text on the *Yoga Sūtra* attributed to Śaṅkara.

1. Within Patañjali's thought as well as Sāṅkhya philosophy, all rational states are transcended; Patañjali even defines yoga as the restraint of mental activity. But in its highest form of *nididhyāsana*, Śaṅkara's yoga is the full exercise of the intelligence (*buddhi*). Confer footnote 2, pp. 76-77 and references to Satprakashananda. Yet the commentators of the *Yoga Sūtra* have been influenced by Upaniṣadic and Vedāntic thought concerning the triple method. Vyāsa's commentary on *Yoga Sūtra* 1.48, reads : "One attains the supreme state of yoga by developing knowledge (*prajñā*) in a threefold way : hearing the authentic words (*āgama*), reasoning on them, and the ardent practice of meditation." Confer Satprakashananda, p. 195.

experience, against which reasoning and scripture are validated. He even gives to everyday life experience a sort of priority over the authority of scripture.[1] The truth of scripture and discrimination are to be internalized and experienced. Scripture, or the instruction of the guru, is but a "working hypothesis which with the aid of the meditative process must be experienced," writes a modern Advaita philosopher.[2] Advaita Vedānta as an abstract philosophy of life derives its meaning and validation from concrete experience, religious worship and meditation, but at the same time it protests the limitations of the concrete by insisting upon what K. C. Bhattacharya calls the inwardization of religion through experience and intuition.[3]

Several of Śaṅkara's central principles of religious philosophy are based upon ordinary experience : namely, the limitations of religious activity, the superimposition of the non-self upon the Self, and the efficacy of knowledge. Experience in spiritual development, for him, is a direct means of self-realisation. Likewise, knowledge of Brahman is experience relating to oneself that arises from transcending physical and psychic limitations and achieving universality. The classical axioms, "I am Brahman," and "All this is Brahman," are experienced in the human world, but the experiences transcend and universalize both the world and human beings. Theory and practice are not too distant from each other in Advaita, because individual experience is the highest criterion and validates spiritual growth.[4] For this reason Śaṅkara distinguishes the knowledge of scripture and the guru (*jñāna*) from the liberating knowledge of personal experience (*vijñāna*), which is gained in concentration.[5] The means to new understanding within the meditational process are reasoning and intuition. Both foster growth at various stages of concentration. The process cannot go on without rational discrimination, and it reaches no finalization without meaning from intuitive experience. Hearing, reflection and concentration are continued until intuitive vision arises. Śaṅkara's commentaries and his conception of

1. Confer Devaraja, pp. 54, 57.
2. Confer Nagaraja Rao, p. 75.
3. Confer Bhattacharya, Vol. I, p. 123.
4. Confer Date, p. 11.
5. S. *B. Gītā* 3.4.

religious development are too rational, however, to be called mystical. Intuitive vision, in his epistemology, is a natural consequence of rational and reflective processes. Likewise, knowledge of the Self is based upon profound human experiences and understandings.

The antinomy mentioned previously, the method of leading from duality to nonduality by means implying duality, may now be seen to be less paradoxical.[1] Stressing the importance of world and of human experiences, Śaṅkara discovers that liberating knowledge is immanently present in the individual's world and within his range of experience. Although the religious seeker concentrates upon the substratum (*adhiṣṭhāna*) of phenomenal reality in the meditational process, liberating knowledge is immanent or present to the very substratum of that reality.[2] Ordinary knowledge, attained through hearing, reflection and concentration, bears an intrinsic relationship to liberating knowledge. The success of the reflective analysis of empirical reality depends upon absolute and transcendent knowledge. Limited consciousness has a base in transcendent consciousness, otherwise an infinite regress would follow.[3] There is no contradiction in the methodology that leads a student, from duality to nonduality by means implying duality, because Śaṅkara posits not only transcendent consciousness but also an intrinsic relationship between

1. I depend for the resolution of this discussion upon De Smet (1956), pp. 5-9.

2. Being is the ground (*adhiṣṭhāna*) on which illusion and ignorance occur. The ground is not different with different things, but it is one for all phenomenal things. An imperfect perception of the ground is the cause of illusion and ignorance. Sarvajñātman draws a sharp distinction between the ground (*adhiṣṭhāna*) and the object to which false perceptions refer (*ādhāra*). The former is the real substratum. Sarvajñātman writes : "An illusion has reference to a substratum (*adhiṣṭhāna*) that is, in relation to the illusion, real. The rope is the substratum of the snake falsely perceived in it; Brahman is the substratum of the world falsely (but necessarily so from the standpoint of sense experience) to be created from it" (Deutsch, p. 310). The substratum is *sat-cit-ānanda*. Brahman is the ground of phenomenon: *sat-cit-ānanda* underlies the phenomenal object. Ignorance and illusion may identify the characteristic of *sat* (real) because its manifestation is perceived while *cit* (consciousness) or *ānanda* (bliss) are not perceived. Confer Deutsch, pp. 257-268; also Dasgupta. Vol. 1, pp. 446, 449, 451-452.

3. Confer S. *Kena* I.6.

liberating knowledge and empirical knowledge. He presumes a community of being and existence between the religious seeker and his world and Brahman.[1]

The final goal of the religious student in educational development, according to Śaṅkara's Vedānta, is to become a liberated person living within society. The educational process neither takes the individual out of this world nor creates a new world for him. It permits instead the birth of a new kind of person. This person is the detached seer (*sākṣī*), the observer, the witness Self who stands in wisdom (*sthitaprajña*) undisturbed within the most disturbing conditions of social life.[2] He is a guru, created out of a teaching tradition, who now offers to others a similar freedom path.

1. De Smet (1956), p. 9.Confer Indich for a recent and thorough study of consciousness in Advaita, especially Chapter II.
2. Devaraja, p. v.

Chapter Four

THE TEACHING HERITAGE AFTER ŚAṄKARA

In Śaṅkara's day there was variety in pedagogical theory and practice; the writings of several of his contemporaries show how they gave direction to the developing teaching tradition. Kumārila Bhaṭṭa, the exponent of Pūrva Mīmāṃsā that accords priority to religious duties, made a successful critique of Buddhism but accommodated his thought to Advaita Vedānta. Among his students was Maṇḍanamiśra, with whom Śaṅkara entered into debate.[1] Maṇḍana holds an important place in the teaching tradition because the Vācaspati school, which diverges from Śaṅkara's thought, is rooted in his conception of Advaita. Although Maṇḍana wrote three works on Mīmāṃsā, his single work on Advaita, *Brahmasiddhi*, influenced and set a certain direction in the history of the late medieval teaching tradition.[2]

Maṇḍana prepared the way for meditation to take the central place in medieval Hindu asceticism, but the priority he gave it was rejected by Śaṅkara and his disciple, Sureśvara, who wrote directly against Maṇḍana. Exalting meditation in religious education, Maṇḍana denies that the verbal testimony (*śabda*) of the Vedas is sufficiently efficacious by itself. Meditation, he believes, is absolutely necessary for Vedic testimony to be effective. According to Maṇḍana, verbal testimony generates only indirect cognition, and both religious activity (*karma*) and knowledge

1. The tradition that Maṇḍana was converted to Advaita and became the second disciple of Śaṅkara who was called Sureśvara is rejected by most modern scholars.

2. Maṇḍana's place in Indian thought is due especially to his exposition of the *sphoṭa* theory, which teaches that a word in a sentence or an individual phoneme is an entity other than sound, and this entity bears meaning. For Maṇḍana the meaning of a word, as an entity, pre-exists in the individual; when a person speaks and is heard, an identical meaning is awakened in the hearer. Maṇḍana believes that the meaning of words or sounds is rooted in the Self. (Confer Subramania Iyer, 1966, pp. 8 ff.) Śaṅkara holds for the eternality of Vedic sounds but rejects Maṇḍana's position, arguing that words and meaning belong to the world of appearance and do not exist in the Self. (S. *B. Sūtra* I.III.29; also *S. C.U.* VII.I.3).

(*jñāna*) are necessary to transform direct knowledge into self-realisation. This position has major consequences for the guru because it reduces his role to a minimum. Placing the responsibility of liberation fully upon the student through his own effort of meditation, Maṇḍana relativizes the teaching role of the guru. The scripture and the teacher are foundational for Śaṅkara; for Maṇḍana it is meditation and the effort of the meditator that form the basic structure of educational development.[1] The principal reason for this difference with Śaṅkara is that Maṇḍana gives supremacy to the conjunction of religious activity and knowledge in the liberation process. Religious activity is integrated with knowledge so that human effort becomes the sole means of realisation, and knowledge results from that effort.[2] Śaṅkara and his first disciples oppose this stand. For the master Advaitin, as he argues in all his commentaries, religious education is the comprehension of Vedic texts. Maṇḍana, arguing that intuitive realisation is the direct result of meditation, raises up the meditative life as the direct and immediate cause of liberation. The distinction between the role of meditation and that of verbal testimony sets the context for the development of the teaching tradition in the post-Śaṅkara period.

The First Disciples of Śaṅkara

Śaṅkara had four intimate disciples : Padmapāda, Sureśvara, Hastāmalaka and Toṭaka (Ānandagiri). The first two, Padmapāda and Sureśvara, were major commentators of Śaṅkara and outstanding writers in their own stead. Sureśvara wrote commentaries on Śaṅkara's exposition of the *Bṛhadāraṇyaka* and *Taittirīya Upaniṣads*, the hymn *Dakṣiṇāmūrti* and the *Pañcīkaraṇam*. His *Naiṣkarmyasiddhi*, a study of the Vedānta, is the major work in which he confronts Maṇḍana, and he quotes the master's *Upadeśasāhasrī* seventeen times in it. Sureśvara understands himself as a true disciple of Śaṅkara, and his description of their relationship markedly indicates his conception of the guru and the teacher-student relationship.

Sureśvara looks to Śaṅkara as the source of his reception of the Vedānta and his own illumination. "Having served with

1. Biardeau (1969), p. 122.
2. Confer Maṇḍanamiśra, *Brahmasiddhi* in Kuppuswami Sastri (1937).

reverence the feet of the blessed Śaṅkara, and obtaining from him this pure knowledge . . . I have spoken," writes Sureśvara.[1] "From him . . . I obtained the science illumined by the Vedānta," he continues.[2] Attributing his realisation to Śaṅkara, Vyāsa and Gauḍapāda whose *Māṇḍūkyakārikā* he freely quotes,[3] he directs singular devotion toward the master Advaitin : "Finding none superior to him . . . the highest breaker of the bonds of primal ignorance," "the omniscient, established in the Supreme Self," "our guru, the teacher of gurus," "who by the role of reason removed ignorance."[4] He compares the guru, in this case Śaṅkara, to Śiva. But Sureśvara is also an independent thinker who does not adhere blindly to his preceptor's teaching but gives different interpretations to Upaniṣadic texts. He has a more flexible understanding of the Vedānta than the other major disciple, Padmapāda.[5] Yet he stands firmly within the Vedānta for he understands the transmission of the tradition to be "for purposes of purifying our understanding by the testimony of those who know Brahman."[6] Sureśvara distinguishes students according to their capacity to hear, to remember and to reason.[7] The triple method structures the student's relationship with the guru. Apart from the preceptor there is no hearing of Vedic texts; the guru induces reflection in the disciple. But the guru remains above Vedic injunctions. Sureśvara's conception of the guru-disciple relationship is basically the same as Śaṅkara's.

Sureśvara establishes both spiritual growth and self-realisation upon understanding the terms and the meaning of the great Upaniṣadic axioms.[8] The primary factor in liberating knowledge is the text as apprehended. In the understanding of Vedic texts, Sureśvara posits intuitive experience. Apprehending Vedic axioms removes ignorance; the Self then stands in Itself.[9] Sureśvara's major attack is against the importance of meditation, as

1. Sureśvara, *Naiṣkarmyasiddhi* IV.75.
2. Ibid., IV.76.
3. Ibid., IV.41-44.
4. Ibid., I.3; IV.74, 77.
5. Seshadri, p. 34.
6. Sureśvara, *Naiṣkarmyasiddhi* I.6.
7. Ibid., II.2-3.
8. Ibid., III.1.
9. Ibid., I.51-52.

advanced by Maṇḍana. He refutes Maṇḍana's arguments for the value of meditation (*upāsanā*) upon the Upaniṣadic axioms, on grounds that there is nothing to assure the effectiveness of such meditation.[1] He limits the role of repetition in the meditative process and considers repetition useful only for those who hear the scripture infrequently or partially.[2] The import of the great axioms comes from perfect hearing. "By cumulative repetition of thought," he writes, "only concentration comes about. The modalities of knowledge like perception do not reveal their objects as a result of repetition."[3] Sureśvara insists upon reasoning for the sublation of ignorance and the emergence of the Self. He gives less importance to repetition and memory than does Śaṅkara, but he stands in continuity with the master concerning the primacy of reason. Sureśvara refers to different kinds of students who achieve realisation in somewhat different ways, but both he and Śaṅkara hold for the efficacy of the text itself for liberating knowledge.

Padmapāda, who is somewhat less flexible a disciple than Sureśvara, is considered the founder of the Vivaraṇa school of Advaita, another late medieval development. Although only fragments of his *Pañcapādikā* exist, the first of such works on Śaṅkara's commentary on the first four aphorisms of the *Brahma Sūtra*, he sets the way for the transmission of the master's method. The Vivaraṇa school of Advaita under Padmapāda's impetus stresses verbal testimony. Like Sureśvara, Padmapāda extols Śaṅkara unreservedly. He considers the master's words equal in authority to the Vedas.[4] Padmapāda gives a rare, first-hand account of Śaṅkara's personality : "He has given up all pomp and power, and true reasoning has chosen to abide with him forever, becoming part and parcel of him. He is calm and serene, having rooted out the mighty *kāla*, time, the all-destroyer. He has no obstructions anywhere."[5] The invocatory verses of the *Pañcapādikā* praise both Bādarāyaṇa and Śaṅkara and mention the entourage of ascetics around Śaṅkara. Toṭaka, another intimate disciple of Śaṅkara, also praises the master and refers to

1. Ibid., III.90 ff.
2. Ibid., III.125.
3. Ibid, III.90-91.
4. Padmapāda, *Pañcapādikā* 2.
5. Padmapāda, *Pañcapādikā*, in Seshadri, p. 21.

him in a hymn as "the glow of the glorious sun of knowledge, my guru," and "the refuge of the teachers of the most excellent teachers."[1]

Padmapāda places religious growth within the context of the triple method. Hearing inquires into the meaning of Upaniṣadic passages concerning the Self; reflection gathers rational support for scripture, frequently through syllogistic argumentation; concentration strengthens personal conviction regarding the meaning of the identity propositions grasped by reflection.[2] Padmapāda retains the intellectual and thoroughly rational nature of the triple method. Meditation (*upāsanā*) in itself is fruitless for him. Reflection and concentration exist as rational and methodical tools to prepare the way for knowing Brahman.[3] The objective of Padmapāda's treatise is to place knowledge of the Vedas through verbal testimony above all else, and in the process he also questions the value of meditation. Meditation is not the cause of immediate perception since it does not result in intuitive percetion. In fact, meditation on Brahman is a superimposition that hinders the process of reflecion.[4] Padmapāda argues that it is against reason that the Self be attained by an act (*kriyā*) of meditation as its cause.[5] Knowledge arising from the Vedas, however, has the capacity to remove ignorance. Only Vedic testimony brings about immediate experience. The classical example that Śaṅkara and his disciples use to illustrate the efficacy of verbal testimony is a story about ten boys who cross a river. When the ten arrive on the further shore, one of them counts but nine in the group, obviously neglecting to include himself. A passer-by, noticing the consternation of the boys, counts them and finds all ten present; verbal testimony immediately dispells the previous ignorance. Verbal testimony brings about a rational comprehension of the meaning of words. The words, in the classic application, are the Upaniṣadic identity propositions; the meaning of these propositions yields new knowledge.[6] Elevating

1. Seshadri, p. 44.
2. Padmapāda, *Pañcapādikā* 4.91. 11.31.
3. Ibid., 4.9. 16.54.
4. Ibid., 4.9. 2.3-4; 4.9. 7.16.
5. Ibid., 4.9. 10.23.
6. Murty, p. 11, defines *śabda* in this manner : "When the purport (tātparya) of a sentence is uncontradicted by other means of knowledge, as

verbal testimony above every other pedagogical tool, Padmapāda at the same time raises the role of the guru in the educational scheme. The conclusion of his work heralds the unique and absolute need for the guru and his direction.

Sarvajñātman, a disciple of Sureśvara, consolidates Śaṅkara's teaching among the early disciples.[1] His major work, upon which six commentaries were written, is a study of Śaṅkara's commentary on the *Brahma Sūtra*. Since Sarvajñātman's preceptor was Sureśvara, continuity between them and Śaṅkara is evident. Showing typical appreciation for the guru tradition, Sarvajñātman praises Vyāsa, Śaṅkara and Sureśvara and accepts the position of his predecessors while advancing their teaching. He expounds the Upaniṣads through the grace of his guru.[2] The import of the Upaniṣads is received successively from the preceptor.[3] In Sarvajñātman's commentaries, the guru examines the student in the typical fashion and teaches the great axioms by eliciting questions, doubts and objections.[4] A student who has attained the four prerequisites need only commit himself to renunciation and the guru. Renunciation forces the student to examine the terms of the Upaniṣadic propositions.[5] Sarvajñātman's contribution is a precise determination of the order of priority among the cluster of means in Advaita pedagogy. The means are pursued by him because as a whole they overcome the experience of agentship, the annihilation of which gives rise to knowledge.[6]

Sarvajñātman distinguishes between the remote and the proximate causes of knowledge. Remote causes are the religious acts that increase desire for knowledge; for example, ritual, sacrifice, penance, devotion to God, duties of social life and control of

well as unknown through other means of knowledge such as perception and inference, then that sentence becomes a *prāmaṇa*, i.e., a means of valid verbal testimony."

1. Sarvajñātman as the disciple of Sureśvara is challenged by Srikantha Sastri, pp. 401-408; yet later research maintains discipleship. Confer Veezhinathan (1972).
2. Sarvajñātman, *Saṅkṣepaśārīraka* 1.5-8; 4.60.
3. Ibid., 4.52.
4. Ibid., 1.92-93.
5. Ibid., 1.71; 3.3-4.
6. Ibid., 3.358.

the mind and senses. Desire for knowledge results from these causes because they remove obstacles and defects in the mind.[1] The proximate cause of knowledge is Vedānta study relating to the Self : "By this alone, you realise the transcendental state of the supreme Self."[2] The proximate causes remove ignorance concerning the sense of the great axioms. Both the remote and proximate causes are auxiliary means, for they have the basically negative effect of removing ignorance. The Upaniṣadic text itself is the only direct and positive cause of liberating knowledge that is instrumentally effective in the developmental process.[3] Sarvajñātman's treatise retains the whole of the tradition while still maintaining the primacy of the Upaniṣadic propositions. Placing the great sayings above all other means, he strengthens the role of the guru as a rational guide.

These three early disciples of Śaṅkara, through their emphasis on verbal testimony and the Vedānta texts and through their consequent relegation of meditation to a secondary role, establish a definite direction in the guru tradition for the following centuries. They stand in continuity with Śaṅkara and the Vedānta because they are gurus in their own right. Although less creative than Śaṅkara, they advance the teaching tradition in Indian education and religion. Absent in the teaching of these early disciples is any major concern for classical yoga because all mental obstacles can be overcome, in the Vedānta of this period, by the discussion, deliberation and discrimination that goes on between guru and pupil.

Works of the Late-Śaṅkara

The writings of the late-Śaṅkara, a term used here to designate the contested works of the master Advaitin, receive separate treatment in this place not only because they became popular from this period onward but also because this literature contributed to the diversity of the late medieval development. The twenty-volume memorial edition of the works of Śaṅkara, consisting of over 400 titles of commentaries, hymns and short treatises, contains only about 24 works deemed authentic by

1. Ibid., 3.334; 3.340; 3.352.
2. Ibid., 3.54.
3. Ibid., 3.341. Confer Veezhinathan (1972), Intro., pp. 128-134.

modern scholars.[1] The remaining works, 384 or 409 depending upon the method of tabulation, are still relevant to the study of Śaṅkara and the Advaita teaching tradition. The works of the late-Śaṅkara give the impression of catholicity to both philosophical and devotional developments in Hinduism. They extend beyond the central concerns of the master Advaitin and sometimes seem to conflict with his fundamental ideas. This vast body of literature embraces both change and continuity within Advaita Vedānta. The role of the guru is enlarged rather than diminished in the late-Śaṅkara, for these works reflect an even greater dependence upon and need for the teacher. Devotionalism, which dominated the guru tradition from the time of the popular *smṛti* literature but was restricted in Śaṅkara's major commentaries, has no boundaries in these works.

There is a popular story in the writing of the late-Śaṅkara that is widely retold, about his encouter in Benares with an outcaste (*caṇḍāla*) who manifested the highest illumination and oneness with the Self. In poetic and philosophical language, the author describes the character of the *caṇḍāla*-guru, employing in a five-stanza hymn the refrain, "This is my conception of a guru." The guru is described in terms of consciousness, consciousness beyond the phenomenal, which is witness to the universe. "He whose mind is thus firmly rooted in the extremely blessed, eternal, highest reality free from all taint, is my guru, be he *caṇḍāla* or twice-born one."[2] The guru is one with Brahman who directly intuits the inner "I" as pure consciousness. According to the late-Śaṅkara literature, identification with God, especially Śiva, predominates the conception of guru. In a penetrating example of discrimination titled "Who Am I," the poet sings such refrains as these : "I am the Eternal Witness, the Inner Self, Śiva Himself;" "By the Master's gracious instruction I am no *jīva*, but Śiva Himself."[3] The guru is proclaimed in terms of illumined consciousness and identity with God, as captured in the refrain of another hymn : "I am Śiva, Pure Consciousness and Bliss, I am Śiva Himself."[4] The guru is described as that reality which

1. Confer Piantelli, Appendix 1; also Belvalkar (1929), pp. 217ff; also the work of Mayeda and Gussner.
2. Late-S., "The Guru or the Master," in Subrahmanya Sarma, p. 22.
3. Late-S., "Who Am I," ibid., pp. 37-39.
4. Late-S., "The Self as Pure Consciousness and Bliss," ibid., pp. 51-55.

remains after all superimposition is removed.[1] In the *Śivānandalaharī*, Śiva is addressed as the world-teacher (*lokaguru*), an appellation of the realised preceptor. One is a teacher only if he has the capacity to liberate another. The same hymn extols the supreme God who is the source of benevolence (*Śambhu*), who does what is benevolent (Śaṅkara), and who is benevolence itself (Śiva).[2] In another treatise popular among Advaitins, discourse between guru and disciple, the author cautions the disciple not to make any distinction between Śiva and the guru. The preceptor is Śiva incarnate who assumes the form of teacher when he is pleased with the devotion and worship of the religious seeker.[3] A Tantra text of the late-Śaṅkara conceives guru, God and *mantra* to be one and the same.[4] Since the guru is beyond superimposition and ignorance, there is distinction of neither teacher, scripture, pupil nor teaching.[5] The guru is beyond duality; he destroys duality.[6]

Two dominant characteristics of the guru's life are that it is ascetic and that it is an instrument of grace. The ideal guru, pure and compassionate of mind and skillful in teaching, is in need of nothing.[7] "Blessed indeed are the persons who wear only the loin-cloth," is used to introduce each stanza of another hymn.[8] Although the teacher is versed in scripture and has the capacity to lead a student through discrimination, the grace of the teacher is the reason one transcends saṃsāra.[9] Other concepts that are infrequent in the authentic works of Śaṅkara occur more often in this literature; two of these are the notion of guru as an Inner Guide, that is, the Self as teacher, and the notion of the guru's silence as teacher.[10] The guru's relationship with a student is

1. Late-S., "The Indescribable Divine Principle in Man," ibid., pp. 55-62.
2. Late-S., *Śivānandalaharī* in Mahadevan (1963).
3. Late-S., *The Quintessence of Vedānta*, in Tattwananda, pp. 254-256.
4. Late-S., *Tantrik Texts*, in Avalon, p. 26.
5. Late-S., "The Indescribable Divine Principle in Man," in Subrahmanya Sarma, p. 60.
6. Late-S., *Svātmanirūpaṇa* v.1, in Venkataraman, p. 198.
7. Late-S., *The Quintessence of Vedānta* 253, in Tattwananda.
8. Late-S., "The Glory of Renunciation," in Subrahmanya Sarma, pp. 9-11.
9. Late-S., *The Quintessence of Vedānta* 236, in Tattwananda.
10. Ibid., 1004; also confer Late-S., "Hymn for Forgiveness," 9, in Nikhilananda (1975).

characterized by devotion and the reconciliation of faith objects : Śiva, Viṣṇu, Śakti, Sūrya, Gaṇapati and Kumāra. The Hindu pantheon serves as the context for the creation of the student as a love-personality.

Several factors are typical of the religious seeker in the late-Śaṅkara. The student is urged to seek out a devotee of God, the company of the wise, and a realised master in order to serve him unceasingly.[1] Service to the guru is still the principal *sādhana*, while ritual and other religious duties are eventually put aside. Frequent mention is made of the four prerequisites, discrimination, renunciation, desire for liberation, and the six ascetical virtues.[2] A disciple is one who is enlightened by the words of the guru, through his grace, and who absorbs his mind "in the lotus feet of the guru."[3] The *Gurvaṣṭaka*, a hymn stating that all is in vain without the help of the teacher, counsels devotional concentration on the person of the guru as a prior condition for fixing the mind on the words of the guru. Coupled with this is intense devotion to God, extending to one or all the *avatāra*-s, and expressing itself in interior or exterior worship.[4]

Bhakti receives more emphasis in the liberation process of the late-Śaṅkara than in that described in the authenticated literature. Yet the intellectual nature of the seeker is preserved as well, for the educational method puts equal stress on discrimination and on the removal of superimposition. On the other hand, there is no explicit mention of any equality envisioned between teacher and student, a major contribution in the early Śaṅkara. The late-Śaṅkara's emphasis upon devotion accounts for this omission, because the notion of *bhakti* seems to displace the broader vision of equality through the spiritual growth of the disciple. The primary relationship between teacher and student has become one that blends *bhakti* and knowledge; it is no longer the relationship of sovereign knowledge envisioned by the early Śaṅkara.

Regardless of the *bhakti* emphasis, knowledge and ritual still stand opposed in religious development. The intellectual nature

1. Late-S., "Steps to Realisation," in Subrahmanya Sarma, pp. 4-5.

2. Confer Late-S., *Ātmānātmaviveka*, in Chaterjee, pp. 36-37; also confer *The Quintessence of Vedānta* 14 ff, 94 ff, in Tattwananda.

3. Late-S., *Gurvaṣṭaka*, in Mahadevan (1959), pp. 45 ff.

4. Confer "Bhagavatpādas' Hymns on Vishnu," K. K. A. Venkatachari, in Ramaratham, *Śaṅkara and Shanmata*.

of the educational method is evident especially in the prose works of the late-Śaṅkara. The triple method is amply advocated. Discrimination through analysis of the states of consciousness and the coverings of the Self is pursued in order to overcome superimposition.[1] The preceptor leads the student by questions and answers, overcoming doubts and objections, to a firm understanding of the scripture. There is negligible difference in the rational methodology between the early Śaṅkara and this body of literature. In fact, many of these hymns are more vivid and emphatic in negating superimposition than the original Śaṅkara. They force sublation of all that is ephemeral. In the hymn "Who Am I," the author writes : "I am not the body, nor the senses, nor the mind, nor even the ego: neither the vital airs, nor the intellect...I am no *jīva*...I am neither born, nor grown up, nor become dead."[2] While there are a great number of devotional hymns in the late-Śaṅkara, an equal number closely resemble the Upaniṣadic texts in that they extoll the rigorous discrimination of Self from non-self. Although the vocabulary of classical yoga is sometimes used, the eight-limbs are understood substantially as in Śaṅkara, with the mentalization of each stage. For example, the *āsana*-s are described as states of mind aiding concentration, and *prāṇāyāma* is the mind restrained by one powerful idea.[3] Even though this body of literature perceives scripture as a means of liberation, it does not conspicuously isolate the Upaniṣadic axioms as the early Śaṅkara and his first disciples do. The path of knowledge is still there, but within a devotional context.

Devotion gives a different quality to meditation. This literature makes a remarkable attempt to express devotion of Viṣṇu, Śiva or Govinda without losing the rational pursuit of the early Śaṅkara. Sentiments of high devotionalism coupled with belief in *nirguṇa* Brahman are common. At the same time, the author of the *Hastāmalakastotra* says : "The Self is discovered by himself for

1. Confer Late-S., *Svātmanirūpaṇa*, in Venkataraman; also *Hastāmalakastotrabhāṣya* in Dhole; *The Quintessence of Vedānta* 809-814, in Tattwananda.

2. Late-S., "Who Am I", in Subrahmanya Sarma, pp. 38-40; also confer "The Taintless Atman," "The Eternal Consciousness," "The Self as Pure Consciousness and Bliss," "The Indescribable Divine Principle in Man."

3. See Late-S., *The Quintessence of Vedānta* 910-921, in Tattwananda.

which he (the devotee) stands in no need of others."[1] This body of literature deals with many of the identical problems found in the master Advaitin but seeks a reconciliation of the issues. A clear accommodation takes place between nonduality and the pluralism in ordinary experience, between worship and concentration, between devotion and knowledge.[2] Once the guru is accepted as God and equated with God within a devotional framework, the consequences affect religious growth, the educational method and the epistemological questions which undergird the teaching tradition.

Although there is a more direct relationship between the late-Śaṅkara and the epics, Purāṇas and subsequent devotional literature, the former stands in closer continuity with Ādi Śaṅkara than in a full *bhakti* tradition. The *Mahābhārata*'s introduction of the grace (*prasāda*) of the guru, the Purāṇas' stress on the humanistic personality of gods and gurus, the religious seeker's affection for and submission to the guru dominating the *smṛti* literature—are all represented in the late-Śaṅkara. But such notions stand within the Advaita experience and not in isolation from it. The grace of the guru is a salient feature of the *bhakti* mystical tradition. The preceptor's grace increases the receptivity and capacity of the student; the late-Śaṅkara accepts this. But whereas the *bhakti* tradition looks to the guru as the sole liberator, one who may fully liberate in a moment of favor, spontaneously and instantaneously, such does not occur in this body of Advaita literature. During the epic period with the rise of religious sects, such as Śaiva, Śākta and Vaiṣṇava, there is a parallel shift that capitalizes on the spiritual personality of the guru to the detriment of the intellectual aspects of his personality. This is not evidenced in the late-Śaṅkara, but a balance between the spiritual and intellectual aspects of the guru's personality, established in the Upaniṣads, is retained. In modern times the followers of Śaṅkara speak of *bhakti* within an Advaita context; such a formulation fits well the late-Śaṅkara.

1. Late-S., *Hastāmalakastotrabhāṣya* in Dhole, p. 7.

2. Confer Suryanarayana Sastri, pp. 69-70. In this place Sastri speaks of the "reconciliation" between earlier and later Advaita; but I find the interpretation of S. Kuppuswami Shastri (confer bibliography) more convincing and thus use "accommodation" with intent.

Diversity Within Advaita Vedānta

A broad diversification took place in the development of Advaita Vedānta in the late medieval period. Discussion centered about the causality of intuition, that is, the nature of the proximate and direct cause of liberation. Upon the resolution of this problem rested the role of the teacher in the following centuries. Either the Upaniṣadic texts or meditation or the mind itself was considered by different Advaita thinkers to be the direct cause of liberating knowledge. In each case, the function of the guru held different importance. The consequent debate established within the Advaita tradition the Vivaraṇa school, which upholds as primary the Upaniṣadic texts from the teacher, and the Bhāmatī school, which follows the lead of Maṇḍanamiśra and upholds meditation and the mind as causative of intuitive knowledge. Both schools, however, deny the possibility of perceiving supersensuous knowledge through popular yoga techniques.

The fundamental difference between the schools consists in the importance each gives to the triple method collectively, and the degree of emphasis of each upon hearing, reflection and concentration individually. Both schools recognize and practice the triple method, but the different emphasis determines the specific function of the guru, the weight of his lineage and the duration of his influence upon the student. In the Vivaraṇa school, hearing, reflection and concentration are indirect causes of enlightenment, but the great Upaniṣadic axioms that come into contact with the sense of hearing are the direct cause. The importance of the guru and his lineage from Upaniṣadic and Advaita seers is paramount. He functions as teacher throughout the triple process, until the student achieves equality with him through liberation. For the Vivaraṇa school, meditation is an auxiliary means based upon the understanding of Upaniṣadic texts. In the Bhāmatī school, however, concentration is uninterrupted meditation that results from *upāsanā* and produces an intuition of Brahman. The guru is restricted to teaching the Upaniṣadic texts at the initial stage of hearing, and he is not necessary for the further development of the student. The divergent positions between the two schools is their conception of the triple process. The Vivaraṇa tradition conceives it as one integral process, while the Bhāmatī tradition conceives the triple method as successive and temporal stages and eliminates the role of the guru after the first stage. The Bhāmatī school gives an essential place to religious activity (*karma*), a deviation from the teaching of Śaṅkara.

Both *karma* and *bhakti* were incorporated into Advaita Vedānta during the post-Śaṅkara period. Devotion is a less common topic among the great commentators, since it enters into philosophical discussion infrequently. But during this period a parallel devotional literature developed in Advaita that is comparable to the devotional development in the late-Śaṅkara.

Vācaspati, a mid-ninth century Bihar Bengali, wrote the *Bhāmatī*, which along with the works of Maṇḍana kept alive a line of Advaita beyond that of Śaṅkara. This work has been the subject of many commentaries both within and outside Advaita Vedānta. Although Vācaspati wrote commentaries on most of the works of Maṇḍana, he depends largely upon the latter's *Brahmasiddhi*. He introduces the *Bhāmatī* with homage to Vyāsa and Śaṅkara. His description of the preceptor follows Purāṇic lines : "...he explains the meaning of the sacred teaching, confirms (his pupils) in the observances, and himself conforms to these observances."[1] Guided by Śaṅkara, however, he argues that the teaching of the preceptor is "knowledge free from the direction to activity."[2] Again following the master Advaitin, Vācaspati calls ritual observances remote means of spiritual growth that destroy sin and purify the mind but do not contribute to the goals of concentration.[3] Desire for knowledge and inquiry into the nature of reality commence the religious path, which depends upon reflection and concentration. Even though intuition is accompanied by inquiry and reflection, it does not result from verbal testimony "but from perception, that (intuition) being the invariable result of that (perception) alone."[4] Knowledge is from perception rather than from verbal testimony of the scripture and the teacher. The fruit of spiritual growth is intuition, and consequently the mind alone is considered the direct cause of liberation by Vācaspati. Intuition produces knowledge that is not sublatable but absolute; only liberating knowledge is non-sublatable.[5] Some

1. Vācaspati, *Bhāmatī*, in S. Sastri & Raja, p. 181.
2. Ibid., pp. 92-93.
3. Ibid., pp. 83-85.
4. Ibid., p. 78.
5. Ibid., pp. 159, 239.

scholars consider the difference between Vācaspati's position and that of the Vivaraṇa school to be more a verbal than a material one.[1] Yet later Advaita looks to the *Bhāmatī* as the basis for raising meditation above other practices. Vācaspati, moreover, does not give the same urgency to the role of the guru as Śaṅkara and the Vivaraṇa school do.

By mid-fourteenth century, two significant teachers of Advaita emerged, Bhāratītīrtha and Vidyāraṇya; the former was the teacher of the latter. The texts of these figures are still contested, but the *Dṛg-Dṛśya-Viveka* is thought by some scholars to be the principal work of Bhāratītīrtha.[2] Both writers show a liberalizing trend in Advaita. The *Dṛg-Dṛśya*, whose author was the *jagadguru* of the Sringeri *maṭha* for fifty years, counsels a double path : namely, inquiry for the more intelligent and contemplation of Brahman for the less intellectually astute. Bhāratītīrtha suggests meditation with sound, word and image, but he also recommends meditation in the heart with no symbol whatsoever.[3] He advocates meditation on symbol where the distinction of the knower, the act of knowing and the known exists (*savikalpa samādhi*); yet he also speaks of meditation in which there exist neither symbols nor the distinction of knower, the act of knowing and the known (*nirvikalpa samādhi*).[4] For Bhāratītīrtha, meditation strengthens the conviction in and understanding of the Upaniṣadic axioms.

Vidyāraṇya's *Pañcadaśī* states its purpose to be the teaching of Brahman to those who have been purified by the worship of the guru.[5] Instruction is from a teacher with lineage.[6] Knowledge from such a teacher is an indirect means of liberation for Vidyāraṇya, but teaching joined together with inquiry results in a

1. Ibid., p. 269, note by trans.

2. This work has been attributed to Śaṅkara, Vidyāraṇya, and Bhāratītīrtha; likewise the *Pañcadaśī* of Vidyāraṇya has been attributed to Bhāratītīrtha. Confer Nikhilananda (1949), Mahadevan (1962), and Mahadevan (1969).

3. Bhāratītīrtha, *Dṛg-Dṛśya-Viveka* 22, in Nikhilananda (1948). Confer Mahadevan (1969), p. 262.

4. Ibid., 23-25.

5. Vidyāraṇya, *Pañcadaśī* 1.2., in Shastri.

6. Ibid., 1.32.

direct means of knowledge.[1] Since the guru stands outside religious development, he may either meditate or not; nothing is obligatory to him. The student, on the other hand, must listen ceaselessly to "the drumbeat of the Vedāntic scriptures."[2] Vidyāraṇya, who probably headed the Sringeri *maṭha* after Bhāratītīrtha, quotes Vāsiṣṭha as to what should occupy the mind of a student. For those who have made no spiritual progress, one half of the mind is for enjoyment and one fourth of the mind each for philosophy and devotion to the teacher; but for the student who has advanced even slightly, one half of the mind is for enjoyment and philosophy equally and one half for devotion to the teacher.[3] Vidyāraṇya implies that there is a transfer of spiritual power (*śaktipāta*) from the guru to the disciple.[4] The teacher, possessing complete knowledge of reality, out of compassion brings about true comprehension in the student.

The subject of Vidyāraṇya's *Jīvanmukti-Viveka* is renunciation in which both desires and duties are overcome. Although the author does not deprecate *japa* and repetition of a *mantra*, in the *Pañcadaśī* he recommends ritual and meditation to those still bound to external objects and the path of knowledge to those with but average intelligence.[5] Yoga, likewise, is prescribed for those without the capacity for reflection; yoga has a temporary effect while knowledge of Brahman is permanent.[6] Vidyāraṇya teaches within the triple method. Direct knowledge by reflection (*manana*) does not occur spontaneously and thus hearing (*śravaṇa*) must be continued.[7] Inquiry includes both reflection and concentration ((*nididhyāsana*) because the key obstacle to direct knowledge is lack of inquiry.[8] Vidyāraṇya uses inquiry as the cohesive factor in the triple method in the same manner as Śaṅkara. Memory is also part of the triple method, for it prevents

1. Ibid., 7.31; 9.25; 9.30.
2. Ibid., 9.97; 9.102-103.
3. Vidyāraṇya, *Jīvanmukti-Viveka*, in Dvivedi, p. 124.
4. Ibid., in Poona (1916) edit., p. 48.
5. Vidyāraṇya, *Pañcadaśī* 12.3-4, in Shastri.
6. Ibid., 9.131; 4.38-49.
7. Ibid., 7.101; 7.97.
8. Ibid., 9.29-31. The word vicāra (inquiry) is used throughout the text and includes both reflection and right apprehension.

understanding from escaping. Hearing, reflection and concentration are referred to Vedāntic texts alone while all else is put aside. But rational discrimination is the single thread that holds the educational method together and makes it efficacious.

Meditation is not ignored in the *Pañcadaśī*. Symbolic meditation overcomes the belief that the world is permanent, while concentration (*ekāgratā*) overcomes the idea that the body constitutes the Self.[1] The difference between knowledge of Brahman and meditation on Brahman is that the former is governed by the nature of Brahman while the latter is governed by the will of the meditator.[2] Yet this does not render meditation futile, for in Vidyāraṇya's terms meditation effects a productive error : "An actual error, therefore, may be productive in that it produces a desired result. In this way worship of Brahman (under illusory form) may produce the result of liberation."[3] Just as a productive error may lead to correct knowledge, so too meditation may lead to knowledge.[4]

Vidyāraṇya does not encumber the student with rules, restraints and prescribed methods. He stresses the immediacy of experience.[5] His *Jīvanmukti-Viveka*, which quotes Śaṅkara's *Upadeśasāhasrī* at length, advocates liberation by means of the mind and within the mind. The lineage of Śaṅkara is sustained in the writing of Vidyāraṇya by the role assigned to self-inquiry and the guru in promoting effective self-inquiry.

Sadānanda Yogīndra, a member of the Sarasvatī order of ascetics, in the middle of the fifteenth century, wrote the *Vedāntasāra*. a compendium of orthodox Advaita that closely follows the thought of Śaṅkara. It became a popular summary for Vedānta training among young ascetics because of its clarity in exposing orthodox discipline and methodology. Sadānanda extolls his guru, Advayānanda, who, he says, is free from duality.[6] When the teacher explains the meaning of the Upaniṣadic axioms and

1. Ibid., 7.104. Attributes may be applied to Brahman for meditation, but the attributeless Brahman is meditated upon "by covering Him with mental *vṛtti*." Ibid 9.55-58.
2. Ibid., 9.74.
3. Ibid., 9.13.
4. Ibid., 9.123.
5. Ibid., 7.113; 7.118; 7.122.
6. Sadānanda, *Vedāntasāra* 2, in Nikhilananda (1941).

refutes superimposition, he says, the import of the texts is understood.[1] Sadānanda defines Vedānta and the specific role of the guru in terms of scriptural testimony (*śabda*).[2] The single aim of the Vedānta and the guru is to eliminate ignorance and falsification (*māyā*). This goal guides the preparation and training of the student.

Sadānanda gives special attention to the competency of the student. In addition to the four common prerequisites, he emphasizes a comprehensive knowledge of the Veda. He encourages the study of secular knowledge, grammar, etymology, prosody and astronomy, as well as auxiliary literature in order to gain a general view of the entire Veda. Although he cautions against performing ritual with a view toward attaining specific results, he commends the performance of obligatory rites, penances and devotions as the daily prayers and sacrifices of the higher castes and householders.[3] Such works purify the student's mind, while meditation concentrates his mind.[4] Then the student approaches a teacher for service. The instruction of the preceptor is received until consciousness of the Self arises.[5] Sadānanda accepts Śaṅkara's exposition of the triple method, but his description of the eight-limb yoga path is akin to the classical yoga system. The *Vedāntasāra* does not possess the creativity or depth of other medieval works on Advaita, but it stands as an example of Śaṅkara's teaching in brief outline with few accretions. It is a sign, appearing centuries after the master, that Śaṅkara's lineage has passed through generations of teachers with relatively little change.

Madhusūdana Sarasvatī, a mid-sixteenth century ascetic of a Śaṅkara order, stands in stark contrast to Sadānanda for his degree of accommodation and deviation from Śaṅkara.[6] He ranks with Maṇḍana and Vācaspati as an independent thinker

1. Ibid., 171.
2. Ibid., 3.
3. Ibid., 6.
4. Ibid., 13. *Upāsana* is used in the text for meditation.
5. Ibid., 181.
6. The dating of Madhusūdana is still uncertain. One contemporary scholar places him between 1490-1580, while another places him somewhat later, 1540-1647. Confer Modi, Divanji. His most important work in which he refutes the *Dvaita* school is the *Advaitasiddhi*.

and initiates yet another line of Advaita development. His major work supports *bhakti* as an equal means along with knowledge for the realisation of *nirguṇa* Brahman. This position, of course, diminishes the role of the preceptor. Yet he salutes his own guru, Viśveśvara Sarasvatī, as an *avatāra* of Śaṅkara and ends the *Siddhāntabindu* reprimanding Vyāsa, who did not "put together the complete sense of the Vedānta."[1] He extolls Śaṅkara and Sureśvara, who he says collected the whole meaning of the Vedānta. Calling his own teacher a peripatetic guru, Madhusūdana attributes to him whatever merit there is in his own work. His conception of the preceptor is one who gives only moral advice to the pupil with the scripture serving as the instrument of imparting such advice.[2] He does not view scripture and the guru as an integral cause of instruction. The Upaniṣads, *Brahma Sūtra*, *Bhagavad Gītā* and *Bhāgavata Purāṇa* stand side by side with equal authority. Yet revelation of scripture comes through the Upaniṣadic axioms and their elucidation.[3] Madhusūdana speaks of two types of liberation : the first is instantaneous through the simultaneous use of hearing, reflection and concentration, while the second is gradual illumination through devotional meditation on Brahman. This thinker believes not only that *nirguṇa* Brahman may be an object of *bhakti* but also that devotion leads to realisation more quickly.[4] Madhusūdana epitomizes the effective use of devotion within the Advaita teaching tradition. Although he diminishes the role of the preceptor in the salvation process, his pragmatic assimilation of *bhakti* indicates that even Advaita teachers draw extensively upon *smṛti* literature and especially devotional experience as it flourishes in medieval religious life. Advaita, in its broadest sense, is not an isolated intellectual tradition but stands at the center of Hindu experience. Madhusūdana may reflect more accurately than the majority of the Advaita writers the Śaṅkara heritage as it is encountered and experienced within the various sectors of Indian society.

A century later the *Vedāntaparibhāṣā* of Dharmarāja Adhvarīndra, who came under the influence of the Vivaraṇa school,

1. Madhusūdana, *Siddhāntabindu*, in Modi, pp. 1, 147.
2. Ibid., p. 95, 147.
3. Ibid., p. 7.
4. Ibid., pp. 12 ff.

reflects once again Śaṅkara's thought. This text, popular even in this century for its orthodox Advaita metaphysics and epistemology, establishes the educational method and realisation upon the guru and the succession of teachers. Dharmarāja believes that the personal origin of knowledge is fundamental to Upaniṣadic and Vedāntic wisdom.[1] He devotes an entire chapter to the competency of the student. One is equipped with competent knowledge when the content of understanding is not sublatable.[2] Competency is always in terms of valid knowledge that is common to experience and recollection.[3] Attributing only an indirect role to rites, Dharmarāja points to hearing, reflection and concentration as the instruments of knowledge. The triple method consists in mental acts that achieve full understanding. Each moment of the triple method causes a subsequent step that removes ignorance, until a transformation of mind, generated by reflection and concentraticon, occurs.[4] In this brief work, Śaṅkara's conception of the guru and the path of discipleship is brought into the modern period.

The Threshold of the Present

The majority of Advaita authors from the time of Śaṅkara to the present century, especially those previously treated, were ascetics in a Śaṅkara order and occasionally headed one of his major *maṭha*-s. In this century Candraśekhara Bhāratī (1892-1954), the guru of the Sringeri *maṭha*, brought the post-Śaṅkara development to the threshold of the present. Even though he was not a writer of scholastic commentaries, his public talks and personal dialogues have been recorded.[5] At the age of twelve, Candraśekhara came under the influence of the reigning *ācārya*, who initiated his education in logic, Pūrva Mīmāṃsā and the Vedānta, in that sequence. The youth cultivated extraordinary devotion to his guru. When he became a reigning guru himself, he travelled and taught widely throughout India, but he spent the final third of his life in total seclusion.

1. Dharmarāja, *Vedāntaparibhāṣā*, 5.54, in S. S. Sastri (1942).
2. Ibid., 4.8 reads "Competency consists in the non-sublation of a relation that is the content of purport."
3. Ibid., 7.8.
4. Ibid., 9.20-37.
5. Confer Krishnaswami Aiyar (1956), (1961).

Candraśekhara upholds Śaṅkara as the Lord who came among humankind for the preservation and propagation of religion.[1] He stresses the necessity of the guru and surrender to him. The guru's specific role is to teach the scripture, especially the Vedānta, and a particular course of action suited to the individual. Only a proper guru can convey the significance of the injunctions, prohibitions and meaning of the Vedas. With an intense faith in the guru, the meaning of scripture becomes more accessible.[2] Speaking against contemporary education and especially Westernization, this classical teacher defines service to the teacher as the preservation of caste duty, maintaining traditional family practices and performing duties allotted to the individual in life.[3] Thus a special place is given to *karma* yoga. Urging complete faith and surrender to the guru, Candraśekhara calls the teacher a guiding light, a spiritual master, one not blinded by darknes.[4] The primary role of the guru is to impart Vedic testimony. A guru can be discovered by anyone who has a desire for liberation and a relative degree of competency, and who makes a search for a teacher : "He is ever available and is but waiting for symptom of real earnestness in you."[5] This attitude contrasts with a story that is told of a student who once sought out Candraśekhara and asked the guru to teach him Advaita. The sage responded, however, that Advaita is neither something to be learned nor something to be taught : "It is essentially something to be realised by oneself. I cannot therefore undertake to teach you."[6] Since nonduality exists on a level of experience beyond the phenomenal, it transcends words and concepts.

Working from Śaṅkara's notion of the possible equality between teacher and student, Candraśekhara speaks of the guru's imparting his own state of Brahman-existence to the student, which brings about an equality in order that the student can in turn

1. Aiyar (1956), p. 101.

2. Aiyar (1961), pp. 3, 7, 33, 59, 73-74.

3. Ibid., p. 46; also confer Aiyar (1956), p. 35. In the second citation, the author speaks of performing daily Vedic rites and attending to the dictates of the *Dharma Śāstras*; also confer p. 53.

4. Aiyar (1956), p. 70.

5. Ibid., p. 15.

6. Aiyar (1956), p. 160.

impart instruction.[1] Competency becomes a favorite theme of the Śaṅkarācārya, who accepts the guru and scripture together as perfect in competency. The guru and his testimony contribute to the competency of the disciple so that he discovers knowledge for himself.

Candraśekhara's personalized method is evident in his talks and dialogues. His lectures are highly logical, eliciting systematic reasoning from the audience at every step until understanding is reached. He progressively unveils teaching of the most simple and mundane realities until an audience is able to accept the finer levels of philosophical discourse. He permits his disciples to come to self-understanding through the logic of dialogue wherein they themselves discover meaning. The teacher exists as an instrument for one's own discovery of knowledge. The capacity of Candraśekhara to speak with benefit to different kinds of people, from a variety of communities and social positions, also emerges from his discourses.

The role of Vedic testimony, the four prerequisites for studentship and the threefold method are present in the instruction of this guru. He ignores neither *bhakti* nor *karma*, but he reconceptualizes them in concrete situations. Devotion is not a substitute path, but religious activity is true devotion. He teaches, for example, that communal devotion (*bhajana*) is intended for moments of leisure in the midst of duties. If a *bhajana* is divorced from activity, it is not true devotion.[2] To carry out the commands of the Lord, he observes, is a greater act of devotion than singing divine praises. "Real devotion lies in carrying out his (the Lord's) dictates implicitly."[3] From another perspective, Candraśekhara gives an Advaita interpretation to devotion when he speaks of progressive stages in a love relationship with God. The devotee first experiences something consonant with an expression of "I belong to the Lord," which grows into a response of "The Lord belongs to me," but culminates in "The Lord is verily myself."[4] *Karma*, *bhakti* and *jñāna* are present as successive stages

1. Aiyar (1961), pp. 9-10.
2. Aiyar (1956), pp. 146, 149.
3. Ibid., pp. 150-151.
4. Aiyar (1961), p. 124.

in his teaching, and even though devotion is turned into salvific activity, knowledge and self-discovery remain the primary religious path and goal. This twentieth century preceptor brings the ancient lineage to present times by drawing upon both the master Advaitin and the broad development of the post-Śaṅkara period. He places the guru-*śiṣya* tradition into the present. His teaching resonates with that of the living Śaṅkarācāryas in India today.

PART TWO

PRESENT DAY ŚAṄKARĀCĀRYAS

CHAPTER FIVE

THE ŚAṄKARĀCĀRYAS AND THE SEATS OF LEARNING

Śaṅkara reorganized Hindu ascetical life along monastic lines by establishing *maṭha*-s to propagate *sanātana dharma* and the Advaita tradition. Ānandagiri, an early biographer of the master, confirms the fact that Śaṅkara had many disciples who headed many *maṭha*-s as teachers.[1] Four or five of these religious centers were headed by his foremost pupils, Sureśvara, Padmapāda, Toṭaka and Hastāmalaka, from whom the lineage of the Śaṅkarācāryas evolved through the centuries. Tradition establishes the major *maṭha*-s at Sringeri, Kanchi, Dwaraka, Puri and Badrinath as the principal seats of learning founded by Ādi Śaṅkara, from whom they claim direct lineage. Those Śaṅkarācāryas who are recognized today by the faithful as *jagadguru*-s, world teachers, head these five centers. Ādi Śaṅkara placed the *maṭha*-s in geographically strategic areas of the far north, the east, the west and the south of India, thus linking all India with Advaita teachers.

Although much has been written in this century about the historic character of the *maṭha*-s and the succession of Śaṅkarācāryas, it is improbable that any critical and definitive history embracing all five centers and their gurus can be achieved. The ancient texts dealing with the institutions, called *maṭhāmnāya*-s, date from the post-Śaṅkara period; they are inconclusive and are challenged by some modern historians as gratuitous.[2] The *ācārya-paramparā*-s, which list the successors within each institution, are also questionable documents because with the one exception of the Sringeri *paramparā*, they are based on the traditional dating of Ādi Śaṅkara in the fifth century B.C.E.[3] Historians also

1. Confer Aiyer & Sastri, pp. 46-47.

2. Examples of these texts: *Śaṅkarācārya-Jagadguru-maṭhāmnāya Śaṅkaragranthāvali; Unpublished Upaniṣads; Yatisandhyāsamuccaya*. Manuscript copies exist in the Oriental Institute, Mysore, and the Bhandarkar Oriental Research Institute, Poona. For a challenge to the *maṭhāmnāya* scheme, confer Aiyer & Sastri, pp. 106 ff.

3. Confer Aiyer & Sastri for an attempt to establish Śaṅkara's life between 509-477 B.C.E., pp. 6 ff and 147 ff.

mistrust these texts because they are religious records showing signs of having been altered through the centuries. Some of the historical evidence was destroyed or tampered with because of rivalries among the religious centers. Since most of the history was written by devotees of particular gurus, the principle of alteration, which gives liberty to writers to change details of history as long as the dignity of a person's life is not diminished, was generously employed.[1] Recently, however, historical study has improved at centers like Sringeri and Kanchi, where past rivalries have precipitated critical research. There is ample material to reconstruct the lives of some past teachers, for example at Sringeri from the time of Vidyāraṇya, as well as to reconstruct the *maṭha*-s themselves as institutions.[2] Even though the need for critical historical research is accepted, the principle of tradition still holds validity among these institutions and their followers.

There is no reason to nullify the basic tradition of these *maṭha*-s as Vidyāpīṭhas, seats of learning, founded by Śaṅkara with importance over and above his other foundations and possessing a succession of teachers from him.[3] The authority of a particular reigning teacher has sometimes been challenged in court cases, or challenges have been made when the seat is not occupied. The concern for historical affirmation, especially in this century among devotees, is fundamentally a concern for apostolic succession, so to speak, which is to say for a teaching tradition possessing personal and unbroken lineage. Tradition is the basis of lineage and validates it unless proved mistaken.

The history of the Vidyāpīṭhas is a history of the Śaṅkarācāryas. Although the *ācārya-paramparā*-s may appear fanciful to a modern historian, they highlight the fact that a *maṭha* or a *vidyāpīṭha* rests solely upon its teacher and his relationship to previous gurus. As already noted, four of the five centers trace their teachers to Ādi Śaṅkara with the archaic dating of 509-477 B.C.E., rather than the 788-820 C.E., the date accepted by modern scholars.[4] Three of the *maṭha*-s claim Sureśvara, Śaṅkara's greatest student, as their

1. Devasenapathi, p. 42.
2. Jnanananda Bharati (1969 A), p. 1.
3. The clear exception in teaching lineage is the Jyotirmaṭha which ceased to exist for some centuries but is now revived; other *maṭha*-s have had less serious breaks in lineage.
4. Confer Sastry & Kumaraswamy; also Aiyer & Sastri.

first guru, with one *maṭha* listing him as regent. The Puri *vidyāpīṭha* had difficulty filling a vacancy between 1960 and 1964 because the previous guru, instead of selecting one successor, left a will with the names of twenty-seven individuals whom he considered worthy of the seat. Some of those named refused the position while others persevered but briefly in the seat before Śrī Niranjan, the eleventh of the twenty-seven nominees, began his reign in 1964.[1] The Sringeri, Kanchi and Dwaraka *maṭha*-s of the Śaṅkarācāryas have the most thorough records with dates for each guru; the list of past gurus at the Puri *maṭha* lacks dates; and a *paramparā* record is unavailable from the Jyotirmaṭha in the Himalayas.[2] In this century, three of the *maṭha*-s, Dwaraka, Puri and Sringeri, have had their teachers challenged as legitimate holders of the seat. The Dwaraka case was pursued for thirty-five years before it ended in a favorable court decision for the reigning guru in 1951; similarly, the court resolved the Puri case in 1950 by giving the then-reigning and renowned teacher, Śrī Bharati Krishna, a favorable decision. The Jyotirmaṭha, twenty-seven miles from Badrinath in the Himalayas, had the most radical break in lineage.[3] According to some records it ceased to exist for nearly three centuries, but authorities of the institution today admit a break of only 165 years. It was suppressed by political authorities, but in the last century there took place a renaissance among the *maṭha*-s existing in the same area, during which the Jyotirmaṭha also was revived.[4] The reinstatement of this northern Śaṅkara

1. Confer Aiyer & Sastri, p. 180. In one printed *paramparā*, Śrī Yogeswarananda Tirtha is listed as the 144th successor of the Govardhana Pīṭha, who reigned sometime between 1960 and 1964, but the official *paramparā* of the *maṭha* dropped his name because he did not continue as Śaṅkarācārya; his name was replaced with Śrī Niranjan who is now reigning.

2. Ibid., pp. 142 ff. I was also unable to secure a *paramparā* from Jyotirmaṭha.

3. The Dwaraka Pīṭha had breaks in succession and dislocations into branches of considerable consequences, but it is now fully restored. Confer Aiyer & Sastri, pp. 173 ff; also Bodas, pp. 64-66. Breaks in succession also occurred in the Govardhana Pīṭha, but it is also fully restored. See Aiyer & Sastri, pp. 173 ff; also Bodas, pp. 48-51. For a challenge to the head of the Sringeri *maṭha*, see Aiyer & Sastri, pp. 188 ff.

4. Sastry & Kumaraswamy discredit this renaissance, p. vii. These writers claim that Jyotirmaṭha was extinct for nearly three centuries. *Shri Jyotirmath : A Brief Introduction*, p. 5, gives a 165 year gap between reigning *ācāryas*.

foundation was brought about by the provincial government, the encouragement of devotees, and the work of its first Śaṅkarācārya in this century, Swami Brahmanand Saraswati. The Śaṅkarācāryas and their devotees have a heightened concern for apostolicity. This concern has an obvious theological implication, for unbroken lineage in Advaita symbolizes the eternal in humankind, in history and in the cosmos. The teaching of the Śaṅkarācāryas is the continuation, it is believed, of *sanātana dharma* in its Advaita expression from generation to generation.

The Vidyāpīṭhas Today

The *Vidyāpīṭhas*, seats of learning, at present are a formidable institution; their degree of organization shows itself in the physical complex with temple, *maṭha*, library, *pāṭhaśālā* and guest house. These foundations are connected to or in proximity to major Hindu temples, which increases the prestige of the *maṭha*-s. The temples are usually pilgrim centers and are generously supported by the faithful. The present Śaṅkarācāryas have given major attention to the educational institutions, the *pāṭhaśālā*-s, associated with each *maṭha*. I found them contemporary buildings, well kept and conducive to serious study. Reflecting the least concern are the *maṭha* residential buildings, usually old, unpretentious and in need of restoration. The seats of all the Jagadgurus are strikingly similar in their simple, ascetical and scholarly character. The actual seat is usually in an average-size room with a wooden platform elevated a few inches from the floor and in some cases covered with a tiger skin. Upon this the Jagadguru sits when he teaches his devotees, grants audiences to visitors, conducts private business, studies and meditates. The seat is frequently surrounded with books, manuscripts, journals, newspapers, correspondence and, in one case I observed, an all-India train schedule.

The Sringeri Vidyāpīṭha is situated on the banks of the Tunga River in the western ghats of Karnataka, comprising temples, *pāṭhaśālā*, library, *maṭha*, and several large guest houses. In early times the Śaṅkarācāryas and their disciples lived in forest hermitages scattered throughout the Karnataka countryside, but in the fourteenth century Vidyāraṇya constructed a residential building and the Śāradā temple in Dravidian style. An adjoining Vidyāpīṭha was a *jagir*, exercising jurisdiction and supported by taxes collected from its jurisdiction, but today it is fully self-sustaining.

The Sringeri Vidyāpīṭha governs over forty educational institutions and temples throughout India with another major *pāṭhaśālā* in Bangalore, where I met the Śaṅkarācārya. A similar pattern is observed in the Kanchi Kāmakoṭi Vidyāpīṭha in Tamil Nadu outside Madras. The Kāmākṣī temple of Kanchi, undergoing restoration when I first saw it, is typical of this old temple city. Yet the Kāmakoṭi *maṭha* is modest, with a place for public worship, offices and simple residential quarters for the guru and his attendants. The *maṭha* in Kalavai, where the senior *ācārya* is now in retirement and where I met him, consists of a few rooms built in south Indian village style with adobe walls and thatched roof. The *pāṭhaśālā*-s of this *maṭha* at Kumbakonam, Puri, Tiruvannamalai and New Kanchi have received greater attention. The Govardhana Vidyāpīṭha in Puri, situated on the Bay of Bengal in Orissa, is the most unassuming of all. Over the centuries it became surrounded by hills of sand swept along the Orissan coast; today the entrance to the *maṭha* is several stories above its original, and the pilgrim walks down into old stone rooms buried in sand. It took me several days to actually find it. Yet the *pāṭhaśālā* attached to the *maṭha* is a recent structure with all the amenities for effective scholarship. The Dwaraka Vidyāpīṭha is attached to the famous Dvārakādhīśa Temple, a major pilgrim center in western Gujarat on the shore of the Indian Ocean. The temple stands on a site commanding all Dwaraka and its environs, while the *maṭha* adjoining it could easily be missed by the pilgrim. The present Śaṅkarācārya has built a college and research institute, both modern, large and efficient structures, outside the old town of Dwaraka. At Dakor, a short distance from Ahmedabad, there is another *maṭha* of the Dwaraka Vidyāpīṭha, which the present guru uses more frequently because of its accessibility within Gujarat. Although it is a modern building, with a temple in the shape of an ascending lotus, the seat and the residential quarters for the *pāṭhaśālā* and attendants are modest. Finally the Jyotirmaṭha, overlooking the market village of Joshimath, is 6,000 feet above sea level in the northwestern Himalaya Mountains. It is a handsome structure which reminded me of a Swiss chalet of the last century. The Badrinath temple, a major Hindu pilgrim site, is twenty-seven miles beyond at 11,000 feet above sea level and rests beneath 21,630-foot Mt. Neelkanth. The seat of the Jyotirmaṭha and its *pāṭhaśālā* in Allahabad, where I first met its

Śaṅkarācārya, is somewhat more ostentatious than those of the other Vidyāpīṭhas. The guru of this religious center is the spiritual head of the Daṇḍa *Sannyāsīs*, numbering over 1,000 Brāhmaṇas, and as such engages in the role of a *rājaguru* which, as we shall see, distinguishes him from the others.

The reigning gurus have been only minimally interested in their *maṭha*-s, while the educational foundations receive their foremost concern. The Vidyāpīṭhas present a mere institutional aspect to the uninformed visitor, but to their supporters they witness to the search for religious knowledge. Education is institutionalized as an effective sign not only of lineage but also of an intellectual tradition.

Concern for lineage is the basis for increased interrelations among the Śaṅkarācāryas in recent times. Meetings among the gurus were initiated by Śrī Narasiṃha Bhāratī, a Sringeri Śaṅkarācārya, at the turn of the century. Continued by his successors, the meetings were brought to fruition with the present heads of the Vidyāpīṭhas. In 1958, for example, on the bank of the Gaṅgā in Kanpur, the Jagadgurus of that time met at a Vedic *sammelana* in which they commissioned Swami Swanandashram of the Kashmir Gaddi to travel beyond the Indian sub-continent. The Sringeri and Dwaraka *ācārya*-s met in 1964, and the next year at a Śaṅkara Jayantī festival in Kalady, Śaṅkara's birthplace, the gurus of Sringeri, Dwaraka and Puri gathered to issue a common message. The head of the Dwaraka Vidyāpīṭha installed Śrī Nirañjana in the Puri seat in the presence of the Śaṅkarācārya of Badrinath in 1964. This resulted in the issuance of a joint communication from the three assembled.[1] Thus the *ācārya*-s of this century attempt to reflect a common endeavor and a united tradition. The devotion they have for each other is also apparent. The gurus, however, of the four *āmnāya maṭha*-s are not generally cordial to the Kanchi Vidyāpīṭha. Rivalry with Kanchi continues and the followers of the other *maṭha*-s, even younger students who were my informants, do not accept Kanchi as a foundation directly established by Ādi Śaṅkara. This rivalry is not carried on only among the zealous devotees whom I observed; an assembly of learned *paṇḍita*-s of the four *āmnāya maṭha*-s, held in Puri in 1964, resolved in rigorous terms that only four seats were established

1. *Four Amnaya Pithas*, pp. 12 ff.

by Ādi Śaṅkara. This resolution, which has been repeatedly published, obviously received the confirmation of the three attending *ācārya*-s[1] of the north, east and west. The devotees continue this agelong debate because of a righteous concern to preserve and reserve the legacy from Ādi Śaṅkara. Nonetheless, over the years the senior *ācārya* of Kanchi has been in contact with heads of other Hindu *maṭha*-s throughout south India and has issued a number of public statements with them. Moreover, he visited Puri with its many *āśrama*-s and the Lord Jagannath Temple, and in the early 1970's established in Puri a Śaṅkara temple and *pāṭhaśālā* for Sanskrit study, which I found highly operative. There is evidence that the former head of the Puri Vidyāpīṭha met with the senior *ācārya* of Kanchi in the late 1930's.[2] The good relationships between the Vidyāpīṭhas and even their rivalry give evidence of a united teaching legacy.

The influence of these foundations today as pilgrim centers and educational institutions is significant. The five sites are pilgrim centers in their own right because major Hindu temples of historical importance are either attached to them or nearby. At Badrinath in the north, where one tradition has Śaṅkara leaving the body, and at Puri in the east with its revered Jagannath temple to Lords Jagannatha, Balabhadra and Subhadra, pilgrims gather in huge numbers. Dwaraka in the west, one of the seven sacred cities of Hinduism, with the Dvārakādhīśa temple of Lord Kṛṣṇa, is believed to be the ancient capital where Lord Kṛṣṇa ruled. Kanchi in Tamil Nadu is another sacred city where in ancient times devotees from both Hinduism and Buddhism assembled. Likewise, Sringeri in the Karnataka ghats with its Śāradā temple has been a favorite pilgrim site for several centuries. The Vidyāpīṭhas benefit from the pilgrims to these temples, who not infrequently become devotees of the Śaṅkarācāryas. Devotees come for religious retreat and sometimes, as I discovered, spend days and weeks giving service to the institution while seeking *darśana* from a Śaṅkarācārya.

Worship in both temple and *maṭha* also draws pilgrims and devotees. A broad variety of Hindu worship is found in the temples and the *maṭha*-s. Traditional forms of worship are evident; for

1. Ibid., pp. 19-20.
2. Ramaswami Sastri, p. 86.

example the Śaṅkara temple of Sringeri integrates Śaiva, Śākta, Vaiṣṇava, Saura, Gāṇapata and Īśvara worship in both form and formless aspects. The Puri *maṭha* has a Śiva *liṅga*, Kṛṣṇa with flute and an ensemble of *mūrti*-s gathered in one place. The popular eclectic worship is based upon the tradition that Ādi Śaṅkara revived and gave stability to six alternate ways of worship, the *ṣaṇmata*-s.[1] Ascetics from the Śaṅkara orders have consistently worshipped personal gods. Śaṅkara in his commentary on the *Gītā* speaks of the six attributes of God that correspond to the six Gods, Śiva, Viṣṇu, Śakti, Sūrya, Gaṇapati and Kumāra. The *ṣaṇmata* tradition is equally reflected in the hymns of Ādi Śaṅkara in which every aspect of the *saguṇa* Brahman is praised and adored. The temple worship consists in all *saguṇa* forms of devotion, which are considered necessary for the religious development of ordinary householders. It is conducted by a few selected priests who devote themselves to ritual. I observed that the devotees of the *maṭha*-s are usually more involved in *pūjā* than the students or teachers in the *pāṭhaśālā*-s, who generally restrict themselves to Gāyatrī *japa* and the daily *sandhyā* prayers.

The *maṭhāmnāya* texts have Ādi Śaṅkara instituting in each *maṭha* a female deity (*devatā*) and a crystal *liṅga* brought from Kailāsa.[2] The worship resulting from this tradition is in full evidence today. The goddesses Kāmākṣī, Śāradā, Vimalā, Bhadrakālī and Pūrṇāgiri are popular in Kanchi, Sringeri, Dwaraka, Puri and Badrinath respectively. Tradition is highly specific; for example, it is believed in Sringeri that Ādi Śaṅkara installed Śāradā, who represents *brahmavidyā* and Śrī Cakra, and gave to Sureśvara a crystal *liṅga* of Candramaulīśvara and a *mūrti* of Gaṇapati. *Liṅga* worship is in evidence in each *maṭha*, and I even observed that the gurus when on tour usually carry the crystal *liṅga* with them. The present *ācārya* of Dwaraka installed 1,331 *Śivaliṅga*-s in a Jñāna Mandira along with 1,220 *śāligrāma*-s of Nārāyaṇa around a *mūrti* of Viṣṇu. The place of the *liṅga* in *pūjā* is in accord not only with Śaṅkara's Śaiva background but also with Advaita ideology. One modern devotee writes :

Liṅga means a symbol; here it stands for the pillar of light

1. Confer Ramaratnam.
2. Confer *Āmnāya Upaniṣad* in *Unpublished Upaniṣads.*

> that the "knowers of the Self experience in the cave of the heart." The *liṅga* cannot be said to have a form, nor is it quite formless; in its shape neither a beginning nor an end can be marked; the *sphaṭika liṅga* has no colour but takes the colour of the object presented before it; and hence it is the most appropriate symbol of the Infinite Brahman without form or attirbutes, but by the play of *māyā* assumes various forms to bless the devotee.[1]

Ablutions of and offerings to the *liṅga* are an essential part of *pūjā*. In Dwaraka, for example, a silver cow is placed over the green-stone *liṅga*, and as milk is poured into an upper orifice it flows out from the udder of the cow upon the *liṅga*.

Pūjā in the Śaṅkara Vidyāpīṭha-s consists of both Vedic and Āgamic elements, and even draws upon the Tantra. The Āgama *śāstra*-s especially the twenty-eight Śaiva Āgamas, are the basis for a great portion of the *pūjā*. This mixed *pūjā*, as it was characterized to me by a *paṇḍita*, is usually carried out by resident Brāhmaṇas in the morning and evening and by the *ācārya* at noonday worship. I witnessed a guru greeted by both Vedic recitation and *bhajana* music. Cow-*pūjā* and elephant *pūjā* are common in several Vidyāpīṭha-s as introductory rites. The Śaṅkarācārya himself conducts his own worship behind a curtain, hidden from the devotees, who are not permitted to view a Jagadguru lowering himself before deities. When a guru is on tour, there is little or no *pūjā* performed publicly in the *maṭha*, but when the guru is present punctuality marks daily ritual.

The *maṭha*-s are place for *pūjā*, *darśana* and teaching. The experience of *darśana* by devotee is at least as important as, if not more important than, an *ācārya*'s *pūjā*. Devotees come for the blessing and experience of the guru himself. The guru meets publicly each day with those on pilgrimage and grants private interviews to those who request them. These are intense moments of experience for the devotee or pilgrim, and they also afford an opportunity for the guru to teach. Although some of the present Śaṅkarācāryas do extensive public teaching while residing in the *maṭha*, others limit their teaching to a *śiṣya* or a few intimate attendants.

The Pāṭhaśālā-s and Traditional Education

A Śaṅkara *maṭha* is principally a seat of learning. The

1. Venkataraman, p. 116.

pāṭhaśālā and its education tradition give a distinct character to a Śaṅkara Vidyāpīṭha. The senior *ācārya* of Kanchi has spoken of a return to the spirit of the *gurukula*, the ancient forest school, and a gradual reintroduction of the *gurukula* as a superior form of education.[1] There is an element of the *gurukula* system in all the *pāṭhaśālā*-s of the Śaṅkara *maṭha*-s. The students are supported by the *maṭha*, which supplies their education, food, clothing and housing. They frequently live and study in quarters adjacent to the *maṭha*, but the teachers, who are usually Brāhmaṇa house-holders, live outside the *maṭha*. I observed in Sringeri that a few older students with their *paṇḍita*-s live together around the bungalow of the Śaṅkarācārya. Older students who ask to attend the guru live in closer proximity to him and receive instruction more directly from him. The *gurukula* system, however, has not been preserved fully in modern times because the majority of teachers are householders living with their families, so that the students usually are without the intimate association of their teachers that was customary in ancient times.

Most characteristic of the *pāṭhaśālā*-s is the traditional system of learning. Education is limited to males. The Sringeri school usually enrolls eighty students, from age ten to the late teens, and approximately thirteen *paṇḍita*-s each specializing in a particular Veda or branch of Sanskrit study. The *paṇḍita* of the *Yajur Veda* in Sringeri told me that he has spent forty-five years with this text alone. The *paṇḍita*-s there are Smārta Brāhmaṇas whose students have been sent by Smārta families. If a youth arrives without having received *upanayana*, it is given in the *maṭha*. The basic course of study in Sanskrit learning, such as literature, grammar and the Vedas, usually extends over seven years but can take as long as ten years. Instruction is also given in logic, Mīmāṃsā and Vedānta philosophy, and astrology. The more advanced students of this *maṭha* go to the Bangalore *pāṭhaśālā* to specialize in Pūrva Mīmāṃsā and Vedānta. There were six students and two *paṇḍita*-s there when I first visited, and the course of philosophical studies lasts for six or seven years. The Kanchi *maṭha* supports many *pāṭhaśālā*-s with a few young students in Sanskrit studies at New Kanchi. The major school at Kumba-

1. Confer Mahadevan (1975), p. 81; Ramakrishna Aiyer, pp. 14-15; Ramaswami Sastri, p. 33.

konam, which was the seat of the Kanchi Śaṅkarācārya for some decades in the past, usually has fifteen to twenty students and three to four *paṇḍita*-s.

In the Govardhana *maṭha* at Puri, the school has courses other than Sanskrit studies, namely in history, mathematics, geography and several modern languages for a few younger students. The Vedas, however, are still introduced to the young students. The Sanskrit Academy of this *maṭha* has in recent times around four hundred students and fifteen teachers in a ten-year program, which may be followed by two or more years with specialization in Sanskrit literature, grammar, the Vedas and the Vedānta. The Dwaraka *pāṭhaśālā* at Dakor teaches traditional Sanskrit studies but has made an attempt to integrate Sanskrit and modern education. In 1960 the present Śaṅkarācārya of Dwaraka established a Sanskrit Academy and Arts College and an Indological Research Institute for graduate study, under the direction of the *maṭha* but affiliated with a major Gujarat university. The Arts College had four hundred students specializing in Sanskrit, Gujarati and economics under twenty teachers. In 1976, in my initial visit, twenty-eight students were studying for the traditional Sanskrit titles of *śāstrī* and *ācārya*, and thirty-five students were pursuing a modern M.A. degree in Sanskrit. There were also eight or ten students at the doctoral level in Sanskrit studies. Female students participate in college and graduate education. The two major professors for doctoral students were a traditional *paṇḍita* and a modern research scholar in Sanskrit studies. The *pāṭhaśālā* of the Jyotirmaṭha is located in Allahabad, where the present Śaṅkarācārya frequently resides.

A major education endeavor at several of the Śaṅkara Vidyāpīṭhas is the training of the junior swāmī, the designated successor of a reigning Śaṅkarācārya. The junior swāmī of Sringeri, who is in his late-twenties, was selected by the senior *ācārya* as a youth of fourteen from Andhra Pradesh. The Śaṅkarācārya teaches him in some areas of study, but other experts also participate in his education. Since logic is a speciality of the Sringeri line of gurus, this is a domain of the Śaṅkarācārya himself. The junior swāmī of Kanchi, who is now the reigning *ācārya*, was educated along similar lines, namely in the Sanskrit schools under the supervision of the Śaṅkarācārya but drawing freely upon experts in various fields. Two disciples are in line for the head of the Jyotirmaṭha;

both are older men. The older of the two is Swāmī Viṣṇudevānanda Saraswatī, who looks upon the present Śaṅkarācārya and his predecessor, Swāmī Brahmānanda, as his gurus since he has been a *śiṣya* of both. A second *śiṣya*, fifty-year-old Swāmī Nārāyaṇānanda, is the direct disciple of the reigning Śaṅkarācārya. Both of these individuals receive frequent instruction from the *ācārya* since they are with him almost daily. All these men are *śiṣya*-s in the classical sense, for they live intimately with the Śaṅkarācāryas who directly instruct them and even take them on tour.

The *pāṭhaśālā*-s preserve a learned tradition, especially an oral tradition. The *paṇḍita* legacy is still present. Each teacher has received traditional Sanskrit education and is an expert in one area of Sanskrit study or one specific text. The students in their conversations with me easily distinguish between their *paṇḍita*-s and the Jagadguru as transmitters of an intellectual and a spiritual legacy respectively. The *pāṭhaśālā*-s are remnants of a past educational system. The head of the Sringeri school told me with pride that there is nothing modern in education in his school. Few *paṇḍita*-s use a Western language, since all classes are conducted in Sanskrit with recourse to the regional Indian languages when necessary. The ancient *maṭhāmnāya* scheme allotted to each Vidyāpīṭha secialization in a particular Veda : *Sāma Veda* for Dwaraka, *Atharva* for Badrinath, *Ṛg* for Puri and *Yajur* for Sringeri. Although this is followed even now, there is a preference for the *Sāma Veda* in at least three of the Vidyāpīṭhas.

The average student is exposed to the entire area of Sanskrit and Vedic literature, but specialization may be initiated at an early age. A student of sixteen in Sringeri, for example, informed me that he had studied the *Yajur Veda* for six years and intended to devote two more years to the task. Specialization in the Vedānta is restricted to a few students, never more than three or four at one time. Vedic study is stressed more than specialization in the Vedānta, because there are in the *pāṭhaśālā*-s only a few older students in their twenties, the age at which serious Vedānta study is undertaken. By this age some youths have opted for other areas of Sanskrit literature or priestly lore and practice. Higher studies usually take six or seven years beyond the basic course, and by that time the majority of students have entered contemporary institutions or other paths of life. Student interest and capacity, from my observations, have limited serious study of the Vedānta. The way the Vedānta is taught differs from the traditional teaching method used with the Vedas and Sanskrit literature. There is more emphasis on understanding in the former and on memorization in the latter. In the Bangalore school for Vedānta studies, the *paṇḍita* lectures on the Vedānta in the context of the six orthodox philosophical systems, Jainism and Buddhism, and then proceeds to classical Upaniṣadic texts and works of Śaṅkara. Memorization of these texts is not part of the method as it is with the Vedas. Although Śaṅkara's commentaries on the *Brahma Sūtra* and the *Taittirīya Upaniṣad* are preferred, other texts like the Bhāmatī and authors like Sureśvara and Vidyāraṇya also are examined. A Sanskrit school under traditional *paṇḍita*-s is not the place for creative Vedānta scholarship, but Vedānta research is pursued in the Indological Research Institute of Dwaraka. The Sringeri Vidyāpīṭha has also established a research center for Advaita studies in Kalady.

The traditional method of learning for younger students of the *pāṭhaśālā*-s is based upon the oral transmission of literature, received by them with an attitude of devotion and in an environment of austerity. The classes for Sanskrit recitation are small, ranging from two to eight students. At the beginning and end of each session, the students prostrate before the *paṇḍita*. In one class I heard each *śloka* repeated twice by the *paṇḍita* and then recited twice by the student in melodic patterns that depend on the particular text being memorized. The *paṇḍita* responds swiftly to mistakes and demands a corrected recitation. In another class in the *Ṛgveda*, I observed that *śloka*-s of fifty words were recited at one time and the students counted the words on their fingers. Fifty such groups of fifty words comprised a lesson, which constituted a forty-five minute class. The ideal is to spend four hours each day in such lessons and six hours in private recitation. Although there is time for explaining a text and eliciting questions from the students, recitation and training of memory appear more important among young students, who have a limited understanding of a passage. This is in accord with the classical pedagogical principle that understanding comes after memorization. Both pupils and teachers told me that they look upon the capacity to memorize as a grace and blessing. Some students commented that the Gāyatrī *japa*, thrice daily, is a key to strengthening the memory.

The Present Śaṅkarācāryas

The Śaṅkarācāryas under investigation here are learned men, effective administrators of religious institutions and mature religious personalities. The importance of their place in the Hindu world today can be gauged by assessing the quality of their lives and their ministry.

The *ācārya-paramparā* of Sringeri lists thirty-five Śaṅkarācāryas, including the present one. Before the guru reigning now, the *maṭha* had two extraordinary leaders, renowned for holiness and teaching, in Śrī Narasiṃha Bhāratī (*ācārya* between 1878-1912) and Śrī Candraśekhara Bhāratī (*ācārya* between 1912-1954). The present guru was born in Bangalore in 1917 as Srinivasa Sastri, and as a youth received *upanayana* in the *pāṭhaśālā*.[1] In 1931, at the age of fourteen, he was selected by the Śaṅkarācārya as his successor and given *sannyāsa* by him and named Śrī Abhinava Vidyātīrtha. Gifted in the intricacies of logic, he was taught by the then-reigning guru and resident *paṇḍita*-s. The senior *ācārya* became a recluse during the last twenty years of his life and, consequently, turned over to the young *sannyāsī* important work in the Vidyāpīṭha. He was entrusted with major *pūjā* and the daily administration of the *maṭha*. When he succeeded to the seat in September 1954, he was already a seasoned teacher and religious leader in spiritual and secular affairs. A natural intellectual, speaking Sanskrit, Hindi, Kannada and Tamil, he began to promote significant sacrifices and *pūjā*-s and became an outstanding religious speaker on his lengthy tours throughout India. His talks drew upon the Upaniṣads and *Gītā*, and he frequently quoted from Śaṅkara's *Vivekacūḍāmaṇi* and *Śivānandalaharī*. Although he wears ochre robes, this Jagadguru is occasionally viewed in regal dress. Arrayed in royal robes, adorned with a diadem, and carried in a golden palanquin with royal insignia, this teacher is experienced as a kingly Jagadguru. One devotee commented about these rare moments: "His Holiness in his person represents to us the supremacy of *sanātana dharma*."[2] This *ācārya*'s reign has been characterized by scholarship and efficient administration. Descibed by devotees as an

1. Confer Jnanananda Bharati (1969 A), pp. 46-49; Venkataraman, pp. 90 ff; Krishnaswami.
2. Rajgopal Sharma.

intellectual giant, he nevertheless appears to be a simple person, approachable, friendly to everyone and possessed of a quiet charm. One devotee writes that he is "outwardly very busy but at heart very calm and quiet."[1]

The senior *ācārya* of the Kanchi Vidyāpīṭha was born in 1894, 100 miles south of Madras in the village of Viluppuran, as Svaminathan Sastri.[2] Although a prodigy youth, he attended regular school and at the age of ten entered the Arcot American Mission School where he studied the Bible as well as other subjects. He received *upanayana* in 1905, and soon visited the 66th Śaṅkarācārya of Kanchi who expressed to his attendants the desire to install the youth as his successor. Yet upon the death of the guru, Sastri's cousin was installed in early 1907; he was a sickly youth who died shortly after. On his way to attend the obsequies, the young Sastri was informed that he had been chosen to succeed to the seat. In 1907 at the age of thirteen, the youth became Śrī Candraśekharendra Sarasvatī, the 68th Jagadguru of the Kāmakoṭi Pīṭha. For some years the child-guru studied Sanskrit and the Vedānta with learned teachers of the *maṭha*. By 1919, still a young man, he began public ministry that continued vigorously for half a century. He became an exemplar of the peripatetic guru, spending over thirty years on tour throughout India. With scholars at Benares, Calcutta and Puri he discussed the Vedānta and Vedic questions, but to his followers and the masses his daily life was marked by meditation, *pūjā*, and religious instruction in *dharma* to public audiences. He was a *sannyāsī* whose wide interests even included photography; he spoke many languages and conversed with scientists, scholars, royalty, ordinary workers and villagers alike. His ministry, his administrative acumen and his influence upon the people of Tamil Nadu as head of a religious institution remain unparalleled by any figure of this century. He and Śrī Ramana Maharṣi and Śrī Aurobindo Ghose have dominated south India as religious personalities in modern times, but the Śaṅkarācārya had the broadest appeal and effectiveness among the people. He was recognized in all sectors as a *jñāna*-yogī and a man of extraordinary austerities. While touring Madras, he held lectures in Sanskrit on the *Brahma Sūtra* and at the same time gave popular religious

1. Ramalingeswara Rao, pp. 38 & 40.
2. Confer Mahadevan (1975); Ramaswami Sastri; Ramaratnam.

discourses. In 1954 he selected his successor, a nineteen-year-old youth, who remained his personal *śiṣya* for the next twenty-five years. Śrī Candraśekharendra began a life of seclusion and silence in 1970, and placed the Vidyāpīṭha completely in the hands of his successor. He first secluded himself in Andhra Pradesh, then moved to a hut adjoining a Śiva temple outside Kanchi in 1972. Presently he resides in the tiny village of Kalavai, a few miles from Kanchi. The silent guru still gives daily *darśana*. He is considered to be one of those few figures who combine religious administration, leadership in *pūjā* and devotion, and serious philosophy. He has been described in terms of the ideal in the *Gītā* where temperance in speech, self-control and a sense of detachment are the hallmarks of the religious personality.[1] Even devotees of other sects and other gurus consider Śrī Candraśekharendra a person with an Advaita consciousness.[2]

The junior swāmījī, as he is called, who is now the reigning Śaṅkarācārya of Kanchi is Śrī Jayendra Sarasvatī. Born in 1935 and educated in the *maṭha* schools before being selected for the seat, he was given *sannyāsa* at Kanchi in 1954 by the Śaṅkarācārya. The next sixteen years were spent at the side of the senior guru whether on tour, in *pūjā* or meditation, absorbing the public and private teaching of his guru. He became reigning Śaṅkarācārya in 1970, and his first "tour of victory" followed in 1972, with visits to Delhi, Varanasi and other sites in north India. The 1500-miles tour was done on foot. Although this was popular in ancient times and remains so even today among the wandering ascetics, the tour of victory on foot captured the hearts and imaginations of many. Titles like "tour of victory" or "conquest in all directions" are given to the journeys of the Śaṅkarācāryas to signify the religious understanding awakened by their presence, worship and teaching. Śrī Jayendra spoke to large audiences along the way in Hindi, Telugu, Tamil and Sanskrit. In Delhi he delivered a series of lectures on *sanātana dharma*. At the same time, he drew crowds to *pūjā*-s and temple consecrations. In March 1976, he called a World Hindu Conference in Madras to revive practical religious life within Hinduism. In May of the same year, he brought together scholars at Kanchi for an all-India *sammelana*.

1. Veezhinathan, in Mahadevan (1975), pp. 86, 90 ff.
2. Chandrasekharendra Saraswati, p. 3.

The 144th Śaṅkarācārya of the Govardhana Vidyāpīṭha of Puri is Śrī Nirañjana Deva Tīrtha who was nominated as one of many in the will of his predecessor, the reverend Śrī Bhāratī Kṛṣṇa. From Gujarat originally, he was born Chandrashekhar Shastri and became a householder with three sons and two daughters. He spent his life in the teaching profession before heading the Puri *maṭha*. As a traditional *paṇḍita*, he was a professor of Vedānta and principal of the Gurukula Āśrama, Haridwar, the editor of "Sanmārga," and finally principal of the Sanskrit College of Jaipur for the nine years preceding his *sannyāsa*. He earned a host of academic titles and honors.[1] The Śaṅkarācārya of Dwaraka gave him *sannyāsa* and installed him in the seat on July 1, 1964.[2] Most of the gurus in the Puri line were former householders, which explains the large number of successors in the *paramparā* of the *maṭha*. The Puri gurus customarily take what is called *daṇḍa sannyāsa*, that is, ascetical vows with immediate authority. The staff (*daṇḍa*) of the *ācārya* signifying authority over a *maṭha* is automatically received. Approaching his mid-fifties when he bacame Śaṅkarācārya, Śrī Nirañjana is presently in his early seventies. Within this relatively short period, he has achieved a reputation as an outstanding intellectual leader, an ascetic and a political figure. Speaking six languages including Sanskrit and English, he is often called upon to address learned groups to settle Vedic questions. In 1966 he fasted for seventy-three days in the cause of cow protection, which swiftly brought him notoriety throughout India; again in 1972 he rose to national attention with the establishment of an organization against family-planning.[3]

Śrī Abhinava Saccidānanda Tīrtha, the 77th *ācārya* of the Śāradā Vidyāpīṭha of Dwaraka, was born in 1919 of a Brāhmaṇa family in Karnataka. At the age of fifteen he was given *sannyāsa* by Srī Krishnananda, the head of a Saṅkara *maṭha* in Karnataka, and soon became the head of the same institution upon the death of its guru. In 1945 at the age of twenty-six, he was installed in the Dwāraka seat by Śrī Bhāratī Kṛṣṇa of Puri. He became a

1. He earned the titles *vidyālaṅkāra* and *vidyābhāskara*; from the Śaṅkarācārya of Dwaraka he was awarded *paṇḍita-mārtaṇḍa* and *darśana-vāgīśa*.
2. For the proceedings of this ceremony, confer Saraswati & Upadhyaya.
3. Lutt, p. 418.

versatile scholar and a peripatetic guru-ascetic. Although he is a Sanskritist and an intellectual, his interests embrace social, educational, political and spiritual works as well. His academic interests and the educational institutions established by him clearly mark his achievements. Śrī Abhinava's public talks, usually philosophical in content, possess a universal appeal in their simplicity, inculcating a deep humanism and the integration of thought and culture.[1] He is one of the few Śaṅkarācāryas who freely speaks to foreigners in English. When he is residing in Dwaraka, his noonday *pūjā* extends for several hours and is preceded by a discourse on Upaniṣadic or Vedic themes. His regularity in meditation, *pūjā* and *japa* is well known. Versatility also marks his ministry. One devotee calls him a profound scholar, a polyglot, an embodiment of ancient culture.[2] Blending asceticism with practical morality, he quickly encourages confidence and perseverance in devotion among his followers.[3] A professor has written of him : "To see Him, or to have His Darshan is an event of one's life and to live with Him is education."[4]

Swāmī Śāntānanda Saraswatī, the reigning *ācārya* of the Jyotirmaṭha, of Badrinath and Joshimath, was installed in 1953, after the death of his predecessor, Swāmī Brahmānanda, who reinstated the northern foundation in 1941. Little public information is available concerning the life of Swāmī Śāntānanda before *sannyāsa*. This guru, along with Maharṣi Mahesh Yogi, the international teacher of transcendental meditation, and Swāmī Viṣṇudevānanda, was *śiṣya* of Swāmī Brahmānanda. The seat, however, was not open to Maharṣi because he was not a Brāhmaṇa but a Kṣatriya. Even presently the two gurus speak of each other as *gurudeva*. I witnessed Swāmī Śāntānanda celebrating guru *purṇimā* publicly for Maharṣi in Delhi. The Jyotirmaṭha head, like the other Jagadgurus, travels widely throughout north India. Speaking on common religious themes, he presides at public *pūjā* frequently but does not do much *pūjā* personally. In public and even in

1. Upadhyaya (1967), p. 3; also confer Saktidassan & Subramanian; also Raval & Upadhyaya.
2. Upadhyaya (1967), p. 4.
3. Saktidassan & Subramanian, pp. 9 ff.
4. Upadhyaya (1967), p. 4.

private, he is usually enthroned much like a *rājaguru*, as leader of the Daṇḍa Sannyāsīs. He both dresses and marks his body differently from the other Śaṅkarācāryas. His clothing is more saffron than ochre, and there is neither grey ash nor the triple horizontal Śaiva markings on his forehead and body. Rather, he covers his forehead completely in bright yellow ash with a single red *tilak* mark. Swāmī Śāntānanda is gradually acquiring non-Indian devotees because of his close association with Maharṣi Mahesh Yogi. He spends extensive time, probably more than some of the other Śaṅkarācāryas, instructing his two *śiṣya*-s, his attendants and those who live with him. I observed that in public teaching he elicits visible devotion, as followers present him with flowers and prostrate before him. His teaching is time-consuming but interspersed with anecdotes and a great amount of humor and light-heartedness. Like the other gurus, Swāmī Śāntānanda draws devotees from all sectors of society, educated and wealthy, middle-class and villagers, male and female, young and old. This *ācārya* has close ties with the two Śaṅkarācāryas of Puri and Dwaraka in that they have similar outlooks and have come together for common causes.[1]

The Ministry of the Śaṅkarācāryas

The work and concerns of India's present Śaṅkarācāryas have a striking similarity of purpose. As religious leaders they try to revitalize Indian education, temple life and social life. They infrequently enter political life. Besides establishing, supporting and administering Sanskrit schools, they are spokesmen for classical Hindu education. They advocate the kind of education that could revive ancient culture and the Vedas. The senior *ācārya* of Kanchi has called for the training of young men in the Āgamas and Vedas, in arts, crafts and temple worship from the Āgamas. This form of education would draw upon the participation of parents and it would also meet the needs of villages. He has spoken of the need for Oriental schools more comprehensive than the *pāṭhaśālā*-s.[2] The Dwaraka *ācārya*, who has combined traditional and contemporary methods in the Arts College and the Indological Research Institute, has urged modern

1. Lutt, p. 419.
2. Mahadevan (1975), p. 49; Aiyer, p. 153; *Sixty Years*, pp. 8 ff.

educationists to give serious consideration to religion and philosophy in the curriculum of all schools and colleges.[1] This guru has developed ties with Indian universities as in Dwaraka, where the institutions he heads are associated with and accredited by the University of Saurashtra. Both Kanchi gurus have strong associations with scholars at Madras University, and the Sringeri *ācārya* has established and heads a Śaṅkara Research Institute and a Sanskrit College affiliated with Kerala University.

Among periodic assemblies of Hindu *paṇḍita*-s, the Śaṅkarācāryas have become leaders of this particular intellectual community. The *paṇḍita* community has been greatly reduced in numbers in modern times, so that many fear that it may disappear in this century. Nevertheless, the *ācārya*-s call the *paṇḍita*-s together yearly if not more frequently. In Sringeri there is held twice yearly a Vidvat Sadas over which the Śaṅkarācārya presides, and doctrinal conferences are also convoked at different centers for Hindu scholars. The intellectual role of a Śaṅkarācārya is most evident at these times, for he sits as leader among the *paṇḍita*-s. A Sringeri historian writes that it was a revelation to many, including devotees, when the present *ācārya* presided over his first Vidvat Sadas, for he conducted himself as the *paṇḍita* among *paṇḍita*-s, excelling in grammar, metaphysics, logic and ritual.[2] Even those *paṇḍita*-s who were teachers of a particular Śaṅkarācārya, and I had an opportunity to speak with several of them, concede an intellectual superiority to him, not only out of respect for the institution but also because they look upon the guru as the full embodiment of a particular intellectual legacy.

Numerous societies have been formed for *paṇḍita*-s and priests. Societies founded by the Dwaraka Śaṅkarācārya coordinate the educational work of his *maṭha*. The Kanchi Vidyāpīṭha, with an Advaita Sabhā, works for the propagation of Vedānta through publications and meetings. Both Śaiva and Vaiṣṇava scholars gather there for discussions of Vedānta. *Sammelana*-s sponsored by the Śaṅkarācāryas have for their aim the revitalization of Vedic studies. On these occasions the presiding Śaṅkarācārya gives awards and academic titles to outstanding scholars. The preservation of the *paṇḍita* tradition by the Śaṅkara *maṭha*-s goes

1. Abhinava Sachidananda Tirtha, p. 3.
2. S. Y. Krishnaswamy, p. 48.

beyond the preservation of the philosophical heritage in the Indian universities today. Although university professors of Hindu philosophy and culture may be devotees of the Śaṅkarācāryas, they do not enter the assemblies of the *paṇḍita*-s, for they recognize the uniqueness of this line of learning.

The *maṭha*-s issue publications promoting the work and thought of the institutions and their gurus. The Dwaraka *maṭha* has published over 60 pieces of literature in recent times, along with the popular journal "*Navabhāratī*" in Gujarati and the research journal "*Śāradā-Pītha Pradīpa*" in English, Sanskrit and Gujarati. In Sringeri the "*Śrī Śaṅkara Kṛpa*" in Tamil, Kannada and Telugu was founded by the present *ācārya*. Having established the "*Ārya Dharma*" as early as 1915, the Kanchi *maṭha* also supports the "*Kāmakoṭi Vāṇī*" from Madras which reports the activities of the *maṭha* and offers articles on Hindu culture and religion. The Jyotirmaṭha supports the Śrī Śaṅkarācārya Publications Bureau of Allahabad.

The Śaṅkarācāryas prefer to speak, even to foreign visitors, in Sanskrit, indicating their desire to advance the study of this classical language. Along with the *paṇḍita* community, they have been the foremost spokesmen for the study of Sanskrit in modern times. Their interest in Sanskrit has few parallels in India, and their support of the *pāṭhaśālā*-s is indicative of this. They support Sanskrit educational societies and the study of the language for beginners and advanced students, because they see an intimate connection between Sanskrit and the preservation of Indian culture and religion. The Śaṅkarācārya of Dwaraka says that "Sanskrit is India and India is Sanskrit," because it is a means for Indian unity and a means to recapture past ideals and fundamental beliefs.[1] One devotee of the Puri *maṭha* told me that the whole purpose of that institution was to teach the Vedas through Sanskrit. While the senior *ācārya* believes that Sanskrit study will awaken a spiritual advance in India, the junior *ācārya* speaks about Sanskrit education for character formation and the purification of the mind.[2]

The gurus are religious leaders whose social concerns are clearly evident in their public ministries. Throughout his long

1. Upadhyaya (1967), pp. 68, 90 ff.
2. Aiyer, p. 22; Śrī Jayendra Saraswati, pp. 29, 31.

life, the senior *ācārya* of Kanchi has exhorted the higher sectors of Hindu society to alleviate the plight of the poor. He has tried to heighten the social awareness of the Hindu community by suggesting that urban people do manual work in the villages one day a week as a form of social service and by teaching the *śāstra*-s in rural areas. He has also encouraged service to the sick, the hospitalized and the imprisoned, as well as death rites for the poor and unclaimed. Popularising a "rice-gift" scheme, he has suggested that each family put aside money to feed the poor of the local temple.[1] He has asked the Hindu community to question itself daily in such concrete terms as, "Have I done any service today ?"[2] The Dwaraka *ācārya* is popular in Gujarat for his humanitarian efforts. He collects funds for flood and disease victims and those struck by similar tragedies. The Arts College of Dwaraka has only two specializations, Sanskrit and economics, for the Śaṅkarācārya has said that "economics and ethics must move hand in hand."[3] The teaching of the Sringeri *ācārya* does not distinguish between service and worship; the former is a type of the latter.[4] This is *dharma* teaching in the most concrete sense.

Another interest of the Śaṅkarācāryas is the restoration of Hindu temples and active temple life. Funds are often directed toward temple renovation. The Kanchi *maṭha* has restored many temples in south India, especially in villages and the countryside where neglect has left them in ruins. The Sringeri *maṭha* has built a memorial to Ādi Śaṅkara in Kalady, the birthplace of the master, while the Dwaraka Vidyāpīṭha has built a temple to Śaṅkara at Kedarnath in the Himalaya Mountains. The gurus also collect funds to restore India's ancient and revered temple sites. A goal of the Viśva Hindu Pariṣad of Dwaraka is to rid temple and pilgrim sites of commercialism. The Śaṅkarācāryas on tour are called upon to consecrate new temples and to preside over the reconsecration of old temples that is performed every twelve years. By performing *pūjā* and sponsoring major sacrifices, they have tried to focus the attention of the people upon vital temple life.

A Śaṅkarācārya is traditionally a detached ascetic (*tyāgī*) and

1. Mahadevan (1975), pp. 26, 50 ff.
2. Mahadevan, "Meeting with Perfection," in *Śaṅkara and Shanmata*.
3. *Śrī Sharadapeeth Vidyasabha*, p. 14.
4. S. Y. Krishnaswamy, p. 222.

a wandering ascetic (*parivrājaka*). Generally speaking he spends little time in the *maṭha*, and most of his ministry takes place on tour throughout India. I met each *ācārya* on tour outside his residential *maṭha*. An *ācārya* is to be itinerant, so that residence for long in one place is not countenanced. The staff that he always keeps with him is a sign both of authority and of itinerancy. Such a life means detachment and homelessness, qualities cultivated in ancient Indian asceticism. The Śaṅkarācāryas, moreover, follow the path of Ādi Śaṅkara, who spent most of his life travelling on foot throughout India.

Their tours are neither highly organized nor bound by rigid schedule, for the gurus usually move about by request of their devotees. The Sringeri *ācārya* made two extensive tours, one from 1956 to 1962 in south India as a sort of jurisdictional survey, and the other from 1964 to 1968, an all-India tour which took him as far north as Nepal. In addition, he is frequently in Bangalore or smaller cities in Karnataka. On tour the *ācārya*-s are not only preceptors, giving practical advice and encouragement to people in *dharma*, but also leaders of *pūjā*, exemplifying to the faithful the need to fulfill daily duties. The senior *ācārya* of Kanchi has spent most of his life on tour. His first tour of victory lasted from 1919 to 1938, an all-India tour mostly on foot which ended with six months of silence. Other tours by him extended from 1943 to 1950 in south India with long periods in and around Madras. The ceremonial activity that public tours elicit demonstrates the unicity of the Hindu community, for it brings together people from all sectors of society, rich and poor, high caste and low caste, Śaiva and Vaiṣṇava. Although the teaching of the Śaṅkarācāryas on tour increases Vedic and Vedāntic understanding, instruction takes a significantly practical direction in norms of religious life and service. The Dwaraka guru, on tours called conquests-in-all-directions, has gone to the Himalayas, visiting the sacred sites of Kedarnath and Badrinath in 1953, 1963 and 1970, as well as cities and towns throughout Gujarat. The Puri *ācārya*, following the example of his predecessor, Śrī Bhāratī Kṛṣṇa, the only Śaṅkarācārya to travel to the United States of America in 1958, is also a peripatetic teacher to such a degree that Puri has never become home to him.

Only the Śaṅkarācārya of Puri, among the present teachers,

has allied himself with volatile political issues.[1] Once before in this century and also from the Puri *maṭha*, Śrī Bhāratī Kṛṣṇa Tīrtha had close ties to political movements; in fact, immediately prior to his ascendency to the Puri seat in 1925, he was a candidate for president of the revived Hindu Mahāsabhā. This same *ācārya* later came to oppose Mahatma Gandhi by taking a strict orthodox position on the Untouchability Abolition Bill and the Temple Entry Bill which Gandhi was advocating. The present Śaṅkarācārya of Puri was a leading figure in 1966 in the mobilization of over 200,000 protestors who stormed the Parliament in New Delhi because of the government's inability to ban the slaughter of cows. Following the protest which resulted in violence, the Śaṅkarācārya began a fast-unto-death as further public protest and was jailed for some time while continuing the fast. He formed an organization against family-planning in 1972, previously mentioned, and he also attended a national conference against family-planning called by political figures the same year in New Delhi. These incursions into the public arena concerning issues both political and religious have earned him a reputation for rigid orthodoxy in the eyes of many, an image not shared by the other Śaṅkarācāryas.

The Capacity of a Jagadguru

The Śaṅkarācāryas are recognized in India by devotees and even non-devotees as world teachers (*jagadguru*-s). Their popularity as religious figures rests upon their conduct in *pūjā* and effectiveness in teaching. A self-realised guru is, of course, beyond *pūjā*, but the Śaṅkarācāryas foster and participate in customs, ceremonies and worship for the welfare of the people. If they neglect *pūjā*, as it was articulated to me, the people for whom it is beneficial also will neglect it. These preceptors, moreover, have inculcated devotion as a fundamental aspect of their personalities. The devotionalism of the Śaṅkarācāryas at *pūjā* and during other ceremonies inspires devotees. Their intense and visible *bhakti* is well recorded,[2] and even outsiders to the tradition

1. Lutt, p. 418. I owe the following to the research of Lutt, who substantiates the analysis.

2. Confer Saraswati & Upadhyaya, p. 13, which describes the devotion and trance of an *ācārya* during ceremonies of his installation.

testify to it. In the noonday *pūjā* in the *maṭha* or on tour, they appear absorbed in devotion. Although they are looked upon as ritual leaders by many of the faithful, some devotees see the *ācārya*-s only as intellectual and spiritual preceptors. Yet the belief that the real sage is beyond name and form continues. The elderly guru of Kanchi, who no longer performs *pūjā*, was described to me by one devotee as performing *ātman-pūjā* (Self-*pūjā*). Nonetheless, in *pūjā* the Śaṅkarācāryas raise the level of spirituality among people and exemplify the need to fulfil daily duties. Behind this practice is the traditional belief that the extraordinary figure charges the *pūjā* with new life and power.

The Śaṅkarācāryas are not public wonder-workers and are not sought out for the manifestation of yogic powers. The only exception to this was the previous guru of the Jyotirmaṭha who displayed wonders, such as lighting ritual fires and producing *prasāda* offerings, which disquieted the priests of the Badrinath temple. Consequently, the present *ācārya* of the northern *maṭha* is not tempted to repeat these acts. Wonder-stories are infrequently recorded, but devotees freely relate how a particular *ācārya* has affected their lives.[1] They recall especially to outsiders instances of being graced by the guru and experiencing the power of his austerities (*tapas*). The simple quality of the accounts is striking, for the graces recounted range from success in employment or in an examination to the birth of the first male child within a family. One devotee of the senior *ācārya* of Kanchi related to me several occasions when insoluble personal problems found immediate resolution because of the *tapas*, sixty years of it, of the *ācārya*. The Śāṅkarācāryas neither publicly nor directly manifest mysterious powers. One is frequently told that display of yogic power for a Śaṅkarācārya would be merely the play of *māyā* within the world of duality and would serve no lasting purpose. Hence miracle is not a characteristic among these gurus.

But the major factor bringing popularity and recognition to a Jagadguru is his capacity to teach. The Śaṅkarācāryas are sought only by devotees, *paṇḍita*-s and others for their intellectual leadership. Yet their public discourses are marked by simplicity and practicality, with talks on orthopraxis more than orthodoxy. Using analogy, parable and a great amount of secular knowledge

1. Saktidassan & Subramanian, pp. 17 ff.

and common sense, the Jagadgurus speak with broad appeal and charm. At the same time, they have the capacity to lecture ascetics on the Upaniṣads, to discuss the *Brahma Sūtra* with university professors, and to give *paṇḍita*-s solutions to knotty problems from the *śāstra*-s. But for the masses of people, the public discourse on *dharma* is the principal medium and theme. It is also evident that the Jagadgurus can teach through example and silence.

The followers of the Śaṅkarācāryas have an uncanny capacity to distinguish *paṇḍita*, guru and Jagadguru. A world teacher is an instructor in liberating knowledge (*vidyāguru*) with distinctive spiritual excellence. Devotees recognize his excellence and knowledge. The Jagadgurus under consideration here have a capacity to teach all sectors of society, and in fact do so. Their teaching, likewise, has an equally broad spectrum extending from ritual and devotionalism to the path of knowledge. The Śaṅkarācāryas are Jagadgurus because they possess a capacity to teach comprehensively, which is indicative of a religious personality of similar range. They are devotionalists for some, self-realised intellectuals for others, and ritual or ascetical figures for those following these particular religious paths. They possess an all-India appeal because of their multilevelled teaching and their multifaceted personalities. Because these Jagadgurus have wider responsibilities than the typical guru or spiritual guide, they represent an institution and are themselves an institution in India's religious life.

Chapter Six

THE TEACHING OF THE ŚAṄKARĀCĀRYAS

Unlike Ādi Śaṅkara but following in his tradition of teachers in the great *maṭha*-s, the Śaṅkarācāryas of this age teach publicly and orally and are not authors of a written tradition. From the early post-Śaṅkara period to modern times, relatively few teachers of the Vidyāpīṭhas were outstanding writers of the Vedānta. In this century only the late Śrī Bhāratī Kṛṣṇa, author of *Vedic Metaphysics,* could be counted among the writers in the line of modern Śaṅkarācāryas. Hence I am treating in these chapters the oral teaching of the living Śaṅkarācāryas, teaching that in some cases began over fifty years ago and in one case only ten years ago. Although their public discourses have been recorded at times, they have produced neither philosophical nor systematic religious treatises. Their audience, as will become evident, includes not only large public gatherings of devotees and non-devotees but also more limited groups of *paṇḍita*-s, friends, visitors and personal students. There is no thorough way to present their complete teaching either individually or as a group. The researcher has two alternatives. He may look for dominant themes in recorded materials, albeit limited, and check these perceptions for accuracy with the *ācāryas* themselves and a wide range of informants such as devotees, *paṇḍita*-s and students. Or he may from his own interest and perspective in this case the nature and function of the guru, go to the recorded materials and the range of informants for clarification, further articulation and systematization. I have followed both paths in this study with great dependency on my informants, especially the teachers of whom I write. Thus my treatment in the following pages is a reconstruction of their teaching from dominant themes that especially pertain to their understanding of the role of the guru.

The Śaṅkara Vidyāpīṭhas have as their common goal the revitalizing of *dharma* in Hindu life. Śrī Abhinava Saccidānanda of Dwaraka calls Ādi Śaṅkara's work a rejuvenation of *sanātana dharma,*[1] and frequently discourses of the other Śaṅkarācāryas are

1. Upadhyaya (1974), p. 6.

titled *sanātana dharma*. As teachers of *dharma*, these men see themselves as protectors and propagators of traditional teaching and custom.[1] The late Śrī Bhāratī Kṛṣṇa spoke of learning eternal *dharma* from a guru, for the *dharma* taught by a guru precedes instruction in the diverse paths of spiritual development.[2] Eternal *dharma*, for the Dwaraka *ācārya*, is not limited to scripture (*śruti*) but embraces the Purāṇas and *smṛti grantha*-s.[3] He mentions the responsibility to work out a practical scheme in modern times to implement the oneness of humankind as propounded in eternal *dharma*.[4] Thus to propagate eternal truth is to teach the life of *dharma* as found in both the scriptural and the classical tradition. The sage of Kanchi alerts his devotees to the fundamental principle of Hindu *dharma* which, for him, is adherence to an ancient and sanctified legacy.[5] Śrī Jayendra, also of Kanchi, defines the life of *dharma* as the capacity to follow the right path at all times without deviation.[6]

The Dharma Path

To teach the path of *dharma* is to teach the Vedas. The purpose of a Śaṅkara Vidyāpīṭha is to continue the Vedic legacy. The Sringeri Śaṅkarācārya observes that earnestness is not enough to ensure an individual's religious development and holds that one must also determine whether the individual's path is true to Vedic tradition.[7] On the other hand, Śrī Abhinava Saccidānanda calls for the renovation of all Vedic schools because he believes that Indian culture will survive only if the Vedas survive[8]. The gurus give to the Vedas a universality that not only transcends Śaiva and Vaiṣṇava tenets but also extends to all people. "Accept the teaching of the Vedas. Then one can worship any particular deity," observes the Sringeri Śaṅkarācārya.[9] If the Vedas are accepted as the source of all moral law, scripture then becomes

1. Upadhyaya (1967), p. 2.
2. Bharati Krishna Tirtha, pp. 2, 111.
3. Upadhyaya (1967), p. 41.
4. *Shri Sharadapeeth Vidyasabha*, p. 10; *Bhavan's Journal*, pp. 69-71.
5. Ramakrishna Aiyer, p. 6.
6. Jayendra Saraswati (1973), p. 154.
7. Krishnaswamy, p. 56.
8. Raval & Upadhyaya, p. 15.
9. Krishnaswamy, p. 56; confer Mahadevan (1975), p. 57.

applicable to all people and at all times.[1] In reiterating, moreover, the classical notion that the Veda is beginningless, the Sringeri teacher affirms that "it (Veda) inheres in God at dissolution and evolves back during creation."[2] Since the Vedas are believed to contain understanding of all human objectives, Hindu *dharma* does not lead to deviations; rather, the proper fulfillment of one's *dharma* leads easily to liberation.[3]

Following the Vedas in order to fulfill individual *dharma* is an activity, an orthopraxis. To correspond with praxis, the gurus teach practical norms of daily life with the Vedas as their chief norm. They encourage daily study of the Vedas and daily performance of customary Vedic rituals. The sacred writings deal with religious disciplines, activities and rites that have universality for all Hindus.[4] They establish an ordered and disciplined life, along with duty, virtue, worship (*upāsanā*) and wisdom.[5] Just as their public ministry promotes the life of *dharma* in a practical vein, the Śaṅkarācāryas' discourses treat other traditional subjects and themes from a practical perspective. In a series of talks in Madras, for example, the senior *ācārya* of Kanchi explained forty Hindu sacraments, while the junior *ācārya* spoke in Delhi on the worship of popular deities, the Indian epics, the Purāṇas and the Dharma Śāstras. Śrī Jayendra encourages devotees and addresses their personal anxieties; he explains that the first quarter of the Kaliyuga, which is the present age, is a period neither of darkness nor of dissolution as some may think.[6] Śrī Jayendra also discourses upon themes drawn from practical customs; for instance, the elimination of dowry, early initiation for the twice-born, the dangers of eating cow meat, the benefit of religious prostrations and the meaning of sacred ash.[7] He sees a need to teach concretely because so many believers are either uninformed or misinformed; otherwise, he believes, the sin of not explaining the correct positions would attach itself to him

1. Krishnaswamy, pp. 56, 144.
2. Ibid., p. 153.
3. Jnanananda Bharati (1969 B), p. 57; confer Jayendra Saraswati (1976), pp. 47 ff.
4. Raval & Upadhyaya, p. 15; Krishnaswamy, p. 144.
5. Mahadevan (1975), p. 57.
6. Jayendra Saraswati (1973), p. 7.
7. Ibid., pp. 137, 215-249; confer Jayendra Saraswati (1976).

as guru.[1] In a similar vein, Śrī Abhinava Saccidānanda takes a moralistic approach when he expounds "the four feet of religion" as truth, nonviolence (*ahiṃsā*), penance (*tapas*) and purity.[2] The teaching of the sage of Kanchi reflects his judgment that the goal of religious education is a broad spiritual vision in the development of mental discipline, humility and self-control.[3] The gurus' propagation of the Vedas and their teaching of the *dharma* path have wide and pragmatic appeal. It became clear to me, even from initial impressions of their public teaching, that these *ācārya*-s are far more comprehensive in their teaching than the boundaries of Advaita Vedānta.

The Śaṅkarācāryas have become, consequently, exponents of Indian culture and customs. They possess an appreciation and a strong sense of Indian civilization. A common theme of their discourses is the rediscovery of India's past. "Let us rediscover the soul of India," exhorts Śrī Abhinava Saccidānanda, who believes that modern India can achieve integration through its culture. India cannot afford to lose its spiritual foundations, he continues, and Sanskrit, religion and the Vedānta are the means to preserve its heritage.[4] India's mission, according to this guru, is to spread its cultural and spiritual vision.[5] Śrī Jayendra speaks of regaining pride in India by preserving and nourishing the classical culture and its institutions. He points to specific cultural habits, such as tank bathing, which modern society need not reject.[6] Educating the Hindu community in age-old customs is not necessarily cultural fundamentalism; instead it can be viewed as an attempt, to establish continuity with the life of *dharma* and Vedic ideals that were efficacious in the past.

When the Śaṅkarācāryas lecture publicly on the religious life of householders, they stress obligatory vocational and family duties, worship and *bhakti*. Their talks are principally lessons in the traditional duties of the householder set within the context

1. Ibid., pp. 235-236.
2. Upadhyaya (1967), p. 40.
3. Ramaswami Sastri, p. 33.
4. Saraswati & Upadhyaya, p. 1; *Shri Sharadapeeth Vidyasabha*, p. 1; Abhinava Sachidananda Tirtha, p. 3.
5. Upadhyaya (1967), p. 73.
6. Jayendra Saraswati (1973), pp. 27, 250 ff; confer Jayendra Saraswati (1976), pp. 1-11.

of devotionalism. This devotionalism which is thoroughly theistic, accords with the larger framework of the diversity of the spiritual paths (*mārga*-s). Their teaching on obligatory duty resonates with the notion of *karma*-yoga as articulated in the *Gītā*. While one guru says that religion will arise if duty is done properly with faith, another encourages householders to be devoted to duty and to recognize duty everywhere.[1] Dedication of one's activity to God is a state of mind, an attention of the mind, which is desirable even though duty is performed in the interest of all.[2] The Śaṅkarācāryas articulate the efficacy not only of such activity as *sandhyā* prayers but also of practices that control mind, speech and activity.[3] Customs, rituals, duties and discipline are not ends in themselves but symbolize some transcendent fact. "What do they intend to bring to mind ?" asks Śrī Candraśekharendra.[4] Devotion does not absolve one from scriptural duties, for the fulfillment of *dharma* is a fundamental means of grace. Devotion comes afterwards. In fact, only by right conduct does one attain the fruit of devotion.[5]

Worship is the most significant duty encouraged by the Śaṅkarācāryas; daily *pūjā* is their consistent advice. Śaṅkara did not overturn Pūrva Mīmāṃsā, which exalted ritual for its own sake, but he integrated ritual into a vast theistic and nondualist framework. The present Śaṅkarācāryas stand firmly in this tradition. I found daily worship the most visible sign of religious expression among the Śaṅkarācāryas not only in the Vidyāpīṭhas but also while on tour. Just as the Śaṅkara temples and *maṭha*-s employ various forms of worship, so too any form of God can be assimilated into daily life. The choice of a personal deity (*iṣṭa-devatā*) or a particular form of God depends upon the temperament, need and family customs of an individual. Observing that one must begin in worship with a particular manifestation of God, understood as such and not as an absolute, the gurus do not necessarily advocate worship of any one deity. The sage of Kanchi promotes a devotional harmony of deities among his

1. Ibid., p. 46; Krishnaswamy, p. 352.
2. Jayendra Saraswati (1973), p. 113; Ramakrishna Aiyer, p. 79.
3. Ramakrishna Aiyer, p. 74.
4. Mahadevan (1975), p. 77.
5. Jayendra Saraswati (1973), p. 63; Jnanananda Bharati (1969 B), p. 65.

devotees; devotion toward one manifestation is devotion toward every other manifestation.[1] Temple worship is considered indispensable especially in the early stages of spiritual growth and should remain so until the presence of the divine is experienced everywhere and in everything.[2] The Śaṅkarācāryas clearly distinguish between the *saguṇa* and *nirguṇa* forms of worship, and they are convinced that the difference must be made widely known among householders. Most frequently it is *saguṇa* worship to which they address themselves and recommend to their devotees. The observer frequently notes the worship of personal gods even among ascetics of the Śaṅkara orders today; the practice, it is believed, was part of Ādi Śaṅkara's renovation of ascetical life. Śrī Jayendra reserves contemplative worship for the ripened mind, and suggests the worship of idols and the use of *mantra* and *japa* for the wavering mind, the lot of the majority.[3] Worship, however, is not a mechanical activity; it is always presented as a mental act that is fully conscious. The devotees are taught how to concentrate upon and contemplate the deities. Although ritual activity, the recitation and even the writing of *japa*-s are advocated these are acknowledged to be initial steps preceding more mature worship. The gurus look upon the temple as the place for *saguṇa* worship, the place where peace, joy and communion are evoked. But worship ultimately leads to love and knowledge. In fact, the public instruction of the Śaṅkarācāryas is perceived by the majority of devotees as an exhortation to cultivate *bhakti*.[4]

Love is one of the dominant messages of their ministry, and evoking *bhakti* through teaching, *pūjā* and *darśana* is considered a principal function of a Śaṅkarācārya. Love is the most visible characteristic of a guru's personality and ministry. Although these teachers follow the path of *jñāna*-yoga themselves, most of their followers are *bhakta*-s. Devotion is the basis of the six faiths (*ṣaṇmata*) revived by Ādi Śaṅkara, according to tradition,

1. Mahadevan (1975), pp. 49, 148; Jayendra Saraswati (1973), p. 93; Bharati Krishna Tirth, p. 135; Jayendra Saraswati (1976), pp. 30. ff.

2. Mahadevan (1975), p. 55; Jayendra Saraswati (1973); p. 77.

3. Jayendra Saraswati (1973), pp. 34, 75, 119; confer Jnanananda Bharati (1969 B), p. 64.

4. Confer Ramakrishna Aiyer, pp. iv-v.

and therefore it remains integral to his legacy in modern times. Advocating devotion even from infancy among devotees, the Sringeri Śaṅkarācārya recommends that it be fostered through faith, good company, reading and listening to stories of the deities.[1] Devotion is a natural experience and its expression for Īśvara is within every person, observes the sage of Kanchi.[2] From devotion comes strength, the grace of the guru and finally the grace of God. It gives ordinary people the strength of mind to bear suffering.[3] Although the devotee is encouraged to ask God for this gift, its development is helped along by virtues like earnestness, steadfastness and purity of mind. *Bhakti* is selected as the principal *sādhana* at this moment of history because it is easy to cultivate; but it is not the final goal. The gurus speak of it as a discipline preliminary to knowledge. Quoting from both the *Gītā* and Śaṅkara's *Vivekacūḍāmaṇi*, Śrī Abhinava Vidyātīrtha understands devotion to lead to knowledge.[4] Yet *bhakti* and ritual, the Vedas and the *Gītā*, still are taught within a Vedānta context. The gurus urge concentrated devotion, a single-minded devotion, devotion which becomes internal and rational. Such vocabulary hints at the greater Vedānta context heard consistently in their public addresses. Devotion is a preliminary discipline directed to and aiding in the discrimination of Self and non-self.[5] It culminates in mental discipline while developing a desire for Brahman knowledge.[6] The Śaṅkarācāryas thus stand in the Advaita tradition that intellectualizes *bhakti* and views it as the context for higher knowledge.

The Śaṅkarācāryas, in short, are teachers of the three religious paths. Activity (*karma*) and knowledge (*jñāna*) are perceived to be difficult while devotion (*bhakti*) is an easier path accessible

1. Jnanananda Bharati (1969 B), pp. 61, 63.

2. Mahadevan (1975), pp. 81-82.

3. Jayendra Saraswati (1973), p. 67; S. Y. Krishnaswamy, p. 59.

4. Krishnaswamy, p. 276. Also confer Jayendra Saraswati (1973), p. 130; Jnanananda Bharati (1969 B), p. 61; *Bhavan's Journal*, pp. 65-66; Jayendra Saraswati (1976), pp. 68 ff, 82.

5. Krishnaswamy, pp. 261, 421; Jnanananda Bharati (1969 B), p. 61.

6. Upadhyaya (1967), p. 46; Jayendra Saraswati (1976), p. 81, writes that Ādi Śaṅkara has defined *bhakti* as "that tendency of the mind which goes in a one-pointed way towards the lotus feet of God and gets merged in God. . . ."

to the majority of people.[1] Yet each path can foster liberation : conduct, activity, *upāsanā*, concentration, and most importantly knowledge. The fact that there are different paths is usually attributed to the difference in human needs because of differing capacities, temperaments, minds and bodies. From an exegesis of the *Gītā*, Śrī Jayendra evokes the principle of eligibility (*adhikāra*) and bases the variety of paths upon it. Spiritual progress is progression from *karma* to *bhakti* and then to knowledge as the mind is purified by activity and concentrated by other disciplines.[2] Although these gurus have different ways of articulating the relationships among the three paths, they still reflect the catholicity of the post-Śaṅkara thinking on this question. The Dwaraka guru calls the paths avenues or approaches to the divine that join with one another. The tripartite trend and the conjunction of the paths, in his terminology, lead to a conception of the paths as a parallel process rather than separate stages of spiritual development.[3] The senior Swāmī of Kanchi, likewise, envisions the paths as accompanying each other and not as separate and dissociated processes.[4] Śrī Abhinava Vidyātīrtha interprets the doctrine of parallel growth in *karmakāṇḍa* and *jñānakāṇḍa* as an articulation true to Ādi Śaṅkara,[5] a position that may be questioned in terms of the master Advaitin. Nonetheless, in their understanding of these things, the present Śaṅkarācāryas reflect the broad post-Śaṅkara development. Moreover, their personalities represent a composite of classical spiritualities to both the non-devotee and the devotee alike.

Themes of Special Interest

The Śaṅkarācāryas' teaching ranges over the spectrum of Hindu life and custom. There is little unanimity in their choices of what to highlight in the public but personal instruction. Several subjects, however, have bearing upon their role as Jagadgurus; for instance, caste and sectarianism. I observed that the *ācārya*-s struggle with questions and customs of caste that often raise

1. S. Y. Krishnaswamy, pp. 158, 245; Jayendra Saraswati (1973), p. 175; Jayendra Saraswati (1976), p. 68.
2. Jayendra Saraswati (1973), p. 176.
3. Upadhyaya (1967), p. 43.
4. Mahadevan (1975), pp. 81 ff.
5. Krishnaswamy, p. 273.

problems among youth and disenchant even older devotees. In Sringeri, for example, all teachers, attendants of the guru and students are Smārta Brāhmaṇas; the same is generally true in the Kāmakoṭi Pīṭha in Kanchi. In addition, most of the devotees of these two gurus are south Indian Śaivas. Individual devotees in conversations with me frequently expressed concern with the exclusivity implicit in this state of affairs. The sage of Kanchi has non-Brāhmaṇa and even non-Śaiva devotees, as well as devotees from beyond the world of caste and sect. Yet his attendants are all Smārta Brāhmaṇas, householders and *brahmacārī*-s alike who preserve their caste identity publicly and seem to contain the guru within it. The same is frue of the younger Swāmī of Kanchi. On tour the gurus are visibly protected by caste, although caste is not a barrier for a devotee of a Śaṅkarācārya who as a *sannyāsī* transcends caste himself. Because of the institutionalism that they represent, the Śaṅkarācāryas sustain caste and implicitly propagate its exclusiveness. There is little instruction on the subject in their recorded discourses. The late Śrī Bhāratī Kṛṣṇa of Puri believed deeply in caste and tried to rationalize and advance it.[1] The senior Swāmī of Kanchi has spoken of caste solely in terms of duties it imposes and not in terms of rank or of superiority.[2] The present *ācārya* of Puri brought forth the wrath of Maharashtrian Buddhists in 1969, in Poona, when he said that untouchability was integral to Hinduism. Upon identifying my investigation, I was asked throughout India by non-devotees of the stance of the Śaṅkarācāryas concerning caste. Non-Hindus are excluded from the major temples of Dwaraka and Puri, and from the idols of the Kāmākṣī temple in Kanchi, as well as the Śaṅkara temple within the Puri *maṭha*. I noticed that the Dwārakādhīśa temple has a sign at its portal exhorting pilgrims to rid themselves of caste sins before entering; beside it is a sign prohibiting non-Hindus free access. These instances reflect the institutionalism surrounding the Śaṅkarācāryas. The basic institutional reasoning is that as long as Āgamic customs and the *Manu Smṛti* guide their thought, caste rigidity will continue.

Advocacy of devotion toward all Hindu deities, nevertheless, transcends sectarianism among Śaiva and Vaiṣṇava cómmunities.

1. Bharati Krishna Tirtha, p. 54.
2. Ramakrishna Aiyer, p. 158; Mahadevan (1975), p. 56.

Throughout his life, Śrī Candraśekharendra has conspicuously worked toward eliminating sectarian rivalries. As early as 1950, he brought together Vaiṣṇava and Śaiva scholars, *paṇḍita*-s and heads of south Indian Śaiva and Vaiṣṇava religious institutions. A Madhvācārya Jagadguru of Udipi was invited to address a seminar on "Śaṅkara and *Ṣaṇmata*" for university professors in Madras. The sage of Kanchi in his public discourses frequently employs the couplet Śaiva-Vaiṣṇava in order to emphasize the common stock upon which the whole Hindu community draws. In the early post-Rāmānuja period there was no bias against propagating Śaiva and Advaita tenets in Vaiṣṇava temple society, but toleration dissipated over the centuries within both communities. Today the majority of the Śaṅkarācāryas embrace religious customs and expressions of the Śāktas, Śaivas and Vaiṣṇavas. Their teaching in the main reflects the position that Vedic and Vedānta thought and life are common to both Vaiṣṇava and Śaiva communities. Śrī Candraśekharendra, attempting to heal the separation between Brāhmaṇa and non-Brāhmaṇa, Tamil-speaking and Hindi-speaking, Śaiva and Vaiṣṇava tradition, focuses upon the complementary nature of the differences. For him Śiva and Viṣṇu are one, and the difference between the devotees is not great. The Kanchi guru has devoted careful attention to Vaiṣṇava traditions.[1] It is significant that the temples especially in Puri, Dwaraka and Kanchi are sacred places principally for Vaiṣṇava and Dvaita devotees. Nonetheless, the close association that once existed between the Puri *maṭha* and the Jagannath temple no longer exists, but this Vaiṣṇava temple has excluded not only images of Śaṅkara but also the priests of the Puri *maṭha* to officiate in the temple.[2]

Each guru has favorite themes he addresses in the area of practical ethical life. Śrī Jayendra speaks frequently of ethical discipline before college and university youths. A favorite theme of the sage of Kanchi is the simplicity of life, wherein one does not accumulate more than one needs (*aparigraha*). Ethics is viewed as a preliminary step in the eight-limb yoga path.[3] In an

1. Ramakrishna Aiyer, pp. 40, 50; Upadhyaya (1963), p. 33.

2. Lutt, pp. 412-414.

3. Mahadevan (1975), p. 84; Ramakrishna Aiyer, p. 103; Upadhyaya (1963), p. 32.

attempt to give meaning to Indian customs. Śrī Jayendra, for example, observes that cow *pūjā* is performed not merely for the animal but for Lakṣmī, the goddess of wealth, who resides within the animal.[1]

While the Śaṅkarācāryas recognize the universal aspect of Hindu tradition, they have seriously confronted the existence of other religions and its implications for Hinduism. Sringeri's Śrī Abhinava Vidyātīrtha counsels foreigners and non-Hindus, "Practice the virtues that your religion preaches."[2] A common theme of the sage of Kanchi is inter-religious understanding. He advocates toleration of different faiths, observing that there is no need to forsake one religion for another.[3] The late guru of Puri, who addressed non-Hindu groups with some frequency, spoke of any religion that comes in conflict with another as *adharma*, bad *dharma*; and the Dwaraka head cautions against conversion and the usurpation of some foreign religions.[4] These religious leaders were aware of and were generally offended by the proselytizing of non-Hindus in the not-too-distant past, and several have called on the new converts to Christianity or Buddhism to return to Hinduism. It was frequently brought to my attention in Maharashtra that the Puri *ācārya*, especially, has called recent converts to Buddhism back to the Hindu tradition. The Śaṅkarācāryas as traditional Hindu gurus do not have the wide audience of some modern Indian gurus who draw extensively from outside Hinduism and outside India. The Dwaraka and Kanchi Śaṅkarācāryas, however, have Hindu devotees fron outside India, especially from Africa, Southeast Asia and Malaysia. The late Śrī Bhāratī Kṛṣṇa who travelled to the West, the present sage of Kanchi and Swāmī Śāntānanda of the Jyotirmaṭha all have attracted the attention of a few non-Hindu devotees from abroad. Although having a basically Indian and Hindu clientele may seem like a limitation for a Jagadguru, this situation is in harmony with their ties to a specific lineage and an institution.

Yet the Śaṅkarācāryas perceive a universality and exclusivity in Hinduism itself. Śrī Abhinava Saccidānanda has said, "Only

1. Jayendra Saraswatī (1973), pp. 245, 248.
2. Venkataraman, p. 110.
3. Mahadevan (1975), p. 56.
4. Bhāratī Kṛṣṇa Tīrtha, p. 110; Saktidassan & Subramanian, p. 13.

Hinduism stresses that man can become God, he is and can become Brahman."[1] Although many religions hold that there is a unity underlying the diversity of human existence, the Śaṅkarācāryas perceive the affirmation of that unity to be the perennial message of Hinduism. The sage of Kanchi teaches that a universal *sanātana dharma* existed throughout the world before the present historical period, and that in recorded history it emerged in India as eternal truth in Hindu tradition and in other places as the other religions. He hopes that a wiser generation may bring together the best of East and West into a higher and more balanced social unity.[2] Yet the Jagadgurus believe that the universal appeal and place of Indian experience rest with Advaita Vedānta. Several even maintain that Advaita, the message which is uniquely theirs, is also in consonance with all religions.

The Supreme Teaching : Advaita Vedānta

The Śaṅkarācāryas believe that the universality of Advaita rests upon a superiority which is beyond systems of philosophy and cults. One *ācārya* sees in Advaita no fundamental contradiction between religions and cults; another stresses that Advaita excludes no one and has no quarrels with other systems or religions.[3] They hold these positions because they perceive the Advaita experience to be common to all spiritual paths and in the final instance to reconcile all points of view. The Śaṅkarācāryas extoll Advaita as "the crown and glory of Vedic knowledge," "the supreme teaching of Hinduism," "the greatest hope for man Śaṅkara gave to the world," "a reality that can never be denied."[4] "Vedānta *vidyā* and Hindu culture are a hope for all mankind," comments the Dwaraka *ācārya*.[5] These encomiums result from the common understanding of reality that all the Śaṅkarācāryas share and articulate. Advaita stands for the unity of humanity, for the singleness of the human goal, for an entire creation that is one. It has frequently received such praise in the public forum. In the past Advaita was employed to dispel doubt and despair

1. Abhinava Saccidānanda Tīrtha (1976), p. 2.
2. Mahadevan (1975), pp. 33, 77.
3. Krishnaswamy, p. 262; Mahadevan (1975), p. 54.
4. Krishnaswamy, p. 103; Ramaswami Sastri, p. 55; Upadhyaya (1967), pp. 21, 24.
5. Abhinava Saccidānanda Tīrtha, pp. 2-3.

and to shed light on the current problems surrounding previous teachings.[1] The gurus still set it before their devotees as the highest human ideal and goal. It is a goal yet to be achieved, a goal that motivates one to desire liberating knowledge, an objective at the moment achieved by few.

In any series of public talks, a Śaṅkarācārya may deal in depth with Advaita only infrequently. Yet the broad teaching scheme out of which he speaks can only be grasped in the context of Advaita Vedānta. The religious disciplines can be seen as such only within the broader scope of Advaita. On occasion, when engaged with *paṇḍita*-s or ascetics, the *ācārya*-s directly and decisively articulate Advaita themes. When they teach their *śiṣya*-s and attendants, Advaita is again a principal area of exposition. Their public teaching, however, is naturally limited because of the capacity of their audience. Few people are undertaking Vedānta studies in modern times and, likewise, the number of Hindus who are prepared for Advaita as a spiritual path also seems small. As the Sringeri *ācārya* never hesitates to say, one cannot strive for knowledge (*jñāna*) or liberation without the capacity or competency for it.[2] Knowledge as a spiritual path is not suited for all, but it is the ideal for all.[3] Even Arjuna in the *Gītā* is urged to follow *karma* and *bhakti* at a particular time in his life.

Human life is brought to fruition by the attainment of knowledge, Śrī Abhinava Vidyātīrtha comments. Knowledge, which is sacrifice (*yajña*), is the highest ideal.[4] The sage of Kanchi says that the person of wisdom is the ideal person.[5] The Śaṅkarācāryas consistently encourage devotees to strive for knowledge. Reason is equated with knowledge as the best way and the only way, with everything else an antecedent. Śrī Candraśekharendra says, "Everything must be burnt in the fire of *jñāna*," and suggests as a test of knowledge whether each tribulation appears light.[6] Another guru refers to the path of knowledge as that which leads

1. Upadhyaya (1967), pp. 18-19; confer Saraswati & Upadhyaya, "Benediction."
2. Jnanananda Bharati (1969 B), p. 57.
3. Jayendra Saraswatī (1973), p. 175.
4. Krishnaswamy, pp. 138, 219.
5. Mahadevan (1975), p. 57.
6. Ramakrishna Aiyer, pp. 18, 133.

to suppression of sensory desires, for the control of the senses is necessary in order to attain liberating knowledge.[1]

The Śaṅkarācāryas' specific concern is knowledge of the Self as an achievable goal. Setting the direction in terms of self-discovery, the late Śrī Bhāratī Kṛṣṇa observed in typical Advaita fashion that "nothing that was not in existence before has come into existence. Nothing that is in existence can go out of existence."[2] For another Śaṅkarācārya, the underlying unity between macrocosm and microcosm, between the human person and the divine, is the principle of discovery.[3] Recognizing that the Vedānta conception of the divine transcends intellect, the sage of Kanchi says, "When we come to realise that the 'I' we love so much is the 'He,' our mind becomes saturated with Him."[4] Experience of the Self is the object of knowledge, the most challenging of all pursuits. The greatness of India, these gurus believe, is that countless seers have achieved knowledge of the Self. Śrī Abhinava Saccidānanda perceives that humanity is sustained by the divine Self, and consequently "the Self is only to be understood and realised."[5] It is a matter not of putting something new into the human person, but of drawing out what is already present. The search transpires within, and without it nothing is achieved. Śrī Abhinava Vidyātīrtha observes that "this little self must go."[6] The gurus encourage anyone who desires knowledge to resort to education, discipline and good environment in order to eliminate whatever stands in the way of self-realisation. For an understanding of the Self, the study of the *śāstra*-s is recommended with the hope that greater scriptural knowledge will gradually destroy ignorance.

The Śaṅkarācāryas encourage self-effort, for they understand personal experiences and self-inquiry as concrete means to liberating knowledge. They recommend similar pursuits among the *paṇḍitas* and the more advanced older students of the *pāṭhaśālā*-s. One *paṇḍita*, a former teacher of a living Śaṅkarācārya, told me that to do Vedānta as a way of life is to reflect continually on

1. Krishnaswamy, pp. 138-139.
2. Saraswati & Upadhyaya, p. 19.
3. Abhinava Sacidānanda Tīrtha, p. 2.
4. Ramakrishna Aiyer, pp. 64, 95.
5. Upadhyaya (1967), pp. 16-17.
6. Krishnaswamy, pp. 285, 367.

personal experience. He considered Śaṅkara's emphasis on experience to be the master's greatest contribution to the spiritual process. A student of the Vedānta, he explained to me, must perceive how he experiences, what he experiences and finally who is actually experiencing. An analysis of the states of consciousness is made in order to discover the true witness of the human process, the Self. I found this *paṇḍita* giving special emphasis to the experience of others, especially the common experiences of ordinary people, which contributes to the understanding of oneself. When experience is analyzed, the memory holds the impressions, insights and feelings of the past. Self-analysis, therefore, recollects past experience in the absence of the experience. Intellectual comprehension of the Self is not enough, but the Self must be realised as a fact of experience.[1] I discovered among the *ācārya*-s that the effort to understand experience is an essential part of self-inquiry and the Advaita message.

Self-inquiry is understood as the analysis of one's own nature. In a major lecture in 1958 before the Self-Realisation Fellowship in Los Angeles, the late Puri *ācārya* addressed himself wholly to this subject.[2] Deep inquiry into the Vedānta gives rise to this sort of introspection. Śrī Abhinava Vidyātīrtha instructs that self-observation is the only way to achieve the silent mind, a mind free from subjection to past impression. The mind must be observed silently by merely watching the thought processes and the impressions made upon them. Instruction aims to eliminate the domination of the ego. The removal of ignorance means the elimination of I-ness in mind, body and desires, for I-ness is the basic impediment to liberating knowledge.[3] To discriminate the Self from the body is the most difficult of all discriminations, but it is the first one that must be made. When one begins to discriminate habitually, ignorance gradually dissipates. How does the mind become able to discriminate between the real and the unreal ? The sage of Kanchi gives three means : good actions, good company and a prepared mind.[4] In the same vein, the

1. Jayendra Saraswatī (1973), p. 184; Ramakrishna Aiyer, p. 36.
2. Confer Saraswati & Upadhyaya, "Light from Ancient India."
3. Krishnaswamy, pp. 211, 236, 290, 297.
4. Ramakrishna Aiyer, p. 53.

Dwaraka *ācārya* calls for greater use of rationality.[1] The Advaita message attested to by the Jagadgurus is fundamentally a call for rationalization in religious development.

When the Śaṅkarācāryas speak publicly about Advaita, their most prevalent theme is purity of mind and not a philosophical subject from Advaita. The condition of the mind characterizes their discourses and distinguishes them from ordinary religious teachers. In the talks of Śrī Abhinava Vidyātīrtha, for example, this theme is so dominant that it has to be selected as his central message. It is a theme that the Śaṅkarācāryas restrict to no particular audience but preach to the masses, literate and illiterate, householder and scholar alike. Even the *paṇḍita*-s of the *maṭha*-s follow a similar emphasis with their students. For the Sringeri guru, "the conquest of the mind is the conquest of the world."[2] "He is the best man who thinks the best" is the clarion call of the Dwaraka teacher. The same *ācārya* makes frequent visits to jails, and even in these circumstances urges prisoners to be introspective.[3] The exaltation of the mind is brought into the practical order by fostering purity of mind and the proper use of it in discrimination. Purity of mind is thought to prepare the mind for greater understanding. Purity of mind, requisite for devotion and meditation, leads on to religious knowledge.[4] Two classic qualifications for self-knowledge are freedom from desires and purity of mind. Although the latter causes the former, control of mind and control of the senses form one operation. The Śaṅkarācāryas resort to religious disciplines to accomplish it. One teacher suggests association with good and great men and concentration on the "feet of God," while another advocates surrender to God for mental equipoise.[5] Unfailing devotion seems to be a first level of mental purification. The young Swāmī of Kanchi teaches that the first prayer of the devotee should be for peace of mind, purification of mind and strength of mind. The greatest thing to offer to God is one's own mind, he counsels.[6]

1. Upadhyaya (1967), p. 16.
2. Krishnaswamy, p. 367.
3. Upadhyaya (1967), p. 74; Upadhyaya (1963), p. 33.
4. Jnanananda Bharati (1969 B), p. 66; Mahadevan (1975), p. 83; Ramaswami Sastri, p. 57.
5. Krishnaswamy, p. 142; Ramakrishna Aiyer, p. 186.
6. Jayendra Saraswati (1973), pp. 68, 82; Ramakrishna Aiyer, p. 186.

A quiet mind is viewed as a prerequisite for setting out upon the path of knowledge. Mental equipoise can, moreover, be shared with others. Although peace of mind is considered a proximate objective in the educative process, mental purification has for its goal complete mental control. The practice of concentration and mastery over the mind is commonly recommended by the gurus. Such mastery, Sringeri's Śaṅkarācārya observes, cannot come from books but only from a teacher.[1] One's mental attitude is important in perfecting concentration. In all practical things, the individual must determine the particular state of mind evoked. Śrī Abhinava Saccidānanda points to four hurdles that one must overcome in mind control : idleness, absent-mindedness, inattentiveness and inductive thinking. Conscience does not guide effectively, he believes, without good conduct and purity of heart, for without these qualities conscience is not able to distinguish between intuition and the incitement of ignorance.[2] Mental purity and control prepare for the intuitive Advaita experience. Intuition is achieved, according to another *ācārya*, by the suppression of mental transformations (*vṛtti*), which is Patañjali's classical notion of yoga. In commenting upon verses from the *Taittirīya Āraṇyaka*, the Sringeri guru draws upon the commentator Sāyaṇa and makes reference to Patañjali's concept :

> What then, is this discipline ? It is the inhibition of the functions of the mind, as laid down by Patañjali in his *Yoga Sūtras*. With the mind thus controlled, the ascetic is free of all desire for eternal enjoyment. Thus does renunciation through the purity of mind, lead finally to the removal of ignorance.[3]

This is a singular instance where I found a Śaṅkarācārya apparently supporting Patañjali's view of mind control. Since a major portion of the teaching of these gurus concerns the use of the mind, they stand at the center of both the intellectual and the yoga tradition. I must conclude, however, that they publicly advance Advaita concerns in terms of creating a reflective and quiet mind. In closed situations with *paṇḍita*-s and students, they enter more directly into Advaita discourse.

1. Krishnaswamy, pp. 288-289; confer Jayendra Saraswati (1973), p. 5.
2. Upadhyaya (1967), pp. 48, 57; confer Candraśekharendra, p. 35.
3. Krishnaswamy, p. 434.

The Exaltation of Ādi Śaṅkara

Śaṅkara is extolled to the public first as a religious founder and secondly as the major exponent of Advaita. This does not lessen but increases his role in building medieval Hinduism. He is first presented as the one who reinstated Vedic religion and *dharma* by eliminating non-Vedic cults and reforming the ways of worship. His itinerant teaching throughout India, it is believed, rejuvenated eternal *dharma.*[1] Besides articulating Advaita, Śaṅkara's writing coordinated other religious literature with the Veda and placed it before the people. His prayer compositions, moreover, purified the popular devotion toward the deities. The sage of Kanchi calls Ādi Śaṅkara the expounder of the *bhakti* and *jñāna* paths in which no school of thought is excluded.[2] On the other hand, the Sringeri Śaṅkarācārya speaks of the master as a synthesis of Advaita and Tantra wherein *jñāna* and *karma* are conjoined.[3] The Dwaraka teacher speaks of Ādi Śaṅkara as the consolidation of the spiritual paths, who represents the finest spiritual humanism and rationalism in his conception of truth.[4] These diverse perceptions among the teachers are not different philosophical interpretations of Advaita but are different ways in perceiving Ādi Śaṅkara as a comprehensive spiritual personality. Since the Śaṅkarācāryas accept as authentic the disputed literary corpus of hymns, shorter works and secondary treatises of the late-Śaṅkara, they have a textual basis in what they perceive as tradition for presenting Ādi Śaṅkara as a universal figure.

Their devotion to the great master is unparalleled, and they actively promote devotion to him. At Sringeri there is a Śaṅkara temple, while in the Kanchi, Puri and Dwaraka *maṭha*-s, *pūjā* is regularly performed before formidable Śaṅkara idols. The Śaṅkarācāryas have built temples and memorials to the master throughout India. The Ādi Śaṅkara Jayanti Festival, inaugurated in 1833 by the then reigning Sringeri guru, is now an annual celebration. The Jagadgurus are recognized as supreme devotees of Ādi Śaṅkara, and it is not uncommon for their followers to

1. Ibid., p. 391; Bhāratī Kṛṣṇa Tīrtha, pp. 62, 138; Upadhyaya (1974), p. 6.
2. Ramakrishna Aiyer, p. 108; also confer pp. 41, 50.
3. Krishnaswamy, p. 273.
4. Upadhyaya (1974), p. 5.

install Śaṅkara idols in their homes and make the master Advaitin a part of their daily devotional life.

This broad-based devotionalism results from an almost universal estimation of Śaṅkara as *avatāra*. For the Śaṅkarācāryas and their devotees, Ādi Śaṅkara is a manifestation of Brahman. They speak of him as an incarnation, the human form of Īśvara, Lord Śiva incarnate.[1] I was told by one Śaṅkarācārya that he worships Śaṅkara as he does Brahman. The exaltation of Ādi Śaṅkara is acceptable to large numbers of devotees. In fact, it comprises the difference between the devotee, which a Śaṅkarācārya's disciple would be, and an ordinary follower, who would merely esteem the devotional and teaching capacities of the guru. This distinction, brought to my attention by followers of the Śaṅkarācāryas, illustrates the twofold role, intellectual and devotional, which a guru fulfills. Śaṅkarācāryas inherit this twofold leadership role because their specific lineage reaches back to Ādi Śaṅkara. As an *avatāra*, Ādi Śaṅkara restored *dharma*; consequently, today's devotees see in their present Śaṅkarācāryas another restoration of *dharma* taking place in their own lives. The Śaṅkarācāryas represent, in fact not only the Advaita tradition but more importantly the Śaṅkara tradition. The former is the context for its scholastic articulation, while the latter is more comprehensive in actualizing the tradition in history. The teaching of the dharma path and the teaching of Advaita are managed in a similar manner by the Śaṅkarācāryas. The former is the context of the latter. Both are integrated in the one life and personality of Ādi Śaṅkara. Likewise, both are brought together, in various configurations, in the living personalities of those who emulate the master.

1. Mahadevan (1975), p. 83; Ramakrishna Aiyer, p. 63; Ramaswami Sastri, p. 82; Mahadevan (1968), pp. 559-560.

CHAPTER SEVEN

THE TEACHER-STUDENT RELATIONSHIP TODAY

The living Śaṅkarācāryas explain that there are different types of relationships that may exist between a teacher and his student. One Śaṅkarācārya distinguished for me three levels of encounter, each with its own specific goals. The first, he said, takes place with the religious teacher who gives a *mantra* to a youth, initiating him into religious discipline, and who serves as a guide in things religious. The second type of encounter transpires between a traditional *paṇḍita* and the youth whom he educates in a wide range of subjects from the sacred to the profane; and the third is an encounter between the guru and the student he selects to continue a particular lineage and institution in religious wisdom. This threefold distinction is not necessarily exclusive, and a student may pass through several different types of encounter with the same teacher; likewise, the same guru may operate in diverse roles with the same student or with different students. The Śaṅkarācāryas point to the third relaionship as particularly theirs, for they are chosen to continue a lineage of religious wisdom and a religious institution. Nonetheless, they are figures who enter profound relationships with many people for varying purposes. These gurus are products of the *paṇḍita* tradition, one even being a former *paṇḍita*, and as such they establish personal ties with members of this intellectual community. The majority of their followers, however, are devotees in the *bhakti* sense, so that the guru-*śiṣya* relationship in this context is of another quality and purpose. The continuity with the Upaniṣads and Ādi Śaṅkara is especially apparent in the unique relationship between a guru and his chosen successor, as well as in those cases where the teacher is a *jñāna*-guru for one pursuing the path of knowledge. In these two situations especially, Advaita Vedānta is explicitly transmitted.

Sringeri's Śaṅkarācārya describes the threefold distinction sketched above in a different manner. He speaks of the guru who makes one literate, the guru who does good to a person, and finally the guru who releases one from bondage.[1] The first is the *paṇḍita* or the teacher of religious customs and practices; the second is the *bhakti*-guru or public teacher who exhorts people to *dharma* and graces them through *darśana* and *pūjā*; and the third is the *jñāna*-guru who enters into the classical guru-*śiṣya* relationship with a few qualified aspirants. Again, these are not exclusive categories. In fact, a Jagadguru enters all levels of encounter, not infrequently with the same individual. This distinguishes him from an ordinary guru, whose audience and whose own interests and capacities are less inclusive.

The present Śaṅkarācāryas of Sringeri, Jyotirmaṭha and Kanchi have chosen successors who stand within a classical guru-*śiṣya* relationship, and one of whom is already reigning over the Kāmakoṭi Pīṭha. It is evident to me that attendants living closely with Śaṅkarācāryas receive special instruction in the Vedānta from them personally. Swāmī Śāntānanda, for example, is recognized for his frequent instructions to his intimates. Yet when the religious savant Paul Brunton went to the Śaṅkarācārya of Kanchi some years ago in search of a personal guru, he was sent by him to Śrī Ramana Maharṣi, who was not even a member of a Śaṅkara order of ascetics. Śrī Candraśekharendra of Kanchi said at the time : "I am at the head of a public institution, a man whose time no longer belongs to himself. My activities demand almost all my time. ... How can I take personal pupils ? You must find a master who devotes his time to them".[2] Thus the number of individuals who enter into a classical relationship with a Śaṅkarācārya is limited because of the demands that his religious leadership and broader institutional obligations place upon him.

The Śaṅkarācāryas are unequivocal in prescribing a guru for one who seeks liberation through knowledge of Brahman.[3] Śrī Abhinava Vidyātīrtha observes that half the battle is won by receiving the blessings and teaching of a great person.[4] The guru directs one to a salvation path and a program of mental

1. Krishnaswamy, p. 63.
2. Brunton, "With the Spiritual Head of South India," in *Śaṅkara and Shanmata.*
3. Confer Upadhyaya (1967), p. 34.
4. Krishnaswamy, pp. 425–426.

purification.[1] The path must be learned directly from a guru, for less direct methods are usually ineffective. These teachers maintain that God-realisation is possible through the mediation of a proper preceptor.[2] One *paṇḍita* at a Vidyāpīṭha stated in conversation with me that competent gurus are readily available but serve only as guides, who like doctors prescribe a remedy that the individual must effect within himself. The Sringeri Śaṅkarācārya uses phrases like "great men" or "great preceptors" to describe those who are true sources of grace and teaching. It is assumed that such preceptors are self-realised and possess a high level of understanding.[3] A great preceptor knows the Upaniṣads, is free from ignorance, stands in the enjoyment of the Self and is able to impart a path to others.[4] He must be a man of extraordinary intellect, rigorous self-discipline and dedication to God and society, another Śaṅkarācārya observes.[5] Although the sage of Kanchi speaks of God removing ignorance and instilling knowledge, he points to the guru-*śiṣya* relationship as that which brings the individual to a point of receptivity. Faith in the guru makes one more receptive. Complete faith in the guru brings to an individual all that for which he goes to God. God is needed when one cannot find a guru, comments the same *ācārya*.[6] The Śaṅkarācāryas agree that a guru must be a realised person, one equal to *saguṇa* Brahman. As such he embodies liberating wisdom and has the capacity to impart it to others.

As the Śaṅkarācāryas themselves demonstrate, a guru is an ascetic but not a recluse. He is a public figure. The Śaṅkarācāryas take *sannyāsa*, most of them at an early age, live on alms and are surrounded by devoted *brahmacārī*-s and householders. Traditionally the *sannyāsī* and *brahmacārī* were excused from rituals and scriptural duties because of their intense religious and intellectual pursuits. The present day Śaṅkarācāryas, however, are leaders in both ritual and the fulfillment of scriptural duties. There is evidence that occasionally they invite a devotee to *sannyāsa* but will call upon another asectic to give initiation

1. Ramakrishna Aiyer, p. 40; S. Y. Krishnaswamy, pp. 288-289.
2. Krishnaswamy, p. 244.
3. Ibid., pp. 289, 297; confer Ramakrishna Aiyer, p. 78.
4. Krishnaswamy, p. 63.
5. *Four Amnaya Pithas*, p. 15.
6. Ramakrishna Aiyer, pp. 39-40.

(*dīkṣā*). It is only their successors whom they initiate personally into *sannyāsa.* It is understood within Śaṅkara *maṭha*-s and was repeatedly mentioned to me that he who recieves *sannyāsa* from a reigning Śaṅkarācārya has the right of succession. For some of the Śaṅkarācāryas, many years of asceticism preceded their becoming reigning *ācārya*-s. This is true in Kanchi, Sringeri and the Jyotirmaṭha, but the Dwaraka Śaṅkarācārya headed a *maṭha* in Karnataka at an early age. As noted previously, the Puri *maṭha* has a tradition for selecting older men who have been householders, and they receive *sannyāsa* simultaneously with their appointment to head the Vidyāpīṭha. This is not peculiar, for in the classical system the vocation of householder is normally a prelude to asceticism for most people. In the Śaṅkara line of teachers asceticism is necessary, with its consequent practice of celibacy, living on alms, and an itinerant life even as one heads a major Vidyāpīṭha. This tradition of teachers does not permit many gurus to live together in communal life. One Śaṅkarācārya told me that communal life among gurus dissipates the level of asceticism, which in turn dulls their capacity to teach.

A guru embodies the legacy of his predecessors, which, it is to be hoped, comes to life in him. Once he has ascended the seat, a Śaṅkarācārya represents the living tradition. The present teachers are keenly aware that they inherit a legacy from their predecessors. One Śaṅkarācārya confirmed for me not only his continuity with Ādi Śaṅkara, the lineage of teachers and his own predecessor but also the oneness of their teaching and personalities. The concern over succession to a Vidyāpīṭha is foremost an aware ness of the importance of lineage. When *śiṣya*-s have not been selected and trained by the presiding gurus, as in Dwaraka and Puri today, significant steps are taken for a proper appointment to the Vidyāpīṭha. Moreover, even teachers outside the Śaṅkara tradition are equally concerned to see that the seat is quickly filled with the best qualified person. When there have been several claimants to a seat, the gurus have relentlessly sought a final resolution, even, as mentioned previously, to the extent of seeking a court decision.[1]

An ascetic, it is believed, should know four generations of his preceptors. Devotion to past preceptors sometimes extends this

1. Lutt, p. 416.

far among the present Śaṅkarācāryas. Each tradition of teachers in India believes it a duty to express devotion to past teachers. The living Śaṅkarācāryas clearly show their devotion to their immediate predecessors. In Sringeri, for example, close to the present Śaṅkarācāryas's quarters there is a formidable *mandira* for the two previous gurus, Śrī Candraśekhara Bhāratī and Śrī Satcidānanda Narasiṃha Bhāratī. The reigning teacher performs daily *pūjā* there, and students and attendants devoutly visit each day. The Ādi Śaṅkara temple and the Sureśvara temple are also imposing sites of this Vidyāpīṭha. Within the village of Sringeri, moreover, the recently founded college, Jagadguru Candraśekhara Bhāratī Memorial College, is further testimony to the devotion with which a Śaṅkarācārya regards his immediate predecessor. The present Jagadguru at Sringeri reveres his predecessor as an incarnation of Śiva.[1] The sage of Kanchi, who is now in silent retirement in Kalavai, has taken for his retreat an *āśrama* surrounding the *samādhi*-s of the two previous gurus, Śrī Mahādeva and Śrī Candraśekhara VI. Stone edifices mark the sites within the courtyard of the *āśrama*, and their central position highlights the importance given to them. The most revered room in the Puri *maṭha* contains an idol of Ādi Śaṅkara, and in another room there are enthroned pictures of previous gurus and the reigning one that are venerated. I found that veneration of Ādi Śaṅkara is indistinguishable from that given to the previous gurus. The late Śaṅkarācārya of Puri had such great devotion for his own preceptor that he would talk endlessly about him and worship his sandals daily.[2] Likewise, the *maṭha*-s of Śrī Abhinava Saccidānanda in Dwaraka and Dakor have rooms with enthroned pictures of previous gurus. The Dwaraka Śaṅkarācārya has built the Jñāna Mandira containing idols of the past Jagadgurus along with idols of Hindu gods. The ensemble is centered around Nārāyaṇa in an effort to demonstrate the oneness of Śiva, Viṣṇu and the gurus. The same Śaṅkarācārya of Dwaraka, who was an intimate friend of the late Śrī Bhāratī Kṛṣṇa of Puri, actively promotes his preceptor's memory.[3] Consequently, it is clear that the

1. Krishnaswamy, p. 41.
2. Bhāratī Kṛṣṇa Tīrtha, p. xviii.
3. Saraswati and Upadhyaya, p. 4.

Śaṅkarācāryas revere their entire lineage of teachers but have a special regard for their own preceptors.[1]

Reverence for lineage, of course, is a basic reason for their esteem, but the experience these gurus have of their own predecessors also motivates them. I have already mentioned that one *ācārya* told me he looked with equal esteem upon Ādi Śaṅkara, his own preceptor and the line of teachers. Reflecting on his guru, he further said, "His Holiness is Brahman for me." When questioned about how a Śaṅkarācārya exeriences his deceased preceptor, another *ācārya* responded to me by describing a presence that never left him. His guru, he said, was ever present in his thoughts and desires, and he quickly added that he was also present in his heart, will, words and deeds ! An elderly ascetic of a Śaṅkara order in a *maṭha* in Satara, Maharashtra, responding to the same question, revealed to me that his guru was always present in his consciousness. It would seem that lineage, which is integral to the role of a guru, exists both in the conceptual and experiential orders.

There is a quality imparted to the guru because of the interface of scripture and the guru himself. The *paṇḍita*-s give scriptural testimony through their teaching and commitment to Vedic texts that is recognized by most Hindus. Their mastery of ancient texts is witness to tradition. The Śaṅkarācāryas give a somewhat broader testimony. Their witness extends to the Veda and the Upaniṣads, but also includes *smṛti* literature and the long history of the Vedānta. Unlike a Vedic *paṇḍita*, a Śaṅkarācārya is a living testimony of a whole evolving tradition.

What is the relationship between scripture and the guru for these teachers and their followers ? Students of the *pāṭhaśālā*-s and devotees of the Śaṅkarācāryas are quick to accord the guru a superiority over scripture. A particular Śaṅkarācārya equated his own guru with Īśvara, thereby implying that the guru ranked above scripture. Another teacher, when confronted with the suggestion of a possible equality between guru and scripture, raised to me the point that there can be no understanding of scripture without a guru. This need not imply the superiority of one over the other; it may simply indicate that both function as one integral means of knowledge. Following this line of

1. Confer Mahadevan (1975), p. 68.

reasoning, then, the guru is seen to be an embodiment of scripture, an embodiment that one *paṇḍita* described for me as "the breath of God." Scripture must be embodied for its meaning to be truly heard and conveyed. In the educative process this confirms the need for a guru in the first moment of the triple method, the moment of hearing (*śravaṇa*). An ascetic of the Śaṅkara *maṭha* in Satara, mentioned above, told me that scripture is superior to the guru in terms of *sanātana dharma*. However, as another *paṇḍita* of the Vedānta pointed out in response to this discussion, although guru and scripture are both types of teachers, one's personal experience is the actual source of liberation and knowledge and, thus, the ultimate teacher.

Radhakrishnan, the modern Indian philosopher, has written that "religious education depends far less on the spoken word than on the living examples set by the saints themselves, who live in God, are clothed in love and are immersed in service."[1] He identified exemplarity as an essential factor in the definition of a teacher. The Śaṅkara Vidyāpīṭhas of Sringeri, Kanchi and Puri possessed outstanding gurus from the late 19th century to the present. These were men of wisdom, saintliness and broad discipleship, who exercised strong example upon their followers. The same is generally true of the five major Śaṅkarācāryas today. Śrī Candraśekharendra observes that it is the example of great figures who live religion that sustains the people and exemplifies to them a high level of knowledge.[2] The distinction between a religious teacher (*samaya-ācārya*) and a philosophical teacher (*sanātana-ācārya*), or between a saint and a sage, is neither definitive nor sharply drawn in Hindu experience because the power of example rises above and cuts through all understandings.[3] The senior teacher of Kanchi speaks of the guru's duty to inculcate discipline in his pupils, with such virtues as gentleness, humility and consideration for others.[4] Virtue, like discipline, is taught by example. Much of a guru's public activity is done to edify the people by giving them good example. It is the example of the preceptor that engenders faith. The sage of Kanchi, in a personal

1. Mahadevan (1960), p. 5.
2. Ramakrishna Aiyer, p. 78.
3. Mahadevan (1960), p. 3.
4. Candraśekharendra, pp. 173-174.

farewell upon completing a tour of Madras, said: "I will be able to bring about a change in you only to the extent to which I am able to develop my inner power. If I desire to reform you more, I must purify myself to the extent necessary."[1] This is a significant insight into the power of example. It is generally said in India that the role of the guru is to show others that self-realisation is a human possibility. If the teacher is to cause a change in human development, which is expected of a Jagadguru, his exemplarity is the identifiable source of that change. When the Śaṅkarācāryas tour India, they gather large crowds at public discourses; hundreds line the streets as they pass through towns and villages. Their discourses offer simple instructions, and their participation in *pūjā* is viewed from a distance with mixed attention. Frequently the guru's glance or manner are the more lasting impressions. His appearance embodies religious meaning : namely, the ascetic in ochre robe whose authority and teaching go back to Ādi Śaṅkara. Example is a major factor in defining them as teachers. Their power of exemplarity is frequently as effective as the power of their message.

The Meaning of the Student Today

"My disciples are my family. Where they take me, I go," remarks Śrī Abhinava Vidyātīrtha.[2] Although the Śaṅkarācāryas' discipleship is large, students (*śiṣya*-s) in the classical sense of the word are limited in number. There are few *śiṣya*-s following the path of *jñāna*-yoga under the personal guidance of the living Śaṅkarācāryas. One reason for this is that few people have the religious or intellectual capacity to do so. A student is constituted as such by his personal qualifications for the path of knowledge. When I asked about the qualifications necessary for becoming a student, the Śaṅkarācāryas would unhesitatingly respond with Ādi Śaṅkara's fourfold prescription. I also found that they may even recite directly from his commentary on the *Brahma Sūtra* : discrimination between the real and unreal, aversion to the fruits of personal activity, the cluster of six virtues and desire for liberation. Aspiration for liberation without these qualifications for the pursuit is futile and may even have negative

1. Ramakrishna Aiyer, p. 204.
2. Krishnaswamy, p. 133.

effects such as disillusionment with the religious quest. One *ācārya* spoke to me of the qualifications for self-inquiry, enumerated in the *Gītā* as discrimination, renunciation, study, generosity, meditation, *tapas* and ritual.[1] Only a mature ascetical personality, disciplined and tested, has the capacity for studentship in the path of knowledge. The Śaṅkarācāryas may occasionally isolate particular means that give rise to competency such as devotion or meditation, but the fourfold complex of ascetical achievements must be present to some degree for the successful pursuit of knowledge.[2]

The late Śrī Bhāratī Kṛṣṇa of Puri attributed competency to differences in temperament, tastes, conditions and natural capacities.[3] The same reasons are implied by the present gurus. They refer to a moment of readiness, due to past *karma*, for the pursuit of wisdom under a preceptor. Competency is described by them as a subtle reality; a natural tendency for devotion and religious activity and wisdom may indicate one's potential capacity. A Śaṅkarācārya observed to me that self-inquiry must always be taught according to the capacity of the individual, so that frequently the more effective methods and significant questions are not confronted. He followed this principle in his own discourses to college students, most of whom were studying for secular professions, by not discussing the *ātman* quest or question because it was not the moment in their lives for it. Another informant, a university professor of philosophy, observed that if they lack the four classical qualifications, even professional philosophers of Hindu thought may be practicing a type of pseudo-Vedānta. Hearing, reflection and concentration cannot be performed without the capcity for these operations When one lacks the capacity for knowledge, which is determined by the presence of the ascetical qualifications, a pseudo-Advaita, a merely abstract and intellectual exercise, results in practice. This need not lead to discouragement, however, for the sages teach that the realisation of Brahman is inevitably achieved. The actual existence of ascetical figures who possess the capacity for realisation supports such confidence.

Does competency require a life of *sannyāsa* ? Must one be an

1. *B. Gītā* 10.25.
2. Krishnaswamy, p. 76.
3. Bhāratī Kṛṣṇa Tīrtha, p. 59.

initiated ascetic to pursue the path of knowledge as a student of a contemporary guru ? A *paṇḍita* of a Śaṅkara Vidyāpīṭha was unequivocal with me in pointing out that there was no absolute requirement for *sannyāsa* in order to pursue knowledge, but Ādi Śaṅkara advocated it for easier access to *jñāna*-yoga. The ascetical life releases one from household duties and family ritual. It frees one for a total pursuit of wisdom. While one Śaṅkarācārya may point to the quality of sincerity necessary for asceticism, another may emphasize the high level of mental purification required.[1] The Sringeri Śaṅkarācārya speaks about asceticism as a stepping-stone for both Vedic knowledge and knowledge of Brahman.[2] Some individuals, he continues, qualify for *sannyāsa* by the completion and fulfillment of student life, but others must go through the household stage that is a preparation for detachment, a step toward knowledge.[3] The vocation of an initiated *sannyāsī* is limited by the Śaṅkara tradition even today. One informant, a highly qualified *jñānī* but not a *sannyāsī*, remarked that there are already too many *sannyāsī*-s in India. This position is shared by a growing number in modern Indian society. Asceticism is a state of life naturally restricted to the few because of its rigor and severity.

Celibacy, which is obviously not meant for the majority, is integral to Indian asceticism. It is believed by some devotees that a junior *ācārya* is selected at an early age in order to train him from youth in the discipline of celibacy. The older students of the *pāṭhaśālā*-s are especially conscious of the restrictions of celibacy and of its basis in the Indian tradition for spiritual seekers; sometimes they may even subscribe to ancient notions concerning the spiritual value of seminal retention. According to Śrī Candraśekharendra, only an individual of extraordinary detachment (*vairāgya*) can take *sannyāsa*, and thus the number in society should not be large. He also subscribes to the classical parameters of such a life, which consist in a simple livelihood, going from place to place, and living singly, for if ascetics gather into groups a gradual deterioration of purpose results.[4] At the

1. Ramakrishna Aiyer, p. 72; Jnanananda Bharati (1969 B), 58.
2. Krishnaswamy, p. 103.
3. Jñānānanda Bhāratī (1969 B), pp. 58-59.
4. Ramaswami Sastri, p. 46.

end of their education in the Vidyāpīṭhas, some students naturally desire the life of classical asceticism, but the present Śaṅkarācāryas still restrict it to the few. Those students who complete *pāṭhaśālā* education and wish to remain with a Śaṅkarācārya, becoming his attendants and members of his household so to speak, remain celibate, serve without remuneration, and become *śiṣya*-s in almost the classical sense of the term. The possibility for this style of life varies considerably among the Śaṅkarācāryas according to the customs of the Vidyāpīṭhas. The gurus are surrounded by celibates, usually Brāhmaṇa men, who are dedicated to them and experience a guru-*śiṣya* relationship with them. This does not eliminate, however, the number of householders who also gather about the teacher and perform some form of service. The attendants of the sage of Kanchi, for example, are personally selected by him and although they may be householders, they remain celibate and live on alms while serving him.

The teacher-student relationship is based upon faith and a desire for knowledge. One Śaṅkarācārya affirmed for me that the relationship is intellectual at heart, and although devotion is present, it is not the basis of the relationship. Another told me that the student in faith recognizes his guru. I discovered that this is also the testimony of numerous other devotees. Recognition of one's personal preceptor in faith occurs for some individuals in the first meeting with a guru, while for others it develops over the course of time. Experience of the guru, according to my informants, seems to increase as faith increases so that the relationship grows in faith and as a result of faith. Another Śaṅkarācārya explained to me the relationship between a guru and his disciple using the simple analogy of candy to exemplify the sweetness of knowledge given by a guru. The guru gives the student the gift, the sweetness of knowledge, and upon tasting it the student desires more. Faith, devotion and dependency result. At a mature moment, however, the sweetness of knowledge exists by itself without the need of the guru to offer it. Knowledge thus becomes present in the life and experience of the student. Religious activity and sentiment deepen the faith relationship. Respect for the guru, service and devotion to him advance faith and dispose one to greater knowledge. Respect for the teacher is necessary in order to accept his wisdom, comments Śrī Abhinava

Vidyātīrtha.[1] It can be observed by any outsider, however, that students and devotees speak to the Śaṅkarācāryas with ease and no apparent hesitation. Devotees prostrate themselves before the guru before and after discussion with him, and south Indian Brāhmaṇas approach a Śaṅkarācārya with the upper half of their bodies uncovered out of respect for him. Consequently, the awe so visible among the people during public *darśana* and even during a Śaṅkarācārya's devotion at *pūjā* is absent in private conversation with him. A confident faith and a desire for knowledge seem to supplant any expression of emotion.

Commenting upon the three divine gifts mentioned in the Upaniṣads, a human birth, desire for liberation and habitual contact with great persons, Śrī Abhinava Vidyātīrtha says that each is more difficult to assimilate than the preceding one.[2] Although faith is the foundation of the guru-*śiṣya* relationship, one must persevere in religious service, devotion and desire for knowledge in order for them to become efficacious. Young students usually experience love for the guru that is stronger than their intellectual relationship with him. Respect and devotion are customarily rendered in a special way to father, mother and preceptor in Indian life. The Dwaraka Śaṅkarācārya would extend this reverence to god, Brāhmaṇas, cows, righteous men, saints and teachers.[3] The sage of Kanchi often speaks of guru-*bhakti* and believes that prayer "lies in sincere devotion to the Goddess and the Guru through silent meditation."[4] No essential distinction is made in most of Hindu piety between devotion to the guru and devotion to a deity. Another Śaṅkarācārya exclaims that "to him who is absolute in his devotion to god, and is equally devoted to his preceptor knowledge comes untaught."[5] Devotion not only gives rise to competency, but it also brings the grace of the guru.[6] Devotion to the guru and service to him do not essentially differ.[7] Śrī Abhinava Saccidānanda says that

1. Krishnaswamy, p. 78.
2. Ibid., p. 425.
3. Upadhyaya (1967), p. 49.
4. Ramakrishna Aiyer, p. 22; confer 37 ff; confer Ramaswami Sastri, p. 80.
5. Krishnaswamy, p. 59.
6. Ibid., pp. 59, 76.
7. Ibid., p. 222.

serivce to the guru improves the quality of deeds whether religious or secular. Knowledge from a guru without reverential service, he believes, leads to darkness.[1] Student-attendants may render service to a guru by care of the *maṭha*. The *ācārya* of Sringeri tells his students to give service to the *maṭha* and not to him.

Several of the Śaṅkarācāryas confirmed to this writer that equality is possible in the guru-*śiṣya* relationship. One of them, in conversation with me, considered equality in the relationship to be the goal and perfection of close association. When a Śaṅkarācārya turns a Vidyāpīṭha over to his successor, the implication is that equality has been achieved. There exists, of course, no way for one external to the relationship to ascertain whether a student has attained spiritual equality with his preceptor. What is observable is the reverence that spiritually mature individuals show a junior *ācārya*. Self-realisation, which brings about full equality, does not end the realationship between teacher and student but raises it to a new level of consciousness. The relationship, born in faith, is experienced then as fully conscious.

It has been pointed out that three different types of guru-*śiṣya* relationships are evident among the living Śaṅkarācāryas, each relationship corresponding to a different educational process. The broadest relationship is between a guru and his vast following of devotionalists. A second type of guru-*śiṣya* relationship exists between the guru and his attendants, namely, those residing in the *maṭha* and dedicated to its work. Many of the *paṇḍita*-s and intellectuals associated either formally or informally with a Vidyāpīṭha are included in this group. This second type of relationship includes those who have either begun the discipline of *jñāna*-yoga or are in proximate readiness for it. The third type of relationship is between the Śaṅkarācārya and his chosen successor. This is the guru-*śiṣya* relationship in its most restricted and formal sense. Those following the path of knowledge must have been selected by the guru as his students. The choice of attendants, *paṇḍita*-s, even those giving periodic service to the *maṭha*, and the *śiṣya* with right of succession is made personally by the Śaṅkarācārya.

There is speculation concerning the method of selecting a student

1. Upadhyaya (1967), p. 35.

with right of succession, but the way in which it is actually done is unknown. Devotees have told me that sometimes the goddess in dream guides the guru in his choice. In those cases where successors have not been personally trained by the previous *ācārya*, the most competent adult has been selected by *maṭha* authorities. But in the Sringeri, Kanchii and Jyotirmaṭha traditions, youths have been specifically chosen, initiated into *sannyāsa* and educated for the position of Śaṅkarācārya. Śrī Jayendra Sarasvatī, for example, was selected for *sannyāsa* in 1954, when he was in his early twenties, but it is believed that the senior guru chose him when still a child and had him educated in the traditional manner. He received personal instruction from the senior *ācārya* for sixteen years after his initiation. The junior *Swāmī* of Sringeri, now in his late twenties, was selected as a youth of fourteen for *sannyāsa* and became the *śiṣya* with right of succession in that single act. Sringeri's Śaṅkarācārya spends considerable time personally instructing his protege; it is said that a class does not end until the instruction is completely grasped by the young ascetic. The reigning Śaṅkarācārya of Sringeri was taught by his predecessor for twenty-four years. Swāmī Śāntānanda Saraswatī of the Jyotirmaṭha, although nominated publicly in the will of his predecessor, was a presonal *śiṣya* of the previous Śaṅkarācārya for many years, along with two other *śiṣya*-s, namely, Śrī Viṣṇudevānanda Saraswatī and Maharṣi Mahesh Yogi. Śrī Abhinava Saccidānanda of Dwaraka, commenting on how future Śaṅkarācāryas are selected, enumerates personal horoscope, signs of high spirituality, and the capacity for regular and rigorous spiritual practice.[1]

Attendants within the Vidyāpīṭhas speak openly of the informality of the Śaṅkarācāryas' teaching. A Sringeri student, recalling to me the guru's concern for concentration at all times, related an occasion when, after both had climbed to a hilltop temple, the *ācārya* playfully asked how many steps they had ascended. *Paṇḍita*-s who instructed the Śaṅkarācāryas as youth recall the ambiguity of that situation, saying that they felt that they themselves were being taught in the process of teaching. A *paṇḍita* who instructed Śrī Candraśekharendra in the Vedānta once said to his young pupil, "I play the role of teacher; but really I am your pupil."[2]

1. *Four Amnāya Pīṭhas*, p. 15.
2. Ramaswami Sastri, p. ii.

The Experience of a Guru

What kind of experience one has of a Śaṅkarācārya depends upon whether one relates to him as student, as attendant, as *paṇḍita* or as devotee. I found that the range of descriptions of the experience shows no clear pattern, even with a particular Śaṅkarācārya. A common factor shared by those who experience the gurus profoundly, however, is the significance of the experience itself. Not infrequently, people who have experienced the guru speak of the encounter as the controlling event or the most primal event of their lives. A professor observes that to have *darśana* of Dwaraka's Śaṅkarācārya is the major event of one's life.[1] It is said of the late Śrī Bhāratī Kṛṣṇa that he made those who met him experience themselves as objects of some special love.[2] A *paṇḍita* of the Sringeri Vidyāpīṭha described his experiences to me in language of divine presence and divine knowledge. Students of the same preceptor speak freely about being graced by him. "My highest thoughts come from him," and "He lifts up my mind and thoughts," are responses made to me by a young student who was beginning the path of knowledge. Experiences of the sage of Kanchi have been widely recorded. He confers on his disciples, it is believed, powers of personal purification and personal unification.[3] By a Hindu devotee he is experienced as "the incarnation of Īśvara in human form,"[4] while a Christian devotee quoting from the New Testament in order to gain understanding for herself and probably to aid my understanding, says he exemplifies that "the Father and I are one." A European writes that 'in his presence there was wordless communication, a link with the eternal."[5] A devotee described to me his *darśana* as filled with fear but believed that it rekindled a good heart and a renewed mind in him. A professional educator revealed that she was conscious of the guru guiding and looking after her academic work. Another devotee, reflecting with me shortly after *darśana*, saw his experience as a simultaneous encounter with complete humility and greatness.

Devotees at *darśana* frequently express some visible and audible

1. Upadhyaya (1967), p. 4.
2. Bhāratī Kṛṣṇa Tīrtha, p. xvi.
3. Ramaswami Sastri, p. 23.
4. Ramakrishna Aiyer, p. 111.
5. Mahadevan (1975), p. 93.

emotion, and occasionally a mass catharsis may take place. Yet others experience a Śaṅkarācārya in strictly Advaita terms. Characterizing nonduality as experience, a student of Advaita and a devotee of the sage of Kanchi said, "He is the experience."[1] It is relevant that a Śaṅkarācārya incites nondual experience. An astute description of the sage of Kanchi is given by the *paṇḍita* who, reflecting on his experience, writes : "Though a powerful personality he is most impersonal...He may be called the Personal-cum-Impersonal God."[2] Another individual spontaneously described his experience of the first meeting with a Śaṅkarācārya as "He is not other for me." This seems to be a psychological expression of Advaita experience. Some devotees apparently receive a type of nondual experience through an encounter with the Śaṅkarācārya himself. The Śaṅkarācāryas have extraordinary powers of empathy and compassion that they freely communicate and that help them to quickly identify with devotee and non-devotee alike.

How are these teachers experienced outside the tradition? For a sympathetic observer who is not a devotee of a Śaṅkarācārya, another level of experience and understanding results from an encounter with the guru. Common factors are present among the experiences related by non-devotees, and some generalizations are possible. One is struck, for example, by the Śaṅkarācāryas' simple but full expression of the human. They are warm, light-hearted and totally unpretentious individuals. Although they may be mystical personalities, they are neither mysterious nor aloof. There is no extraordinary mystique about them, so that they are fully men of this world. They share in common a radiant joy, and their joy-filled presence may be the most formidable factor of their personalities. Another common impression is that their body-presence is extremely physical. A particular Śaṅkarācārya may strike the observer as a father-figure in his dealing with those around him, while another may be a brother-figure in his self-projection. As tested sages and saints, they give even to the detached observer the impression that they are a type of ideal human being. The most visible dimensions of their

1. Tatcharian, "The Ideal Prophet of Our Age," in *Śaṅkara and Shanmata.*

2. Confer Balasubramanian, p. 3, for a philosophical consideration of Advaita as experience.

personality, namely, simplicity, joyfulness and common humanity, are instinctively communicated and shared with most sympathetic observers outside the tradition.

The Path of the Student

The advanced aspirant following the path of knowledge even in modern times undertakes study, meditation and the cultivation of mental alertness.[1] Devotion is present, although it is relegated to the background as the path of knowledge is pursued. Generally speaking *haṭha*-yoga, such as physical postures, is not a significant factor in preparing one for the path of knowledge. I detected no significant emphasis on *haṭha*-yoga in the Śaṅkara *maṭha*-s. The recitation of *japa* and *mantra*-s along with the *karma*-yoga of service are the physical forms of yoga clearly in evidence. *Prāṇāyāma*, the regulation of breath, is the single form of *haṭha*-yoga that I found recommended by servral Śaṅkarācāryas. The sage of Kanchi recommends *prāṇāyāma* in order to equalize breathing for the sake of mental equanimity.[2] He especially recommends it to the meditator who has difficulty in concentration.

Meditation and concentration structure the path of knowledge as a liberation process. Śrī Candraśekharendra speaks of *upāsanā*, *dhyāna*, concentration or meditation somewhat synonymously to mean concentration on a form.[3] The place of devotional meditation, as *upāsanā*, has already been discussed, but the real purpose of it is to train the mind for concentration. This is accomplished in devotional meditation by gradually transcending body-consciousness. A rejection of the body is prevalent in some discourses on asceticism of several of the Śaṅkarācāryas. Meditation is a type of devotional reflection (*dhyāna*) on a distinct form of a deity. This is quite common among the devotees of the Śaṅkarācāryas, for higher forms of concentration are restricted to the few. Meditation on name and form develops the four qualifications for the path of knowledge. I found that older

1. Upadhyaya (1967), p. 36.
2. Mahadevan (1975), p. 64.
3. Ramakrishna Aiyer, p. 228.

students of the *pāṭhaśālā*-s understand that concentration must go beyond name and form. Yet formless meditation is both difficult and rare. The junior *swāmī* of Kanchi typically speaks of meditation on *saguṇa* Brahman in his public discourses because it is accessible to everyone.[1]

A Śaṅkarācārya, speaking with me about meditation, used the analogy of an electric light to exemplify growth in concentration. Just as the light is frequently switched on for illumination, so too the powers of concentration are perfected by the repetitive effort of the mind. It is the guru, of course, who initially switches on the light of concentration. In time, however, the steady light of concentration remains without the repeated effort to focus the mind. As progress is made in concentration, differentiation of subject and object begins to disappear.[2] Concentration without an object, that is without name and form, is concentration upon the meaning of the great Upaniṣadic axioms. For this to be achieved, self-inquiry must be effectively sustained. Several students and *paṇḍita*-s expressed to me their view that there is a greater need for self-analysis in spiritual development than in ordinary meditation. Self-inquiry is viewed by most of these practitioners as the unique contribution of Advaita discipline. Since few people have the skill for continual self-inquiry, the practice is limited even though it stands at the center of Ādi Śaṅkara's discipline and his understanding of the Upaniṣads. Yet it is the effort of some Advaita students even today.

Serious self-inquiry, for those who are associated with the Śaṅkarācāryas, may begin either immediately after studentship or subsequent to the householder stage of life. For the occasional devotee of a Śaṅkarācārya, self-inquiry is certainly not the major spiritual practice. Vedānta self-inquiry takes the greater portion of one's day. A *paṇḍita* who was introduced to me as a teacher of Advaita suggested four to five hours a day for effective self-inquiry. This indicates the depth of the commitment that is necessary for the triple method. It is a vocation in itself. Nonetheless,

1. Jayendra Saraswatī (1976), pp. 30 ff. He says, "The chosen form of worship depends on the mind of the person concerned. Thus, each one chooses a God or Goddess according to his mental capacity and state." (p. 62).

2. Confer Mahadevan (1975), p. 49.

Śaṅkarācāryas do not hesitate to speak of self-inquiry and to hold it up as the specific discipline of *jñāna*-yoga. The difficulty of the triple method does not discourage the advanced seeker who is trained in ascetical discipline. There remains, nevertheless, the presupposition that rebirth is necessary for the majority effectively to complete the salvation process. I discovered the teaching of the Śaṅkarācāryas on self-inquiry to be highly orthodox. For example, analysis of personal experience and the use of negation (*neti-neti*) are advocated in order to distinguish the states of consciousness and the coverings of the self. It is the guru who initially guides the students through rigorous discrimination. Discrimination of the real Self from the body is equally recommended in order to transcend the sense of "I" and "mine".[1] A European devotee of the sage of Kanchi told me that since contemporary physics makes a significant contribution toward determining the constitution of the human order and the universe, it could consequently be a useful tool for differentiating the real from the ephemeral.

Meditation in the teaching of the Śaṅkarācāryas is typical of both the Advaita tradition and the Upaniṣads and reveals no significant variance even among the gurus themselves. In the final analysis, meditation on the Self with a mind fully concentrated holds the meaning of the Upaniṣadic truths wholly within the mind.[2] The entire process presumes a rational relationship between the teacher and the student. The triple method, to which the Śaṅkarācāryas generally subscribe, rests upon the hearing, reflection and concentration of the classical truth-axioms. The head of the Sringeri Vidyāpīṭha teaches a classical understanding of the triple method. Hearing (*śravaṇa*) is to listen to the scriptures and their exposition from a preceptor, reflection (*manana*) is deliberative thinking and analysis of what has been heard; and concentration (*nididhyāsana*) is to focus upon the meaning of what has been heard and reflected upon.[3] In concentration, various levels of experience are transcended and new levels of consciousness arise. During the final moment of the

1. Confer Jayendra Saraswatī, pp. 190, 194, 198 ff, 203 ff; also Upadhyaya (1967), pp. 31-32, 37.
2. Upadhyaya (1967), p. 31.
3. Krishnaswamy, p. 244.

triple method, there is no arguing, imaging, reasoning or logical thought, but the condition remains rational because the mind holds within itself meaning of the Upaniṣadic truths. Śrī Candraśekharendra speaks of *upāsanā* as mental action but *jñāna* as mental without the accompanying activity of the mind, which distinction clearly separates devotional worship from Advaita meditation.[1]

The Śaṅkarācāryas imply that the triple method is an integral process. Yet hearing and reflection require years of discipline and discrimination, and it is thus possible to call the triple method an integral process only in its mature stage. Two factors influence the effectiveness of the process : namely, the depth of reflection and its consequent meaning, and the power of the mind to hold the meaning. Several Śaṅkarācāryas confirmed for me that a guru is needed at each moment of the triple method. It is easy enough to understand the guru's role in delivering, exposing and reasoning upon Upaniṣadic wisdom, but it is more difficult to perceive his role in concentration. One Śaṅkarācārya, in conversation with me, suggested that the guru gives the grace of concentration. Another believed that the guru has no direct role in concentration but is uniquely present to the student at this time. This is possibly an oblique reference either to the transference of consciousness or to the power of the guru's consciousness as it impinges upon the student. Yet another *ācārya* told me, without much explanation, that the guru is conscious to the *śiṣya* in both reflection and concentration. It seems, however, that the guru has, at the most, an indirect role to play in concentration. Once the student leaves concentration, the direct activity of the guru resumes in order to deepen hearing and reflection.

It is possible that more detailed instruction concerning the liberation process can only be shared between a guru and his student because of the peculiarities of the individual, and that theoretical discussion outside this context becomes somewhat hypothetical. But from what is observable and attested by informants, it can be stated that a student approaching a Śaṅkarācārya today for the discipline of knowledge receives the legacy of Ādi Śaṅkara and the Advaita tradition. It is highly significant that the Śaṅkarācāryas perceive themselves to have a specific role in the process

1. Ramakrishna Aiyer, p. 236.

of liberation. Both teacher and aspirant testify to immortality through wisdom.[1] This is the goal of education in Advaita Vedânta and the purpose of the guru-*śiṣya* relationship even today.

1. Mahadevan (1975), p. 41.

CHAPTER EIGHT

THE GURU IN THE MODERN WORLD

No single piece of literature articulates the ideal guru in Advaita Vedānta terms more perceptively than Śaṅkara's prayer-poem to Śrī Dakṣiṇāmūrti, the supreme divinity, Lord Śiva, who appears as preceptor.[1] The hymn holds the clarity of nondual experience in tension with the ecstatic devotion and commitment to the divine/human guru. It images the ideal that the great writers of the post-Śaṅkara period tried to express in philosophy and poetry, and which the living Śaṅkarācāryas, as nondualists and devotionalists, try equally to express in day-to-day public life. Part of the hymn is placed here in order to impress upon the reader a vivid ideal before drawing an evaluation from the historical order.

Hymn to Śrī Dakṣiṇāmūrti[2]

I bow to Śrī Dakṣiṇāmūrti in the form of my guru :
I bow to him by whose grace the whole of the world
Is found to exist entirely in the mind, like a city's
  image mirrored in a glass,
Though, like a dream, through *māyā*'s power it appears
  outside;
And by whose grace, again, on the dawn of Knowledge,
It is perceived as the everlasting and nondual Self.
I bow to Śrī Dakṣiṇāmūrti in the form of my guru :
I bow to Him who, by the sheer power of His will,
Projects outside, like a magician or a mighty yogī, this infinite
  universe,
Which, in the beginning, rests, without name or form, like
  the sprout in a seed,
And after creation, by the power of time and space imagined
  through *māyā*,

1. A recent stylometric study of this hymn concludes that it is an authentic work of Śaṅkara. Confer Gussner.

2. Nikhilananda (1975), pp. 239-245. This is reprinted with the kind permission of the publisher, the President, Śrī Ramakrishna Math, Mylapore, Madras.

Appears to be many, possessed of manifold shapes and hues.
I bow to Śrī Dakṣiṇāmūrti in the form of my guru :
To Him whose outward manifestations, though based on the Real,
Appear as illusory, ever changing objects;
Who grants to those who take refuge in Him through the Vedic pronouncement "That thou art,"
The boon of immediate knowledge of Brahman,
To which attaining, a man returns no more to the realm of birth and death.
I bow to Śrī Dakṣiṇāmūrti in the form of my guru :
To him whose knowledge, issuing forth through the organs of sense,
Like the glow of a powerful lamp placed in a pot with many holes,
Vibrates outside in the shape of the thought "I know";
Whose Light it is that illumines the whole of the universe.
I bow to Śrī Dakṣiṇāmūrti in the form of may guru :
To Him who dispels the mighty illusion evoked by *māyā*'s play,
Impelled by which, unseeing, childish, and misguided men
Continually speak, in error, of body, *prāṇa*, senses, and even of the fickle mind, as "I",
Though in reality these are all mere emptiness.
I bow to Śrī Dakṣiṇāmūrti in the form of my guru :
I bow to Him who, as a man, in deep and dreamless sleep,
Exists as Ultimate Truth Itself,
When outer awareness is obscured, like the sun or moon in Rāhu's grasp, and the organs of sense are all withdrawn;
And who, on awakening, tells himself, "It was I who slept,"
And sees again the objects he saw before.
I bow to Śrī Dakṣiṇāmūrti in the form of my guru :
I bow to Him who, in His loving-kindness, reveals to His worshippers,
The eternal Ātman, which—through the changes of waking, dreaming, and dreamless sleep,
Through childhood, youth, maturity, and old age—
Persists as the inexhaustible flow of consciousness,
Revealing Itself in the heart as the ever present sense of "I"

I bow to Śrī Dakṣiṇāmūrti in the form of my guru seated before me,
Who, as a mortal under the sway of *māyā*, and whether awake or dreaming,
Perceives that the world is composed of multiple entities,
Joined in relation to one another
As cause and effect, owner and owned, teacher and pupil, sire and son.
I bow to Śrī Dakṣiṇāmūrti in the form of my guru,
Beyond whom, for a wise and discerning man, no being exists superior;
Who has manifested Himself in an eightfold form
As the tangible and insentient earth, water, fire, air, and ether.
As the sun, the lord of the day, the moon, of soothing light,
And as living man.
This hymn to Śrī Dakṣiṇāmūrti clearly reveals the Ultimate Truth
As the Soul of everything that has life;
Therefore by hearing it and by pondering on it, by contemplating it and by reciting it,
A man attains unrivalled lordship, acquiring the glory of being the Inmost Self of all,
And effortlessly receives, without interruption, the eight unique powers of the Godhead.

The Guru in the Historical Order

The Śaṅkarācāryas are religious teachers and religious leaders. They are both an institution, and bearers of an institution. This latter development goes beyond the Upaniṣadic notion of guru but not necessarily beyond Ādi Śaṅkara's reconceptualization of the guru tradition. His creation of major centers of learning throughout India, headed by outstanding religious teachers, brought about an institution that did not previously exist as explicitly in Hindu life. This is his special contribution to India's
ter teaching tradition. The line of gurus from the time of
to the present century preserved an institution that,
onveyor of Vedic and Vedānta orthodoxy.
le continuity with the teaching, culture and
nturies because a living institution advances
ce the time of Ādi Śaṅkara, the heads of the

Vidyāpīṭhas have been a major support for classical education. In this role they return people to classical foundations. They thus represent one of the more conservative forces within Hindu society. They are an institution that advances institutional religion, including classical education and priesthood, and even traditional caste life. As such they have, moreover, become spokesmen for a broad expression of Hinduism representative of Indian life and culture.

But they are also spokesmen of Advaita Vedānta and its Upaniṣadic foundations. They represent and teach a comprehensive Vedānta that includes nonduality, *bhakti* and ritual. Their teaching, especially their teaching of Advaita, can be understood only within this wider view of the Vedānta and the scriptural tradition. With a few exceptions in the post-Śaṅkara period, the Vidyāpīṭhas have neither been headed by nor produced prolific and innovative writers. Creativity and genius have been sporadic in Advaita articulation over the centuries since Ādi Śaṅkara, and for the last several centuries no individual has emerged to reach the stature of the great medievals who followed Ādi Śaṅkara. The living Śaṅkarācāryas and the present Vidyāpīṭhas are not advancing a significant written tradition either in Advaita or in the wider Vedānta. They remain, however, the center of the oral tradition that has characterized the guru from ancient times. The effort either to revive or to continue a legitimate succession of teachers signals the importance given to oral tradition. The living Śaṅkarācāryas are enhanced in their position by the past teachers whom they represent. Hindus, devotees and even non-devotees of the *ācārya*-s look upon them as the embodiment of Ādi Śaṅkara's legacy. Consequently, people are attracted to them not for the fresh and novel but for the old and tested ways. They have stock answers to most questions, answers reflecting traditional wisdom that the people recognize as such. These perceptions are also confirmed by those outside the tradition.

Although the Śaṅkarācāryas are Advaita spokesmen, Advaita Vedānta is neither their major emphasis nor the reason why they elicit a large following. Contemporary Indians from the academic community and other individuals representing neo-Hinduism in this century probably have done more to advance Advaita as a philosophy and as a spiritual way of life. The wor of K. C. Bhattacharya and T. M. P. Mahadevan are representa of the former, while some teachers of the Ramakrishna order are representative of the latter. This does not diminish the fact that the Śaṅkarācāryas are Advaita personalities for some devotees. For the majority of the devotees, Advaita represents a traditional lineage of teachers more than a specific teaching or path of nonduality. It appears that traditional lineage itself is more important than the particular quality mediated by that lineage. This indicates once again that a Śaṅkarācārya is accepted because he is the embodiment of guru rather than for a particular quality of his teaching.

Devotees regard the Śaṅkarācāryas not as ordinary gurus but as extraodinary teachers, as Jagadgurus. A world-teacher should possess, it seems, a type of universality in both teaching and personality. The responsibilities and capacities of world-teachers are greater than those of ordinary gurus. The former live a more comprehensive life of teacher, administrator, ritualist, and religious leader; their spirituality is a composite of *jñāna*, *bhakti* and *karma* yoga. Their life and spirituality should stand out in the sight of all the world. Jagadgurus should be vital figures for all sectors of society. The present-day Śaṅkarācāryas possess, in some ways, this universal appeal. This line of Jagadgurus is best characterized as having a type of integral personality. The spiritual unity of all beings within a single person distinguishes the saintly tradition in India. T. M. P. Mahadevan writes that one cannot understand the significance of a *mahātmā* or an *avatāra* from the outside because the thoughts, feelings and deeds of such figures embrace the whole world. A Jagadguru, it is believed, effects the world vitally and transforms the world from within in order for it to move forward.[1] There is no access to discover how and whether a Jagadguru inserts new life into the world from within the world itself. Thus it is deemed necessary here to redefine the Jagadguru in terms of his capacity effectively to teach different sectors of Indian society in relatively large numbers. In this sense the living Śaṅkarācāryas are established Jagadgurus.

The range of a Jagadguru's mission follows from the universality of his personality. The living Śaṅkarācāryas are in some respects composite personalities. These intellectually astute men are at the same time effective communicators, generally able

1. Mahadevan (1975), p. 71.

administrators, and individuals of intense devotion and spiritual wisdom. Their outreach is broad, and they embody a form of the classical Hindu personality. Because their personalities are credible to their followers, their teaching is convincing. Yet it is principally for a Hindu community of believers that the Jagadgurus remain so. Unlike many of India's living gurus today, who are world-known and command an international following of Hindus and non-Hindus alike, the Śaṅkarācāryas have a narrower discipleship. With the possible exception of Śrī Candraśekharendra of Kanchi, the Śaṅkarācāryas count only small numbers of non-Indian or non-Hindu devotees among their followers. The Self-Realisation Foundation, based in the United States of America, has on occasion expressed interest in the northern *ācārya*-s of Puri and Dwaraka. Swāmī Śāntānanda of the Jyotirmaṭha is now beginning to attract students of Maharṣi Mahesh Yogi. Likewise, the Sringeri *ācārya* is now looked upon as the spiritual master of a Śaṅkara foundation in the United States.[1] These exceptions may not be highly significant, however. What is the meaning of a Jagadguru, a world teacher, who is seemingly bound to the Hindu community ? Even though their teaching does not now have universal appeal, because of the faith context and the faith symbols it employs, nevertheless their personalities are universal. This is to say that the Śaṅkarācāryas are generally figures of fundamental appeal. The outsider even regards them as exemplars of the truly human. From a theological perspective, a perspective beyond the grasp of observation and empirical analysis, the saint or guru is seen to effect the world from within. This is the sense in which the Jagadguru may well be efficacious in a universal manner. For the believer, of course, this poses no difficulty, for belief usually implies both universality and exclusivity.

Elsewhere I have discussed the insightful contribution of Rabindranath Tagore to the teaching tradition of India as the communication of the truth of the personality.[2] There I demonstrated that the contemporary figures of Tagore, Mahātmā Gandhi and Śrī Aurobindo Ghose were exemplary teachers because the truth

1. This is the Śrī Rajarajeshwari Peetham in Stroudsburg, Pennsylvania. U. S. A., with Swami Saraswati Devyashram as resident guru.

2. Cenkner (1973) and (1975).

of their personalities, in each case qualitatively different, was readily communicated to a general public. Their public included Indian and non-Indian, Hindu and non-Hindu. Although their message was based upon a particular conception of the human person and his future that results from the way each figure lived his life and experienced reality, the characteristic quality of their personalities gave universality to their work and teaching.[1] Yet they were embraced by a limited group of people who were able to identify with their particular personalities. The same is true of the Śaṅkarācāryas, with far more common traits and fewer differences among them. What they say is less important than what they are, at least for the general devotee. Their personalities do not necessarily dominate the way they articulate their message; in fact there is little personalization of the message in their public discourses. However, their personalities dominate their audience. The distinctiveness of the personality of each Śaṅkarācārya, nonetheless, is evident in public and at public meetings. They readily communicate the special quality of their personalities. The Śaṅkarācāryas differ from Tagore, Gandhi and Aurobindo as guru personalities because the former reflect a composite of Hindu religious life—*karma, bhakti* and *jñāna* yoga—while the latter reflect a more individualistic image, certainly more heterodox, in terms of the esthetic, social and gnostic dimensions respectively, of the human person.[2]

The Guru in Modern Life

This has been a century of vitality for the teaching tradition of Ādi Śaṅkara, thanks in part to the leadership of the reigning Śaṅkarācāryas and their immediate predecessors. Most of the Vidyāpīṭhas have had strong leadership from the late nineteenth century to the present time. If this vitality continues through the *śiṣya*-s of the living *ācārya*-s, the Śaṅkara teaching tradition should remain vibrant even into the next century. One cannot, however, discount the quality of traditional orthodoxy transmitted through the Vidyāpīṭhas and the Śaṅkarācāryas as a factor in this vitality. They are spokesmen of Brāhmaṇic Hinduism. The renaissance within Hinduism begun by Ram Mohan Ray and other nineteenth century figures, and continued by Tagore, Gandhi and Aurobindo

1. Cenkner (1970), (1975) and (1976).
2. Cenkner (1976), Chapter XIII and (1975).

in this century, has not perceptibly affected this line of teachers. Swami Vivekananda, the disciple of the saintly Ramakrishna and a popular articulator of neo-Vedānta, perhaps came closest to the orthodoxy continued by the Śaṅkarācāryas, but he neither imitated nor duplicated their type of teaching, mission or guruhood.

A major problem in the future for the Vidyāpīṭhas and the Śaṅkarācāryas is the difficulty of touching the urbanized and the significantly secularized Hindu with classical tradition. At present there is no contemporary response from the Śaṅkarācāryas to this sector of modern Indian society. Present-day Indians, for example, ask both privately and publicly what the Śaṅkarācāryas are saying and doing about social questions like poverty, untouchability and sectarian exclusivity. The response from the gurus to these questions has not been convincing to many for whom the issues are critical. The Śaṅkarācāryas, it appears, consider their role as transmitters of a legacy to be more crucial than the resolution of present day problems or the transformation within contemporary religion. While absorbing the accommodation within the Vedānta of the past centuries, they are not accommodationists in regard to the present. Accommodation usually has been imperceptible when it first takes place; it frequently requires an extraordinary writer who brings new insight to the tradition or renews old insights within it. Since the Śaṅkarācāryas are principally oral teachers, this cannot be anticipated from them.

My investigation has been a contemporary test of a classical notion of guru and the consequent guru-*śiṣya* relationship as found within the legacy of one major guru. A basic continuity has been found to exist between Ādi Śaṅkara and the living Śaṅkarācāryas in their theoretical consideration of these realities. The differences that do emerge are ones of emphasis rather than of essentials. I find that today a distinction must be made between a *śiṣya* and a devotee. A devotee is one who in faith, devotion and service is committed to a guru and is guided by his example and general religious teaching. A *śiṣya*, however, is asceticly qualified for religious education and is accepted by the guru for the path of knowledge. The guru-devotee relationship is certainly more common among the living Śaṅkarācāryas than the guru-*śiṣya* relationship in its strict sense. This may have been true throughout the history of the Śaṅkara tradition, but there is no reliable way to test the assumption historically. The guru-devotee relationship among the living Śaṅkarācāryas transcends Hindu denominationalism, although in south India, for example, the greater number of devotees come from the Śaivas and the Smārta Brāhmaṇas. Yet devotees from other communities are not excluded from discipleship. This is a testimony to the universality of the teaching and personality of these gurus. When on tour the *ācārya*-s have the opportunity to attract a wider cross-section of Indian society than when they reside in the *maṭha*-s. Their teaching on *dharma*, consequently, has broad appeal and cuts across sectarian lines. The guru-*śiṣya* relationship, on the other hand, is kept more within the boundaries of a specific community because the *śiṣya*-s are usually products of the *pāṭhaśālā*-s which are caste bound.

A guru, as understood here, is the focal point of a religious heritage. He embodies its history with all the complexity and growth of the centuries. The guru-*śiṣya* relationship is the unique place where the heritage is transferred from one generation to the next. The guru-devotee relationship, by contrast, is the place where the heritage is assimilated in varying degrees by a faith community. Continuity in the Hindu tradition has a distinctive trait that sets it apart from continuity in other religions; the extraordinary religious teacher, who appears somewhat frequently has been consistently a catalyst for the assimilation of religion by the Indian people.

To identify the guru as catalyst of the religion and faith of a people is to situate his function as superior to the function of a sect within the lives of people. A teaching tradition (*sampradāya*) is more important for engendering and defining faith than sects such as Śaivas, Vaiṣṇavas or Śāktas dissociated from a teaching tradition. *Sampradāya* is usually defined as the chain of masters from which a particular teacher hears and articulates religious wisdom.[1] The term has been understood recently to include not only a teaching tradition but also an ascetical order with devotees forming about a particular monastic or temple establishment.[2] *Sampradāya*, however, is an inclusive term that

1. Satsvarupa, pp. 6-8.
2. Miller and Wertz (1976), p. 4.

comprehends three elements: a teaching tradition with particular doctrine; an ascetical order functioning as an autonomous religious society with devotees; and sectarianism with particular ways of worship toward particular gods.[1] The Śaṅkara tradition includes doctrine, institutional society, and a type of sectarianism that is somewhat eclectic in terms of worship and religious practice.[2] This is not to ignore the fact that Brāhmaṇic Hinduism and Sanskritization are directly fostered by the tradition. The Śaṅkarācāryas at each moment in history gather doctrine, society and sect into a whole, giving devotees a more integral identity than they would have if they saw themselves only as Śaivas, Śāktas or worshippers of the *ṣaṇmata*-s. A *sampradāya*, therefore, includes the notion of sect but touches the faith of people more definitively. It gives more meaning to their lives than the mere sect. The Śaṅkara tradition contains the fullest meaning of *sampradāya*. The catalyst of the *sampradāya* or teaching tradition, understood in the broader sense, is the living guru. He is not only the teacher of doctrine but also the sacred center of a socio-religious institution, around whom people gather to worship the gods and pursue liberation paths. Faith experience is engendered within the context of the *sampradāya*; this always occurs, however, in direct relationship to the living guru.

A *śiṣya* or a devotee of a guru is constituted as such through faith. Faith may be engendered by the guru himself. But an initial faith or trust may also be engendered by someone other than the guru, for example a devotee or *śiṣya* may plant the seed of faith in a neophyte. Faith in the legacy, the tradition, may precede faith in the living guru. There is no way to experience the guru as the living fulfilment of tradition or as the manifestation of the divine without faith in him. Without faith in the teacher, one experiences only a quality of his humanity. In order to encounter the weight of a guru's personality or presence, faith is necessary. The meaning of his presence, knowledge and personality is found likewise, in faith. Just as the understanding of a religion is limited when faith is absent, so too the understanding of a guru is limited when faith in him is absent. Yet as has been suggested, Hinduism is more an orthopraxis than an orthodoxy. Therefore

1. Miller (1977), pp. 528-530.
2. Ibid, p. 530.

the possibility of understanding a guru increases as the life of the Vedānta, such as meditation, concentration and discrimination, becomes more common throughout the modern world.

The guru, as conceived by Ādi Śaṅkara and the Upaniṣads, is a living reality today in India. The *śiṣya*, as conceived by the same tradition, is rare. It is impossible to say whether this situation is any different than in the past, since no historical records attest to how many men in ancient times were *śiṣya*-s in the classical sense, that is, qualified and pursuing the path of knowledge. It must be recalled that although Ādi Śaṅkara himself had many students and followers, he had only four or five pupils to whom he could entrust a major seat of learning with the right to teach broadly. It is not surprising, then, that an *ācārya* of somewhat lesser stature than Ādi Śaṅkara has fewer *śiṣya*-s. It is not uncommon to find in India *ācārya*-s of a Śaṅkara order, even heading a minor *maṭha*, who do not have any *śiṣya*-s in the strict sense of the term. I recall one such guru, well advanced in age, who without embarrassment offered to me that he had not been blessed with a *śiṣya* or a successor.

Although the goal of the guru-*śiṣya* relationship is the spiritual liberation of the student, the continuation of a particular heritage is also of utmost importance to the living Śaṅkarācāryas. In fact, to continue a spiritual tradition of teachers may have been an equally important goal in preserving the teacher-student relationship throughout the centuries. The guru-*śiṣya* relationship has sustained the legacy of Ādi Śaṅkara, a legacy transmitted for twelve centuries. What does this mean for modern society as it moves further away from the wisdom of the past ? The guru of the future may become more an ideal than a practical norm for human life.

In India's religious past, a great personality was a surer standard of virtue than an actual rule of *dharma*.[1] *Dharma* was best comprehended through an exemplar, in this case the enlightened guru who stood within society as the ideal figure.[2] Yet in modern times the *sannyāsī* and guru seem only to reflect the

1. Sarma, D. S., pp. 48, 86; for this discussion I am indebted to Creel (1976), (1977), pp. 106 ff.

2. Creel (1976); Yamunacharya, pp. 33-34, 42-43.

dominant forces of Indian society without directing those forces toward the resolution of critical social and moral dilemmas.[1] But religious figures, especially in modern times, are committed not only to the ideal but also to the actuality of social fulfilment. It is problematic, however, whether the vision or the ideal of *dharma* as embodied by a guru could be translated into public policy.[2] It must be recalled that the classical guru was not the embodiment of social *dharma*; the gurus were not teachers of the Arthaśāstras, and they were teachers of the Dharmaśāstras only to the degree that the wisdom of those tests could be placed within the more fundamental context of scripture (*śruti*). This dilemma points to the metaphysical separation between *sanātana dharma*, from which the guru draws his life and knowledge, and the social *dharma* of public life. Mahātmā Gandhi and Ācārya Vinoba Bhave are exceptions among the hundreds of popular religious figures of this century, most of whom do not have the capacity to either reflect or direct social forces. There has not been a great turn by the more socially conscious Indians of modern times toward either the new gurus or the more orthodox ones because the ideal they embody, a vision of eternal *dharma*, is generally not perceived as immediately applicable to social and political life. The religious vision functions as an ideal in the transformation of individual spiritual life but not in the transformation of general society. The religious teachers may remain norms of religious life, but Indians of the final quarter of the century will likely look elsewhere for norms of daily social life. The vigorous activity of the Śaṅkarācāryas in education, in family life, in community service and in forming a more enlightened social awareness, does not mitigate this impression.

The guru occasions the immediacy of the religious experience of the devotee. For the faith-filled devotee, he is the center of mystery. The sacred center of Hindu life is the living guru. Change and continuity in religious, philosophical and social traditions coalesce in the person of the extraordinary guru; his followers experience him as the restorer of the *dharma* order. Although he may sustain an institution with religious, philosophical and social traditions, he is an institution of tradition

1. Creel (1976) and (1977).
2. Ibid.

himself. The more typical guru, however, is the center for the transmission of the change and continuity wrought by his predecessors. For the devotee the guru may either bring about radical transformation of life in faith or merely facilitate personal identity through faith experience.

The guru is the center of sacredness.[1] In his company the scriptures, idols and even liberation paths pale in importance. The sacred center may be either mystery itself, or the place in which encounter with mystery occurs. In the latter case, the center is the threshold to mystery. Therefore, the sacred center can function as either noumenal or phenomenal reality. Both possibilities exist for devotees and students of a guru. The guru is the context wherein an individual gathers spiritual resources in order to encounter mystery; likewise, the guru is mystery itself in the faith experience of some devotees. The Śaṅkarācāryas who have been described here function in both ways as the sacred center of faith experience.

Rebirth deeply affects religious life in India and may lessen the urgency with which the need for more mature faith experience is felt. For those who still have roots in tradition, figures like the Śaṅkarācāryas will continue to be an influence and source of experience and knowledge. India in this century alone has witnessed a steady march of new gurus, *sādhu*-s and saintly figures. Few of them have been as comprehensive in teaching or in reflecting the richness of Hindu life as the Śaṅkarācāryas. Some contemporary gurus accommodate with ease to the changing times, adopting either eclectic or iconoclastic approaches to religion, but they not infrequently remain thoroughly Hindu in fundamentals. The new gurus often present a narrower expression of Hindu life than those who draw upon the full tradition as the Śaṅkarācāryas are accustomed to do. The novel activity, nonetheless, of the new gurus signals the struggle with contemporaneity in religion experienced among India's holy men and the increasing number of holy women who have become public figures. The genius of the Hindu past has been its capacity to absorb and to produce many types of religious personalities and many forms of religious life. Activity among the new religious figures points to a continuation of this. But the advanced religious personality

1. Miller (1977), pp. 527, 532-534.

in India's history has always been primarily a type of teacher. Teachers emerge from the context of a specific tradition. The importance of the tradition determines the significance of the teacher. The Śaṅkarācāryas are primal teachers because of their tradition. This is the strength of the Śaṅkarācāryas and conversely points to the weakness of more contemporary gurus.

BIBLIOGRAPHY

Major Works of Śaṅkara in English Translation

S. *Ait. U. Eight Upaniṣads with the Commentary of Śaṅkarācārya* Tr. Swāmī Gambhīrānanda. Vol. II. Calcutta : Advaita Ashrama, 1973.

S. *Aparok. Aparokṣānubhūti or Self-Realization of Śrī Śaṅkarācārya.* Tr. Swāmī Vimuktānanda. Calcutta : Advaita Ashrama, 1973.

S. *Ātma. Self-Knowledge.* An English Translation of Śaṅkarācārya's *Ātmabodha* with Notes, Commentary and Introduction. Swāmī Nikhilānanda. Madras : Śrī Ramakrishna Math, 2nd edit., 1962; 3rd edit., 1967.

S. *B. Gītā. The Bhagavad-Gītā with the Commentary of Śrī Śaṅkarāchārya.* Tr. A. Mahādeva Śāstri. Madras : V. Ramaswamy Sastrulu & Sons, 1972 (Madras : Minerva Press, 1st edit., 1897).

S. *B. Sūtra. Brahma-Sūtra-Bhāṣya of Śrī Śaṅkarācārya* Tr. Swāmī Gambhīrānanda. Clacutta : Advaita Ashrama, 1965. *Brahma-Sūtra-Śaṅkara-Bhāṣya.* Bādarāyaṇa's Brahma-Sūtra with Śaṅkarācārya's Commentary. Tr. Vasudeo Mahadeo Apte. Bombay : Popular Book Depot, 1960. *The Vedānta Sūtras of Bādarāyaṇa with the Commentary by Śaṅkara.* Vol. I & II. Tr. George Thibaut. New York : Dover Publications, 1962. (The Sacred Books of the East, Vols. 34, 38. Edit. Max Muller. Oxford : The Clarendon Press, 1890, 1896).

S. *B. U. The Bṛhadāraṇyaka Upaniṣad with the Commentary of Śaṅkarācārya.* Tr. Swāmī Mādhavānanda. Calcutta : Advaita Ashrama, 4th edit., 1965.

S. *C. U. The Chha'ndogya Upanishad and Sri Sankara's Commentary.* Tr. Ganga'nath Jha. Madras : The Indian Printing Works, 1923. (*The Chāndogyopaniṣad,* A treatise on Vedānta Philosophy translated into English with The Commentary of Śaṅkara. Tr. Ganganatha Jha. Poona : Oriental Book Agency, 1942).

S. *Dakṣiṇ. Daksiṇāmūrtistotra. The Minor Works of Sri Sankaracarya.* Tr. V. Subrahmanya Sarma. Holenarsipur:

Adhyatma Prakasha, 1942. (Nikhilananda, 1962 & 1967; Mahadevan, 1970).

S. *Īśa*. *Eight Upaniṣads with the Commentary of Śaṅkarācārya*. Tr. Swāmī Gambhīrānanda. Vol. I. Calcutta : Advaita Ashrama, 1972.

S. *Kaṭha*. Ibid.

S. *Kena*. Ibid.

S. *Māṇḍ. U*. Ibid., Vol. II.

S. *Māṇḍ. Kārikā*. Ibid.

S. *M. U*. Ibid.

Pañcīkaraṇam. *The Panchikaranam of Sri Sankaracharya with Six Commentaries*. Eng. Intro. N. Devashankar Mehta & edit. Gajananda Shambhi Sadhale. Bombay : Gujarati Printing Press, 1930.

Pañcīkaraṇam of Śrī Śaṅkarācārya, Text and the Varttika with word for word Translation, English Rendering, Comments, and the Glossary. Calcutta : Advaita Ashrama, 1972.

S. *Praśna*. *Eight Upaniṣads with the Commentary of Śaṅkarācārya*. Tr. Swāmī Gambhīrānanda. Vol. II. Calcutta : Advaita Ashrama, 1973.

Śataślokī. *Select Works of Sri Sankaracharya*, Sanskrit Text & English Translation. Tr. S. Venkataramanam. Madras : G. A. Natesan, n.d.

S. *Tait. U*. *Eight Upaniṣads with the Commentary of Śaṅkarācārya*. Tr. Swāmī Gambhīrānanda. Vol. I. Calcutta : Advaita Ashrama, 1973.

S. *Upadeśa*. *Upadeśasāhasrī of Sri Sankaracharya*. Tr. Swāmī Jagadānanda. Madras : Sri Ramakrishna Math, 1961.

S. *Viveka*. *Vivekacūḍāmaṇi of Śrī Śaṅkarācārya*. Tr. Swāmī Mādhavānanda. Almora : Advaita Ashrama, 1932. (Calcutta : Advaita Ashrama, 1974).

Major Upaniṣads in English Translation

Hume, Robert Ernest. *The Thirteen Principal Upanishads*. Translated from the Sanskrit. Madras : Oxford University Press, 1965 (1st edit. 1921).

Radhakrishnan, S. *The Principal Upaniṣads*. Edited with Introduction, Text, Translation and Notes. London : George Allen & Unwin Ltd., 1953.

Other Works Cited

Abhinava Sachidananda Tirtha, His Holiness Śrī Śaṅkarācārya of Dwarka, "Hindu Dharma," *Bhavan's Journal*, Vol. XVII, No. 1, 1970.

———. "Summary of Benedictory Address, Bhavan's Seth V. M. Public School, Baroda, February 5, 1976." Junagadh : Doshi P. Press, 1976.

Abhinava Vidyatirtha, His Holiness Śrī Śaṅkarācārya of Sringeri. "Some Thoughts on Bhakti," *Bhavan's Journal*, Vol XVII, No. 1, 1970.

Aiyar, Krishnaswamy C. N. *Sri Sankaracharya, His Life and Times.* Madras : G. A. Natesan & Co. 3rd edit., n.d.

Aiyar, R. Krishnaswami, compl. *Dialogues with the Guru.* Talks with His Holiness Sri Chandrasekhara Bharati Swaminah, Late Sankaracharya of Sringeri Math. Bombay : Chetana, 1956.

———. Edit. *The Call of the Jagadguru*, Teachings of His Holiness Sri Jagadguru Sri Chandrasekhara Bharati Swamigal of Sringeri. Madras : Ganesh & Co., 1961

Aiyer, A. Nataraja & S. Lakshminarasimha Sastri. *The Traditional Age of Sri Saṅkaracharya and the Mathas*. Madras : Thompson & Co., 1962.

Altekar, A. S. *Education in Ancient India.* Benares : Indian Book Shop, 1934.

Apte, Vaman Shivram. *The Practical Sanskrit-English Dictionary.* Delhi : Motilal Banarsidass, 4th revised edit., (1965), 1975.

Aseshananda, Swami. "Meditation According to the Upanishads," *Vedanta for Modern Man*, edit. Christopher Isherwood. London : Allen & Unwin, 1952.

Atmananda, Swami, edit. *Sri Sankara's Teaching in His Own Words.* Bombay : Bharatiya Vidya Bhavan, 1954.

Avalon, Arthur, edit. *Tantrik Texts : Prapanchasāratantram of Shankarācārya.* Vol. XVIII & XIX. Calcutta : Sanskrit Press Depository, 1935.

Baidyanath Saraswati. "Study of Specialists in Traditional Learning : The Pandits of Kashi," *Journal of Indian Anthropology*, Vol. 10, No. 2, 1975.

Balasubramanian, R. "A Critique of Rāmānuja's Objection Against the Advaita Conception of Avidyā," *Journal of Madras University*, Vol. XLVI, No. 1, 1974.

Belvalkar, S. K. *Gopal Basu Malik Lectures on Vedānta Philosophy.* Poona : Bilvakunja Publishing House, 1929.

Belvalkar, S. K. & R. D. Ranade. *History of Indian Philosophy,* Vol. 11, *The Creative Period.* Poona : Bilvakunja Publishing House, 1927.

Bernard, Rev. *Brahma Vidya or Brahman-Knowledge According to Sankaracharya.* Allahabad : St. Paul Society, 1969.

Bhagat, M. G. *Ancient Indian Asceticism.* Delhi : Munshiram Manoharlal, 1976.

Bharati Krishna Tirtha, Swami. *Sanatana Dharma, The Eternal and Everlasting Way of Life.* Bombay : Bharatiya Vidya Bhavan, 1970.

———. *Vedic Metaphysics.* Delhi : Motilal Banarsidass, 1978.

Bhāratītīrtha, *Dṛg-Dṛśya Viveka,* in Nikhilananda (1948).

Bhat, G. K. "The Teacher-Pupil Relationship in the Context of Upanisadic Literature," *Annals of the Bhandarkar Oriental Research Institute,* Vol. LIV, 1973.

Bhattacharyya, Krishnachandra, "The Advaita and its Spiritual Significance," *Studies in Philosophy,* Vol. 1, edit. Gopinath Bhattacharyya. Motilal Banarsidass, Delhi, 1982.

Biardeau, Madeleine. *La Philosophie de Mandana Miśra, vue à partir de la Brahmasiddhi.* De L'Ècole Française *D'Étrême-Orient,* Vol. LXXVI. Paris : Ècole Française D'Étrême-Orient, 1969.

Bodas, Mahadeo Rajaram, *Sankaracharya Sampradaya* (in Marathi), Poona : Keshavraj Godhalkar, 1938.

Brunton, Paul. "With the Spiritual Head of South India," *Sankara and Shanmata,* edit. N. Ramaratnam. Madras : M. L. J. Press, n.d.

Cenkner, William. "Gandhi and Creative Conflict," *Thought,* Vol. XLV, No. 178, 1970.

———. "Tagore and Aesthetic Man," *International Philosophical Quarterly,* Vol. XII, No. 2, 1973.

———. "Religion and Education : Models from Contemporary Hinduism," *Religious Education,* Vol. LXX, No. 4, 1975.

———. "Tagore's Vision of Relationality : Aesthetic and Religious Implications," *Humanitas, Journal of the Institute of Man,* Vol. XII, No. 1, 1976.

———. *The Hindu Personality in Education: Tagore, Gandhi,*

Aurobindo. Delhi : Manohar & Columbia, Missouri, U.S.A.: South Asia Books, 1976.

———. "The Guru : Contemporary Religious Educator," *Living Light*, Vol. XIV, No. 4, 1977.

Chakraborty, Haripada. *Asceticism in Ancient India, Brahmanical, Buddhist, Jaina and Ajivika Societies.* Calcutta : Punthi Pustak, 1973.

Chandra Sen, Sri. *The Mystic Philosophy of the Upanishads.* Lucknow : Upper India Publishing House, n.d.

Chandrasekharendra Saraswati, Sri. *Sixty Years of a Glorious Ministry.* His Holiness Sri Chandrasekharendra Saraswati of the Kanchi Sankaracharya Peetham. Madras : Sree Ramaprasad Press, 1968.

Chaterjee, Mohinee M., tr. *A Compendium of Raja Yoga Philosophy.* Comprising the Principal Treatises of Shrimat Shankaracharya and Others. Bombay : Theosophical Publication Fund, 1901.

Creel, Austin B. "Hindu Seers as Moral Guides." Unpublished paper delivered before the American Academy of Religion, Annual Meeting, St. Louis, 1976.

———. *Dharma in Hindu Ethics.* Columbia, Mo. : South Asia Books, 1977.

Dasgupta, Surendranath. *A History of Indian Philosophy.* Vol. I-V. Cambridge, England: Cambridge University Press, 1922; Delhi, Rept. Motilal Banarsidass, 1975.

Date, V. H. *Vedānta Explained : Śaṅkara's Commentary on the Brahma-Sūtras.* Vol. II. Bombay : Booksellers' Publishing Co., 1959.

———. "Sevenfold Stream of Saintly Life," Gurdeo R. D. Ranade Memorial Lectures. Poona : University of Poona, 1971.

De Smet, R. V. "The Fundamental Antinomy of Śrī Śaṅkarācārya's Methodology," *Oriental Thought* (Nasik), Vol. II, No. 4, 1956.

———. "Theological Method and Vedānta," *Oriental Thought* (Nasik), Vol. IV, No. 1 & 2, 1960.

Deutsch, Eliot & J. A. B. van Buitenen. *A Source Book of Advaita Vedānta.* Honolulu : The University Press of Hawaii, 1971.

Devaraja, N. K. *An Introduction to Śaṅkara's Theory of Knowledge.* Delhi & Varanasi : Motilal Banarsidass, 1972.

Devasenapathi, V. A. *Kāmkoṭṭam, Nāyanmārs, and Ādi Śaṅkara.* Madras : University of Madras, 1975.

Dharmarāja. *Vedāntaparibhāsā*, edit., & English tr. Suryanarayana Sastri, *Vedāntaparibhāṣā of Dharmarāja Adhvarīndra.* Madras : Adyar Library, 1942.

Dhole, Nandalal, tr. *Hastamalakabhasyam.* Calcutta : Heeralal Dhole, 1900.

Divānji, Prahlād Chandrashekhar. *Siddhāntabindu of Madhusūdana with the Commentary of Purushottama.* Baroda : Oriental Institute, 1933.

Dvivedi, Manilal N., tr. *The Jīvanmukti-Viveka* (*The Path of Liberation in this Life*) *of Vidyāraṇya Saraswatī.* Bombay : Theosophical Publication Fund, 1897.

Four Amnaya Pithas. Dwarka : Sri Navbharati Office, 1965.

Ghurye, G. S. *Indian Sadhus.* Bombay : Popular Book Depot, 1953.

Ghurye, K. G. *Preservation of Learned Tradition in India.* Bombay : Popular Book Depot, 1950.

Gonda, Jan. *Change and Continuity in Indian Religion.* The Hague : Mouton & Co., 1965.

———. *Die Religionen Indiens.* Vol. 1 & 2. Stuttgart: W. Kohlhammer Verlag, 1960.

Guénon, René. *Man and His Becoming According to the Vedanta,* tr. Richard C. Nicholson. London : Luzac & Co., 1945.

Gussner, Robert E. "A Stylometric Study of the Authorship of Seventeen Sanskrit Hymns Attributed to Śaṅkara." *Journal of the American Oriental Society,* Vol. 96, No. 2, April-June 1976, pp. 259 ff.

Heimann, Betty. *Facets of Indian Thought.* London : George Allen & Unwin, 1964.

Hiriyanna, M. "The Training of the Vedāntin," *Popular Essays in Indian Philosophy.* Mysore : Kavyalaya Publishers, 1952.

Indich, William M. *Consciousness in Advaita Vedānta.* Delhi : Motilal Banarsidass, 1980.

Ingalls, Daniel H. H. "The Study of Samkaracarya," *Annals of the Bhandarkar Oriental Research Institute.* Vol. XXXIII, 1952.

Jayendra Saraswati, His Holiness Sri. "Towards Dedicated Life," *Bhavan's Journal,* Vol. XVII, No. 1, 1970.

———. *Heritage of Bharata Varsha and Sanatana Dharma.* Discourse of His Holiness Jagadguru Sri Sankaracharya Swamigal of Kanchi Kamakoti Peetham at Delhi, 1973. Madras : Oriental Cultural Education Society, n.d.

———. *Our Heritage.* Madras : Rajan & Co., 1976.

Jnanananda Bharati, Sri Svaminah. *Some Saintly Lives.* Thenkarai, Madurai : Shri Jnanananda Grantha Prakasana Samiti, 1969 A.

———. Comp. *Golden Sayings.* Thenkarai, Madurai : Jnanananda Grantha Prakasana Samiti, 1969 B.

Kantaya, S. Sri, "Date of Śrī Śaṁkarācārya,", "*Quarterly Journal of the Mythic Society.* Culture and Heritage Number, 1956.

Karmarkar, R. D. "Did Śaṅkarācārya Write a Bhāṣya on the Bhagavadgītā,?" *Annals of the Bhandarkar Oriental Research Institute*, Vol. XXXIX, 1958.

Kaviraj, Gopinath, Pt. MM. "Introduction to Hindi Translation of *Brahma-Sūtra-Bhāṣya of* Śaṅkara with *Ratnaprabhā*," *Acyuta*, Vol. 111, No. 4.

———. "Is the Advaita of Śaṅkara Buddhism in Disguise ?" *The Quarterly Journal of the Mythic Society*, Vol. 24, No. 1-2, 1933.

Keay, F. E. *Ancient Indian Education.* Bombay & London : Oxford University Press, 1918.

Kenghe, C. T. "No Antinomy Imputable to Śrī Śaṅkarācārya," *Oriental Thought* (Nasik), Vol. 111, Nos. 2-4, 1957.

Krishnananda, Swami. *The Realisation of the Absolute, A Treatise on Vedānta Philosophy and Its Method.* Sivanandanagar, U. P. : Divine Life Society, 1964.

Krishnaswamy, S. Y. *The Saint of Sringeri in Sacred India.* Madras : Sanatana Dharma Vidya Samiti, n.d.

Kumar Das, Santosh. *The Educational System of the Ancient Hindus.* Calcutta : Mitra Press, 1930.

Kunhan Raja, C. *Poet-Philosophers of the RgVeda, Vedic and Pre-Vedic.* Madras : Ganesh & Co., 1963.

Kunjunniraja, K. "On the Date of Śaṅkarācārya and Allied Problems." *Adyar Library Bulletin*, Vol. XXIV, Parts 3 & 4, 1960.

Kuppuswami Sastri (Shastri), S., edit. & intro. *Brahmasiddhi of Ācārya Maṇḍanamiśra with Commentary by Śaṅkhapāṇi.*

Madras Gov. Oriental Sanskrit Series, No. 4. Madras : Government Press, 1937.

———. *Compromises in the History of Advaitic Thought.* Madras : Kuppuswami Shastri Research Institute, 1940.

Leggett, Trevor. *The Chapter of the Self.* London : Routledge & Kegan Paul, 1978.

Lūtt, Jürgen, "The Śaṅkarācārya of Puri, "*The Cult of Jagannath and the Regional Tradition of Orissa,* Edit. A. Eschman, H. Kulke, G. C. Tripathi. Delhi : Manohar, 1978.

Madhusūdana, *Siddhāntabindu.* P. M. Modi, tr. *Siddhāntabindu, Madhusūdana's Commentary on the Daśaślokī of Sri Sankaracharya.* Bombay : Samaldas College, 1929. Prahlād Chandrashekhar Divānji,tr. *Siddhāntabindu of Madhusūdana with the Commentary of Purushottama.* Baroda : Oriental Institute, 1933.

Mahadevan, T. M. P. *Homage to Sankara.* Madras : Ganesh & Co., 1959.

———. Edit. *A Seminar on Saints.* Madras : Ganesh & Co., 1960.

———. Trans. *Readings from Śaṅkara,* Part One. Madras : Ganesh & Co. 1960.

———. *The Philosophy of Advaita with Special Reference to Bhāratītīrtha-Vidyāraṇya.* Madras : Ganesh & Co., 1962.

———. *Śaṅkara's Hymn to Śiva* (*Śivānandalaharī*). Madras : Ganesh & Co. Private, Ltd., 1963.

———. Edit. *Preceptors of Advaita.* Secunderabad : Sri Kanchi Kamakoti Sankara Mandir, 1968.

———. *The Pañcadaśī of Bhāratītīrtha-Vidyāraṇya, An Interpretative Exposition.* Madras : University of Madras, 1969.

———. Trans. *The Hymns of Śaṅkara.* Delhi, Motilal Banarsidass, 1979.

———. Edit. *The Sage of Kanchi.* Delhi : Arnold-Heinemann, 1975.

Maṇḍanamiśra. *Sphoṭasiddhi.* K. A. Subramnia Iyer, tr., *Sphoṭasiddhi. of Maṇḍana Miśra.* Poona : Deccan College Postgraduate & Research Institute, 1966.

———. *Brahmasiddhi.* S. Kuppuswami Sastri, edit. & Intro., *Brahmasiddhi of Ācārya Maṇḍanamiśra with Commentary by Śaṅkhapāṇi.* Madras Gov. Oriental Sanskrit Series, No. 4. Madras : Government Press, 1937.

Mayeda, Sengaku. "The Authenticity of the Upadeśasāhasrī," *Journal of American Oriental Society*, Vol. 85, 1965.

———. Trans & Intro. *A Thousand Teachings : The Upadeśasāhasrī of Śaṅkara*. Tokyo : University of Tokyo Press, 1979.

Miller, David. "The Guru as the Centre of Sacredness," *Sciences Religieuses/Studies in Religion*, 6/5, 1976-77.

Miller, David & Dorothy C. Wertz. *Hindu Monastic Life. The Monks and Monasteries of Bhubaneswar*. Montreal & London : McGill-Queen's University Press, 1976.

Mishra, B. *Sankaracarya-jagadguru-mathamnaya*. Puri : Balabhadra Press, 1930.

Mitra, Veda. *Education in Ancient India*. Delhi : Arya Book Depot, 1964.

Modi, P. M.. tr. *Siddhāntabindu, Madhusūdana's Commentary on the Daśaślokī of Sri Sankaracharya*. Bombay : Samaldas College, 1929.

Mookerji, Radhakumud. *Ancient Indian Education, Brahmanical and Buddhist*. Delhi & Varanasi : Motilal Banarsidass, 3rd edit., 1960.

Mukherjee, Satindra Kumar. "Śaṅkara on the Relation Between the Vedas and Reason," *Indian Historical Quarterly*, Vol. 6, No. 1, 1930.

Mukhopadhyaya, Govindagopal. *Studies in the Upanishads*. Calcutta Sanskrit College Research Series, No. IX, Calcutta: Sanskrit College, 1960.

Murty, K. Satchidananda. *Revelation and Reason in Advaita Vedanta*. Bombay : Asia Publishing House, 1959.

Nagaraja Rao, P. "Advaita Metaphysics, Its Religious Significance," *Prabuddha Bharata* (Calcutta), Vol. 63, No. 1, 1938.

Nikhilananda, Swami, tr. *Vedāntasāra of Sadānanda*. Almora : Advaita Ashrama, 1941.

———. Tr. *Dṛg-Dṛśya Viveka. An Inquiry into the "Seer" and the "Seen"*. Mysore : Sri Ramakrishna Asrama, 2nd edit., 1948.

———. Tr. *Ātmabodha of Śaṅkarācārya, Self-Knowledge. An English Translation of Śaṅkarācārya's Ātmabodha with Notes, Commentary and Introduction*. Madras : Sri Ramakrishna Math, 2nd edit., 1962; 3rd edit., 1967, (1975).

Padmapāda, *Pañcapādikā*. Eng. tr. D. Venkataramiah. *The Pañcapādikā of Padmapāda*. Gaekwads' Oriental Series. No. CVII. Baroda : Oriental Institute, 1948.

Patwardhan, C. N. *History of Education in Medieval India*. Bombay : Ramji Assar Vidyalaya, 1939.

Piantelli, Mario. *Śaṅkara E La Rinascita Del Brāhmanesimo*. Torino : Editrice Esperienze, 1974.

Radhakrishnan, S. *Indian Philosophy*, Vol. II. London : George Allen & Unwin, 2nd edit., 1929.

———. "Opening Address," *A Seminar on Saints*. edit., T. M. P. Mahadevan. Madras : Ganesh & Co., 1960.

Rahurkar, V. G. *The Seers of the RgVeda*. Poona : Poona University, 1964.

Rajgopal Sharma. "Sri Sankaracharya Dakshinamnaya Sringagiri Sarada Peetham Vyakkyana-cum-Dharma Simhasanam," The Educational & Cultural Activities. Sringeri : Sarada Pitha, n.d.

Ramakrishna Aiyer, comp. *The Acharya's Call, His Holiness Jagadguru's Madras Discourses*, 1957-1960. Part 1. Madras: B. G. Paul & Co., 2nd edit., 1971.

Ramalingeswara Rao, T. *Sri Sureswara Acarya*. Ratnakaram : Vijayawada Bharati Grandha, 1970.

Raman, N. Venkata. *Sankaracharya The Great and His Successors in Kanchi*. Madras : Ganesh & Co., 1923.

Ramaratnam, N. edit. *Sankara and Shanmata*. Souvenir of Conference on Sankara and Shanmata Held in Madras from June 1-June 9, 1969. Madras : M. L. J. Press, n.d.

Ramaswami Sastri, K. S. *His Holiness in Madras*, 1957-1960, *Life and Gospel of His Holiness the Jagadguru of Sri Kamakoti Peetam*. Madras : The Library Press, 1960.

Ranade, R. D. *A Constructive Survey of Upanishadic Philosophy, A Systematic Introduction to Indian Metaphysics*. Poona : Oriental Book Agency, 1926.

Raval, Chandrakant & V. N. Upadhyaya. *On Divine Path*. Dwarka : Shri Navabharati Karyalaya, 1970.

Rayguru, J. K. M. & J. M. S. Tirtha, trans. *Guruparampara of the Samkarananda Math, Puri and Bhubaneswar*. Puri : A. C. Chakarverty, 1926.

Sadānanda, *Vedāntasāra*. Swami Nikhilananda, tr. *Vedāntasāra of Sadānanda*. Almora : Advaita Ashrama, 1941.

Sahasrabudhe, M. T. *A Survey of the Pre-Śaṅkara Advaita Vedānta*. Poona : University of Poona, 1968.

Saktidassan, Jalaya & Saktidassan Subramanian. *Dwarka and Sharada Peeth*. Dwarka : Shri Navabharati Office, 1968.

Saraswati, Vidyananda & V. N. Upadhyaya. *Shree Govardhan Peeth Pattabhishek Souvenir, Puri* 1964. Bombay : Vaishnav & Vyas, 1964.

Sarma, B. N. Krishnamurti. "Śaṅkara's Authorship of the Gītā-Bhāṣya," *Annals of the Bhandarkar Oriental Research Institute*, Vol. XIV, 1932-33.

Sarma, D. S. *What is Hinduism* ? Madras : Madras Law Journal Office, 1972.

Sarmah, Jogeswar. *Philosophy of Education in the Upanisads*. New Delhi : Oriental Publishers & Distributors, 1978.

Sarvajñātman, *Saṁkṣepaśārīraka*. N. Veezhinathan, tr. *The Saṁkṣepaśārīraka of Sarvajñātman*. Madras : University of Madras, 1972.

Sastratakara, Brahmasri. *The Mutts Founded by Sri Sankara Bhagavatpada*. Madras : B. G. Paul, 1973.

Sastry, T. S. Narayana & T. N. Kumaraswamy. *The Age of Sankara*. Madras : B. G. Paul, (1916), 2nd edit., 1971.

Satchidanandendra Saraswati, Swami. *Salient Features of Śaṅkara's Vedānta*. Holenarsipur : Adhyatma Prakasha Karyalaya, 1967.

Satprakāshānanda, Swāmī. *Methods of Knowing, Perceptual, Non-Perceptual and Transcendental, According to Advaita Vedānta*. London : George Allen & Unwin, 1965.

Satsvarūpa dāsā Gosvāmī. *Readings in Vedic Literature*. The Tradition Speaks for Itself. Los Angeles : The Bhaktivedanta Book Trust, 1977.

Seshadri, P. *Sri Sankaracharya*. Trivandrum : University of Travancore, 1949.

Shastri, Hari Prasad. tr. *Panchadashi*. London: Shanti Sadan 1954.

Shri Sharadapeeth Vidyasabha Decinnial Celebrations, August 1971. Dwarka : Shri Sharadapeeth Vidya Sabha, 1971.

Srikantha Sastri, S. "Advaitācāryas of the 12th & 13th Centuries, *Indian Historical Quarterly*. Vol. 14, No. 2, 1938.

Subramania Iyer, K. A. *Sphoṭasiddhi of Maṇḍana Miśra*. English tr. Poona : Deccan College Postgraduate & Research Institute, 1966.

Subrahmanya Sarma, V., tr. *Minor Works of Sri Sankaracharya.* Holenarsipur : Adhyatma Prakasha Karyalaya, 1942.

Sureśvara, *Naiṣkarmyasiddhi.* S. S. Raghavachar, English tr. *Naiṣkarmyasiddhi of Sri Sureśvarācārya.* Mysore : University of Mysore, 1965.

Suryanarayana Sastri, S. S. *The Life and Teachings of Sri Sankaracharya.* Madras : G. A. Natesan, 3rd edit., n.d.

Suryanarayana Sastri. S. S. and C. Kunhan Raja. *The Bhāmatī of Vācaspati on Śaṅkara's Brahmasūtrabhāṣya.* Madras : Theosophical Publishing House, 1933.

———. English tr. and edit. *Vedāntaparibhāṣā of Dharmarāja Adhvarin.* Madras : Adyar Library, 1942.

Tatachariar, Agnihotram Ramanuja. "The Ideal Prophet of Our Age," *Sankara and Shanmta.* N. Ramaratnam, edit. Madras : M. L. J. Press, n.d.

Tattwananda, Swami, tr. *The Quintessence of Vedanta (Sarva-Vedānta-Siddhānta-Sārasaṅgraha) of Acharya Sankara.* Kalady : Sri Ramakrishna Advaita Ashrama, 1960.

Thornton, Edward. "Jungian Psychology and the Vedanta." *Aryan Path* (Bombay), Vol, 35, 1964.

Tiwari, Kapil N. *Dimensions of Renunciation in Advaita Vedānta.* [Delhi : Motilal Banarsidass, 1977.]

Unpublished Upanisads. Madras : Adyar Library, 1937.

Upadhyaya, V. N. comp. *Dwaraka Jagadguru Speaks.* Madras: Ganesh & Co., 1967.

———. Edit. *Life-Sketch of Adi Shankaracharya : A Pictorial Feature.* Dwarka : Shri Navabharati Office, 1974.

Vācaspati. *Bhāmatī.* S. S. Suryanarayana Sastri & C. Kunhan Raja. *The Bhāmatī of Vācaspati on Śaṅkara's Brahmasūtrabhāṣya.* Madras : Theosophical Publishing House, 1933.

Veezhinathan, N. "The Kāmakoṭi-pīṭha and the Sage of Kāñchī," *The Sage of Kanchi.* edit., T. M. P. Mahadevan. Delhi : Arnold-Heinemann, 1975.

———. *The Saṁkṣepaśārīraka of Sarvajñātman.* Madras : University of Madras, 1972.

Venkatarama Iyer, M. K. *Advaita Vedānta According to Śaṁkara.* Bombay : Asia Publishing House, 1964.

Venkataraman, K. R. *The Throne of Transcendental Wisdom, Sri Sankaracharya's Sarada Pītha in Sringeri.* Madras : Akhila Bharata Samkara Seva Samiti, 2nd. rev. edit., 1967.

Venkataramanan, S., tr. *Select Works of Sri Sankaracharya, Sanskrit Text and English Translation.* Madras : G. A. Natesan, n.d.

Vidyāraṇya, *Jīvanmukti Viveka.* Poona : Anandasrama, 1916.

———. Manilal N. Dvivedi, tr. *The Jīvanmukti-Viveka (The Path of Liberation in this Life) of Vidyāraṇya Saraswatī.* Bombay : Theosophical Publication Fund, 1897.

———. *Pañcadaśī.* Hari Prasad Shastri, tr. *Panchadashi.* London : Shanti Sadan, 1954.

Warrier, A. G. Krishna. *The Concept of Mukti in Advaita Vedanta.* Madras : University of Madras, 1961.

Woodroffe, Sir John (Arthur Avalon). *Principles of Tantra.* Vol. I & II. Madras : Ganesh & Co., 1969.

Yamunacharya, M. "The Concept of Dharma and Its Implications to the New Society," *Proceedings of the Twenty-Eighth Indian Philosophical Congress, Baroda,* 1953. ed. T. M. P. Mahadevan, G. R. Malkani, J. N. Chubb and N. A. Nikam. Madras : Indian Philosophical Congress, 1953.

Yatisandhyāsamuccaya. Dwaraka : Dwaraka Pitha, 1967.

Zimmer, Heinrich. *Philosophy of India.* edit. Joseph Campbell. Bollingen Series XXVI. New York : Pantheon Books, 1951.

GLOSSARY

ācārya A teacher who imparts a broad range of socio-religious knowledge; a spiritual guide learned in scripture.

adhikāra Eligibility and competence for spiritual undertakings; moral qualifications for the path of knowledge. *Adhikārin* is one who is competent.

Advaita Non-duality or absolute unicity; the identity of Brahman and *ātman*; *dvaita* is duality, real difference between Brahman and *ātman*. Advaita Vedānta is a school of thought as systematized by Śaṅkara.

Āgama-s Ritual texts from the fifth century onward, expanding upon sectarian rituals but different from the Vedic and Purāṇic traditions; they inculcate principles and practices of the Tantra.

*āmnāya maṭha*s The original retreats or monasteries established by Śaṅkara over which he placed his four major disciples.

aparāvidyā Lower knowledge communicated through scripture and meditation upon objects; distinguished from higher knowledge which is self-revealing.

āsana Physical postures and exercise in the practice of *haṭha*-yoga.

āśrama A place for religious discipline and development within a communal and secluded setting.

ātman The Self, radical subjectivity; identified with Brahman in Advaita Vedānta.

avatāra One who in the course of history is regarded as a descent (literally, a descender) from god in order to renew the human and mundane orders.

Bhagavad Gītā The Song of the Lord; a revered Hindu popular treatise, forming part of the epical *Mahābhārata*, with emphasis on devotion to Kṛṣṇa and divine grace, *karmayoga* and renunciation of the fruits of action.

bhakti Devotion, love; a *bhakta* is one devoted to the Lord. A *bhakti*-guru is a spiritual guide teaching the path of devotion (*bhakti*-yoga).

brahmacarya The first stage of life, the student years, wherein during ancient times the student lived with his teacher and committed himself to both secular and religious discipline;

a time of celibacy. A *brahmacārī* is also a celibate, a religious seeker.

Brahman Absolute Reality; the Transcendent; the Divine.

brāhmaṇa The priestly caste; the highest of the four socio-religious groups; teachers came from this class.

Brahma Sūtra That text which is the first systematic enquiry into the Upaniṣads; aphoristic literature that cannot stand on its own but needs commentary. From the time of Śaṅkara, authorship is usually attributed to Bādarāyaṇa.

caṇḍāla One who belongs to no socio-religious group; one from the lowest sector of society.

darśana Seeing; the sight of the guru which may initiate spiritual awakening; the blessing received from a holy person, a deity, a temple. The word also means a philosophical system.

dhāraṇā The will and intention to concentrate.

dharma Moral duty; the moral and social law as the fundamental norm of human conduct. Divine law. Righteousness, justice, religious obligations. *Sanātana dharma* is the eternal law.

dhyāna The act of concentration.

gurukula A residential hermitage for a teacher and his disciples.

haṭha-yoga The physical postures and discipline of yoga.

Īśvara A name for the supreme lord, usually Viṣṇu or Śiva or one of their manifestations. The supreme controller.

japa The repeated recitation of the name of god, of a *mantra* or other prayers with devotion.

jīva The individual self.

jñāna Knowledge, wisdom. *Jñāna*-yoga is the path of knowledge; a *jñāna*-yogi or *jñānī* is one who follows the path of knowledge as the primary religious discipline. A *jñāna* guru is a teacher of this discipline.

jñānakāṇḍa That part of the Veda which teaches the path of knowledge as the means of liberation.

karma The law according to which every deed has its consequence; a good deed has a good effect and an evil deed an evil effect. Work, activity. *Karma*-yoga is the religious path of activity; a *karma*-yogin is one who follows the path of ritual activity or activity consecrated to God as his principle religious discipline.

karmakāṇḍa That part of the Veda giving emphasis to ritual and sacrificial duties.

kṣatriya The second highest of the four socio-religious groups; the administrative and warrior caste in classical society.

liṅga (*liṅgam*) The phallic symbol representing Śiva in classical Hinduism. *Sphaṭika liṅga* is the crystal stone image in the possession of each Śaṅkarācārya which he personally uses in worship.

manana Reflection; raising questions of and doing philosophical analysis on scriptural statements.

mandira A local temple or shrine.

mantra A syllable, word, verse from the Veda considered sacred and recited repeatedly for its effect in meditation : usually given an esoteric interpretation.

maṭha The complex which houses an ascetic and his disciples or even a group of ascetics; a type of monastery with a principal teacher. *Maṭhāmnāya* are those *maṭha*-s established by Śaṅkara.

Mīmāṃsā Usually understood as *pūrva mīmāṃsā*, the "First Enquiry"; it most generally means the canons of exegesis that explain what duties have to be performed; ritual acts and duties. The *uttara mīmāṃsā*, the "Second Enquiry" is the Vedānta.

mūrti A form or image of a deity used in *pūjā* and sometimes in meditation.

niaidhyāsana Concentration : repeated concentration on the meaning of the Self which results from *śravaṇa* and *manana*; a form of concentration that seeks to apprehend Brahman.

nirguṇa Literally, with no attributes or qualities; *nirguṇa* Brahman is the Absolute without qualities.

paṇḍita Those teachers of the oral tradition who pass along the Veda, other religious texts, and even secular literature. The reciters and transmitters of classical literature. *Pāṇḍitya* : scholarship, learning.

paramparā A document listing the lineage of teachers in a particular sect, *maṭha* or religious order; the guru-*paramparā*-s in the Śaṅkara *maṭha*-s refer to those texts that trace the lineage of teachers beginning with Śaṅkara.

parāvidyā The highest wisdom which liberates; it is not caused by meditation or reflection but reveals itself upon the removal of ignorance.

pāṭhaśālā A traditional Sanskrit school for youths.

prāṇāyāma The discipline of ordered breathing in yoga.

pūjā Worhsip; ritual and prayers offered in the home, the temple or the *maṭha.*

pūrṇimā The day of the full moon used for religious festivals among Hindus. Guru-*pūrṇimā* is a yearly celebration honoring a particular teacher.

*rāja*guru Literally, a kingly guru; those gurus who are esteemed as kingly manifestations of the divine; they are sometimes enthroned and even dressed in a royal manner.

sādhana That which leads to spirituality; the undertaking of a particular religious discipline; religious praxis.

sādhu A general term for an ascetic, a wandering mendicant, a holy man.

saguṇa Literally, with attributes or qualities; *saguṇa* Brahman is the Absolute with essential qualities.

śākta A worshiper of the divine creative power, usually personified as Śakti, the wife of Śiva. *Śakti* is conceived as female and mythically represented in the consorts of the gods. It plays a central role in Tantrism.

śāligrāma A black stone with an image of the disc symbolizing Viṣṇu.

samādhi The higher stages of concentration; sometimes understood as trance, absorption.

Sāṅkhya One of the six systems of Hindu philosophy, usually ascribed to Kapila; a dualistic system believing in a process of involution and evolution; the theoretical basis for classical yoga praxis.

sammelana A convocation and gathering of gurus, *paṇḍita*-s or even *sādhus* in order to strengthen ties, to debate and purify doctrine or to encourage discipline.

saṃnyāsa The ascetical state of life, a state of renunciation; the last of the four stages of Hindu life which follows the separation from all worldly ties. It is often used as a title for a member of a Śaṅkara order of ascetics. A *saṃnyāsī* is an individual, a celibate, who leads the ascetical life.

sampradāya The transmission of traditional teaching from one teacher to another over the course of generations. Although it refers to a monastic order, in an institutional sense, it includes both ascetics and lay people who follow the teaching of a particular guru.

sanātana dharma Eternal law, eternal truth.

sandhyā Literally, twilight; the daily prayers binding a householder and which follows upon the *upanayana* rite; the prayers are customarily said in the morning and evening but may be prescribed even three times a day.

ṣaṇmata Refers to the six alternate ways of worship, corresponding to six gods, Śiva, Viṣṇu, Śakti, Sūrya, Gaṇapati and Kumāra.

śāstra-s Literally, command, book; a revered manual of religious teaching expanding upon *sūtra* literature.

Śiva Literally, the auspicious one; the god of the Śaivas; combines the contradictory but complimentary aspects of destruction and creation, asceticism and eroticism, benevolence and ferocity, good and evil. Symbolized as Naṭarāja, Lord of the cosmic dance, the Nandī bull, and the *liṅgam.* Śiva is the Great Yogī, *mahāyogī*, and patron of yoga who generates power through austerities; he is divine generativity and creativity.

śloka A verse of Sasnkrit literature.

Smārta Brāhmaṇa Member of the Brāhmaṇa caste in South India from *jatis* or subsects who follows the teaching of Śaṅkara and the sectarianism of the Śaivas; especially found among followers of the Sringeri and Kanchi *maṭha*-s.

smṛti Revered religious literature that complements the revealed scripture (*śruti*); especially includes the *Mahābhārata*, within which the *Bhagavad Gītā* holds singular esteem, the Purāṇas and the law books.

śravaṇa Listening to the oral scripture, its exposition and explanation from a guru.

Śrī A title of respect and honor.

Śrī Dakṣiṇāmūrti The supreme divinity as preceptor; the popular hymn of Śaṅkara in which Śiva is identified as god (Īśvara), teacher (guru), and Self (*ātman*).

śruti The revealed scripture; the Veda; the eternal wisdom heard by sages.

sūtra Literally, a thread; hence, a thread of discourse; aphoristic literature that requires exposition and commentary.

Swami (*swāmī*) Literally, a master of the senses; a title given to ascetics and teachers. *Swamiji*, with the honorific *ji*, indicates special affection.

Tantra Derives from a root meaning "to extend," "to expand," a body of literature and religious ritual in yoga, Hinduism and Buddhism. Emphasis on ritual, *mantra*, *yantra*, *maṇḍala*; a form of sacramentalism that tries to elicit the dynamic and divine energy of creation (*śakti*).

tapas Austerities, religious practices; penitential discipline.

upanayana The ceremony of initiation (literally, drawing near) in which the Hindu youth is "twice born" and attains full membership in the higher socio-religious groups; the sacred thread ritual.

Vaiṣṇava One belonging to the sect of the Vaiṣṇavas who worship Viṣṇu, Kṛṣṇa as Lord.

varṇāśrama The ancient Vedic social system of the four classes (*varṇa*), priests and teachers, warriors and public servants, merchants and farmers, and labourers and craftsmen set within the developmental stages (*āśrama*) of life, namely of student, householder, forest dweller and renunciant.

Veda Literally, knowledge; general term for the sacred Sanskrit texts of early Brāhmaṇical Hinduism; revelation (*śruti*); includes hymns, rituals, expository and meditational literature, arranged in four books, *Ṛg*, *Sāma*, *Yajur* and *Atharva*.

Vedānta The end of the Veda or the Upaniṣads; one of the six systems of Hindu philosophy; inspired by the Upaniṣads but also drawing upon the *Brahma Sūtra*. The *uttara mīmāṃsā*, the "Second Enquiry" on the Upaniṣads as articulated by Bādarāyaṇa, Śaṅkara and later Hindu thinkers.

vidyā Literally, knowledge as opposed to non-knowledge (*avidyā*); sometimes refers to the objects of meditation; also signifies liberating knowledge.

vidyāguru A teacher who imparts knowledge (*jñāna*).

Viṣṇu The god of the Vaiṣṇavas; also called Hari and Nārāyaṇa; the preserver god who along with Brahmā, the creator, and

Śiva form a kind of godhead (*trimūrti*); Viṣṇu manifests himself through multiple descents (*avatāra*-s) such as Kṛṣṇa; symbolized frequently with four arms or asleep on the serpent in the primeval ocean; his emblems are the conch, disc, lotus, bow and mace.

vijñāna Right knowledge; for Śaṅkara it implies immediate and direct knowledge that reveals itself once ignorance is removed.

viveka Rational, philosophical discrimination; intellectual analysis.

yāga A ritual sacrifice.

INDEX

Abhinava Saccidānanda, Śrī Śaṅkarācārya, 125ff, 128, 135ff, 138, 145, 148, 151, 155, 165, 167
Abhinava Vidyātīrtha, Śrī Śaṅkarācārya, 122ff, 142-41, 145, 148ff, 155, 161, 165
ācārya 5, 31, 40, 56, 109ff, 114, 117, 119, 122, 127-28, 131, 133, junior-*ācārya* 163, 166-67
adhikāra 13, 47, 142; *adhikārin*, 47
adhiṣṭhāna 74, 82
Āgamas, 117, 127, 143
Ānandagiri, 85
aparāvidyā 76
āsana 79, 94,
āśrama, 27, 39, 158
ātman 20, 24, 43, 162; *ātma-pūjā*, 133; *ātmavidyā* 27
avatāra 93, 102, 153, 179
Bādarāyaṇa, 29, 31, 32, 49, 87,
Badrinath, 109, 115

Bhagavad Gītā 26, 28, 31, 35, 37, 54, 58, 60, 102, 116, 124,139, 141-42, 162; *Gītābhāṣya* 34, 43
bhajana 105, 117
bhakti 18, 24, 26, 27, 42, 54, 55, 93ff, 95ff, 97, 102ff, 105, 138, 140-41, 147, 150, 154; guru-*bhakti*, 165, 178, 179, 181
Bhāmatī 96ff, 121
Bharati Krishna, Śrī Śaṅkarācārya, 111, 125, 131-32, 135-36, 143, 145, 148, 158, 162
Bhāratītīrtha, 98ff
brahmacarya 7, 12-13, 143, 156
Brāhmaṇa, 1, 5, 10-11, 23, 26, 34-35, 118, 143, 183
Brahmasiddhi 84ff, 97ff
Brahma Sūtra 31, 32, 61, 73, 87, 102, 121, 123, 134, 161
Brahmavidyā 9, 12, 116
Bṛhadāraṇyaka Upaniṣad, 18, 21, 32, 85

Chāndogya Upaniṣad 10, 12, 21, 32, 37, 49, 52, 64, 69
Candraśekhara Bhāratī, Śrī Śaṅkarācārya, 122, 136
Candraśekharendra Sarasvatī, Śrī Śaṅkarācārya, 123ff, 128, 139, 144, 147, 155, 160, 170, 173, 180
dhāraṇā 75
dharma 5, 14, 123, 130, 131, 134, 135ff, 136, 145, 152-53, 183, 185-86,
Dharmarāja Adhvarīndra, 102ff
dhyāna 22, 68, 75ff, 170
Dwaraka, 109, 113, 115, 119, 125ff, 128, 129ff, 131, 135, 143, 145-46, 150, 152, 157-59, 165, 168, 180

Gauḍapāda, 22, 29-31, 37, 45, 86
Govinda, 31, 34, 37, 40, 42, 55, 94

Hastāmalaka, 85, 109
haṭha-yoga, 170ff

jagadguru 98, 109, 117, 120, 122, 126, 132-34, 142, 145, 152, 155, 161, 179
japa 73, 99, 116, 121, 126, 140, 170
Jayendra Sarasvatī, Śaṅkarācārya, 124ff, 136-137, 138, 140, 142, 145, 167
Jīvanmukti-Viveka 99ff
jñnna 54, 55, 58, 60, 68, 75, 81, 85, 105, 123, 141, 147, 152
jñānakāṇḍa 19, 30, 142
Jyotirmaṭha, 111ff, 113, 119-20, 126ff, 129, 133, 155, 157, 167, 180

Kanchi Kāmakoṭi Pīṭha, 109ff, 113, 114, 119, 123ff, 124ff, 127-30, 131, 133, 137-38, 140-41, 142-43, 144, 146, 149, 149-52, 155-58, 162, 165, 167, 168, 171-72
karma, 164, *karmakāṇḍa*, 30, *karma* yoga, 49, 60, 84, 97, 104ff, 141-42, 145, 152, 170, 179, 181
Kaṭha Upaniṣad, 17, 48
Kṛṣṇa, 26, 35
Kumārila Bhaṭṭa, 4

liṅga, 116ff

Madhusūdana Sarasvatī, 101ff
muhāvākya, 36, 61ff
manana, 21-22, 24, 66, 67, 99, 172
Maṇḍanamiśra, 30, 71, 84 ff, 87, 96, 101
Māṇḍūkyakārikā 20, 22, 86
mantra, 37, 73, 92, 99, 140, 154, 170
maṭhāmnāya, 109, 116,
Mīmāṃsā, 29-30, 71, 84, 103, 139
Muṇḍaka Upaniṣad, 9, 12, 13, 25, 52
muni 30, 54; *mauna* 54

mūrti 116-17

nididhyāsana 21, 22, 24, 66-68, 76, 79ff, 99, 172
Nirañjan Devatīrtha, 111, 114, 125ff

OM, 23, 24, 69, 74

Padmapāda, 85ff, 109
Pañcadaśī 98ff,,
paṇḍita, 41, 118ff, 120-21, 128ff, 134, 147-48, 150, 154-56, 159, 163, 166-67, 169, 171
pāṇḍitya 54
paramparā, 109ff, 122, 125
parāvidyā, 76
Patañjali, 28, 151
pāṭhaśālā, 112-13, 116, 118ff, 120, 127-28, 148, 159, 163-64, 171, 183
prāṇāyāma 94, 170
pūjā, 116-17, 122, 124ff, 126-27, 130, 132ff, 140, 145, 152, 161, 165,
Puri, 109, 113, 115, 119, 125, 129, 131-32, 143, 144, 145, 149, 154, 157-58, .160, 180

*rāja*guru, 114, 127
rāja yoga, 79
Ṛgveda 2-7, 19

śabda, 84, 101
Sadānanda Yogīndra, 100, 101ff,
sādhana, 73, 93, 141
śakti 93
samādhi, 45, 51, 98ff, 158
sannyāsa, 38-39, 72, 125, 156-57, 162-63, 166; *sannyāsi*, 11, 38-41, 49, 53, 73, 143, 185
sampradāya 183ff
sanātana dharma, 109, 112, 124, 135ff, 146, 160, 186
ṣaṇmata, 116, 137, 140, 184
Sarvajñātman, 89ff,
Śāntānanda Saraswatī, Śrī Śaṅkarācārya, 126ff, 145, 155, 167, 180

Siddhāntabindu, 102ff
śiṣya, 7, 15, 17, 18, 27, 46-47, 55-57, 117, 120, 124, 155, 157, 161, 164, 166, 173-74, 181
Śiva, 43-44, 86, 90ff, 94, 116, 153, 158, 175ff
smṛti, 9, 18, 26-28, 91, 95, 136, 159
śravaṇa, 21-22, 66, 99, 160, 172
Śrī Dakṣiṇāmūrti, 43-45, 85, 175ff.
Sringeri, 109, 113ff, 115ff, 118-20, 122ff, 128ff, 131, 136, 141, 143, 147, 150-52, 154-58, 160
śruti, 5, 8, 136, 186
Sureśvara, 84-85, 89, 102, 109, 121

Taittirīya Upaniṣad, 12, 13, 15, 17, 32, 37, 64, 85, 121, 151
Tantra, 14, 26, 27, 56, 92, 117
Toṭaka (Ānandagiri), 85, 87, 109

Upadeśasāhasrī, 33, 62, 69, 85, 100
upādhyāya, 5, 40; *upajjhāya*, 55
upanayana, 6, 12, 20, 27, 122
upāsanā 23-24, 74ff, 79, 87, 96, 137, 142, 170, 173
Vācaspati, 97ff, 101
vairāgya, 50
varṇāśrama, 38, 49
Vedāntaparibhāṣā, 102ff
Vedāntasāra, 100ff
vidyā, 8-9, 20, 23, 74
*vidyā*guru, 134
Vidyāpīṭha, 111ff, 119, 157, 160, 164ff, 166, 178ff, 181ff,
Vidyāraṇya, 98ff, 100, 112, 121
vijñāna, 58, 68, 76, 81
Vivaraṇa, 87, 96ff, 98, 102
viveka 21, 25, 50, 64, 67, 76
Viṣṇu, 45, 93, 94, 116, 158
Vyāsa, 86, 89

Yājñavalkya, 11, 19, 20
Yoga Sūtra, 28